ESL Teacher Resource Guide

MODERN CURRICULUM PRESS
PHONICS

TEACHER ADVISORY BOARD

ACKNOWLEDGMENTS

EXECUTIVE EDITOR
Magali Iglesias

EDITORIAL DEVELOPMENT
Pinnacle Education Associates, Inc.
Joanne M. Rodríguez, ESL Consultant
Steven-Michael Patterson, ESL Consultant

PRODUCT MANAGER
Christine A. McArtor

PRODUCTION
Julie Ryan, Helen Wetherill

ART DIRECTOR
Terry Harmon

PROJECT EDITOR
Judith C. Stobbe

DESIGN
Bernadette Hruby, Karolyn Wehner

COMPOSTION
Alan Noyes

MANUFACTURING & INVENTORY PLANNING
Karen Sota, Cristina Gomez

All images © Pearson Learning unless otherwise noted.

MODERN CURRICULUM PRESS
An Imprint of **Pearson Learning**
299 Jefferson Road, P.O. Box 480
Parsippany, New Jersey 07054-0480

http://www.mcschool.com
1-800-321-3106

ISBN 0-7652-1257-9

1 2 3 4 5 6 7 8 9   VG   04 03 02 01 00 99

CONTENTS

Consonants

UNIT 1

Short Vowels

Long Vowels

Consonant Blends, *y* as a Vowel

Endings, Digraphs, Contractions

MCP Phonics ESL
Teacher Resource Guides

The **MCP Phonics ESL Teacher Resource Guides** are designed for English-speaking classroom teachers who want additional ESL strategies and tips for using the *MCP Phonics* program with native-English speakers and ESL learners mainstreamed in the same classroom. These Guides are intended to be used in conjunction with the current core *MCP Phonics* components, which include

- ❋ **Student Editions**
- ❋ **Teacher Resource Guides**
- ❋ **Letter Cards (Level A)**
- ❋ **Picture Cards**
- ❋ **Word Cards**
- ❋ **AstroWord multimedia program (17 modules on CD-ROM)**
- ❋ **Rhyme Posters**
- ❋ **Audio Cassettes**

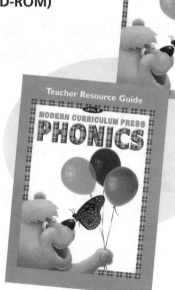

Throughout each two-page lesson tailored for ESL learners in the **MCP Phonics ESL Teacher Resource Guides**, two or more books are recommended in Book Corner activities and correlated to the phonics skill being taught. Selections are identified from the following Modern Curriculum Press series. If you do not have some of these books, substitute other phonics readers, appropriate to your children's level of English proficiency, that you may be using in class.

- ❋ **Ready Readers (Stages 0–5)**
- ❋ **Phonics Practice Readers**
- ❋ **Discovery Phonics**
- ❋ **Winners' Circle**

Organization of Unit Pages

The unit pages of the **MCP Phonics ESL Teacher Resource Guides** for Levels A and B provide activities and strategies for adapting the corresponding *MCP Phonics Student Edition* and *MCP Phonics Teacher Resource Guide* pages to maximize learning opportunities for your ESL learners. Suggestions are offered to modify assessment strategies to make them appropriate for childrens' level of English proficiency. Recommendations are made to allow ESL learners to participate in some activities that otherwise might be too language dense for understanding.

▶ **Assessment Strategy Overviews** identify the phonics skills taught in the unit and offer modification to assessment strategies that ESL learners may require to successfully apply the content.

▶ **Formal Assessment, Informal Assessment, Portfolio Assessment**, and **Student Progress Checklists** modify strategies recommended on the *MCP Phonics Teacher Resource Guide* unit pages. Adaptations are made to activities to honor the native languages of the ESL learners in your classroom. The program provides background into cultural or linguistic issues that may interfere with your children's acquisition of English. An additional recommendation is to provide more visual clues like the ones presented in the Student Edition books, so that ESL learners can concretely connect concepts and words to objects and activities. Suggestions for modifying classroom activities to be more sensitive to the language proficiency of children beginning a study of English are indicated, as appropriate.

▶ **Pretest and Posttest** suggestions recommend to classroom teachers a variety of proven ESL and language acquisition strategies for administering and evaluating both of these assessment tools. Used in conjunction with the *MCP Phonics Teacher Resource Guides*, the **Phonics ESL Teacher Resource Guides** provide practical advice and activity guidelines to allow ESL learners to focus on demonstrating proficiency with specific concepts in phonics.

▶ **Spelling Connections** pages offer a collection of ideas and opportunities to actively incorporate spelling into your phonics program. Many professionals in the field of second language acquisition caution against emphasizing spelling at the pre-production, early production, and speech emergent stages of language acquisition and encourage oral to print activities over traditional written spelling tests. However, you may have children enrolled in your classes who, while identified as ESL learners, have sufficient command of English (intermediate fluency) to be successful with spelling tests. By applying the methods recommended in the **Phonics ESL Teacher Resource Guides**, you can support their early efforts in spelling.

▶ **Phonics Games, Activities, and Technology** pages recommend strategies to allow your ESL learners to participate in dynamic, hands-on learning opportunities. Pre-activity practice, review of key concepts, small-group participation with other ESL learners at similar levels of English proficiency, and revisions to game rules and materials are all content-appropriate and logically sequenced.

Organization of Lesson Pages

As in the *MCP Phonics Teacher Resource Guides*, the **Phonics ESL Teacher Resource Guides** lesson plan follows an established sequence of instruction. Every lesson in the *MCP Phonics Teacher Resource Guides* is supported by a two-page alternate lesson plan designed to maximize instruction for ESL learners.

Lesson plans in the **Phonics ESL Teacher Resource Guides** consist of seven main sections, all offering culturally and linguistically appropriate hints, techniques, and activity modifications for you to use with your ESL learners.

The Informal Assessment Objectives identify the phonics skills taught in the lesson. In addition, language differences in Spanish, Tagalog, Hmong, Vietnamese, Khmer, and Russian are identified, giving teachers the opportunity to be on the lookout for specific differences that may impede pronunciation or may interfere with comprehension.

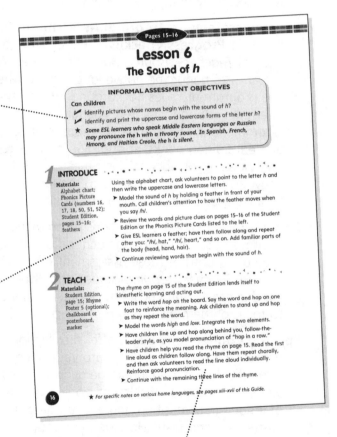

This section provides a twofold opportunity: for teachers to assess ESL learners' current level of language proficiency, allowing for individualized instruction and practice during the lesson and to present to the group the phonics skills to be taught. Rhymes, alphabet charts, Word Cards, Picture Cards, and Alphabet Cards are all beneficial tools for reinforcing English to ESL learners.

This section of the lesson plan provides alternate strategies to maximize instruction. ESL learners may be asked to use the Student Edition pages in a variety of classroom configurations to begin their instruction of the target concepts.

Practice opportunities provide controlled environments in which ESL learners can produce the phonics skill or concept that was introduced and modeled in previous sections. Teachers play a hands-on role, breaking down activities into more manageable tasks and ensuring that children are motivated to succeed.

ESL learners take newly learned skills and apply them as they complete *MCP Phonics Student Edition* pages. Modifications include alternate groupings, simplification of directions and activity tasks, and activities beyond those recommended in the *MCP Phonics Teacher Resource Guide*. Children are asked to complete directed tasks, review their work, and review with the class the key lesson points leading to comprehension and mastery.

3 PRACTICE

Materials:
Student Edition, page 15–16; safety mirrors from a science kit

Involve children in forming the correct sounds of English as they use small safety mirrors (from a science kit) to check their pronunciation.
➤ Write on the board the words from pages 15–16 that begin with the sound of *h*: hat, heart, hand, hill hot, horse, hose, hen, heel.
➤ Using the mirrors, call on children to form the picture name of each picture clue on these pages.
➤ Reinforce pronunciation and meaning by asking such questions as, "How many fingers are on your hand?"

4 APPLY

Materials:
Six familiar objects (or pictures) that model the sound of *h*, six objects (or pictures) that model a different initial consonant sound, two shoeboxes, two index cards, red marker, tape

This variation of the Sorting Sounds activity on page 3k of the *MCP Phonics Teacher Resource Guide* helps children identify and sort familiar objects beginning with the sound of *h*.
➤ Write *Hh* on one index card and a red circle with a slash through it (the international symbol for no) on the other. Tape one card to the front of each box.
➤ Display the objects/pictures, then have children name and sort them into the appropriate boxes.
➤ Verify that each item in the *Hh* box begins with the sound of *h*.

5 ASSESS

Materials:
Student Edition, page 16

Read aloud the direction line for the activity on page 16. Together, review the sound of *h*, and complete items 1–3. Have ESL learners of varying levels of proficiency work in pairs to complete items 4–12. Review the answers aloud to ensure comprehension.

MORE PHONICS PRACTICE
Set aside class time to read trade books with ESL learners. Preview these books and do a first reading to children.

HOW TO MAKE A HEN HOUSE by Bill Holly. Ready Readers, Stage 0 (Modern Curriculum Press, 1997)

UP THEY GO by Stanley Francis. Ready Readers, Stage 0 (Modern Curriculum Press, 1997)

AstroWord
Some children will benefit from additional individualized feedback, such as that provided by the CD-ROMs *AstroWord Consonant Letters and Sounds* and *Phonemic Awareness* (Modules 1 and 2). Encourage native speakers of English and ESL learners to work together to complete activities that interest them using the sound of *h*. Monitor each group's progress.

17

This section provides alternate testing opportunities to evaluate comprehension of the phonics objectives of the lessons. Some of the assessment recommendations are less rigorous than those of the core program; others eliminate potential distractions and complex activities that may lead to confusion.

Two or more recommendations for on-level phonics reading are offered from various MCP series. These, or others in your classroom, may be used to reinforce phonics concepts through choral and independent reading. A preview and first reading of the books to ESL learners is recommended before children read these titles independently.

Seventeen *AstroWord* CD-ROMs practice in-depth phonics skills. Specific modules are referenced at point of use. ESL learners are often paired with more English-proficient peers to use the computer to reinforce the target skills.

Using the MCP Phonics ESL Teacher Resource Guides

The **MCP Phonics ESL Teacher Resource Guides** for Levels A and B follow the same basic lesson structure as the *MCP Phonics Teacher Resource Guides* and offer teachers and students the same program strengths and familiar lesson designs.

▶ **Systematic** The format and design of the program is deliberately consistent, allowing children to become comfortable with recurrent activity types, directions, and strategies. Proven ESL strategies abound in the suggestions offered for modifying activities, providing or accessing background information, conducting lessons, and assessing ESL learners.

▶ **Explicit** Information for both teachers and children is presented in a clear, straightforward manner, using everyday language to present concepts and adapt phonics strategies for ESL learners. Teachers will appreciate the absence of jargon; instead, the focus on moving from simple to more complex activities and concepts and from known information to the unknown provide support for children newly acquiring English.

▶ **Flexible** Classroom configurations abound. This guide offers lesson formats, activities, and games that provide for whole-class instruction, small groups of ESL learners, partners of varying language proficiency, and individual activities for those children who are ready to try independent activities.

The goals of the *MCP Phonics* program are for children to learn to read with fluency and to write using the spelling conventions of English. An additional goal of the **MCP Phonics ESL Teacher Resource Guides** is to appreciate the cultural and linguistic heritage of the children in your classroom.

ESL learners at the pre-production stage of language acquisition may be most successful in native-language or formal English as a Second Language classrooms. This allows children to develop a solid foundation of skills in their native language, then transition those skills to a new language.

Children at the early production, speech emergence, or intermediate levels of language acquisition may be capable of mastering the content and language requirements of a primary-grade English phonics program. The characteristics of the stages of language acquisition described on the following page provide some guidance on what to look for in the development of language acquisition and the behaviors of ESL learners.

WHEN IS A PHONICS PROGRAM APPROPRIATE FOR ESL LEARNERS?

Language learners move through a series of predictable stages as they acquire a new language. Although the terminology and the number of stages vary among language professionals, most recognize four stages of language acquisition. These stages themselves are predictable, but individual language acquisition will vary as language learners develop.

FOUR STAGES OF LANGUAGE ACQUISITION

1 Pre-Production Stage

- ESL learners at the pre-production stage of language acquisition have an extremely limited command of English, although they understand more English than they can produce.
- Children at this stage often use gestures, yes or no answers, nod or shake their heads to communicate.
- ▶ **Instruction** at this level provides abundant opportunities for active listening, using props, visuals, and real objects to surround children with language.

2 Early Production Stage

- Children at this stage comprehend more spoken English, but they still are unable to respond fluently.
- Communication is beginning, but responses are likely to be of the short-answer variety and may be awkard in grammar and structure.
- ▶ **Instruction** typically targets getting children to understand English, rather than actively produce it by speaking or writing.

3 Speech Emergence Stage

- ESL learners at the speech emergence level can follow along for most classroom and daily routines, but they are limited by vocabulary and inconsistent grammatical structures.
- There's an emphasis on acquiring verbal fluency, although linking spoken language to written language through supported activities is common.
- ▶ **Instruction** targets exposing children to more complex vocabulary in the content areas and extending children's repertoire of spoken language.

4 Intermediate Fluency Stage

- Intermediate language learners are well on their way to achieving dual-language fluency.
- These ESL learners comprehend more, can respond more fluently using the conventions of English, and can make themselves understood in a variety of settings, social and academic.
- ▶ **Instruction** at this stage focuses on acquiring content-area or specialized vocabulary and mastering more complex English grammar structures.

Assessing Content Mastery with the MCP Phonics ESL Teacher Resource Guides

Assessment always is a complex issue for teachers of young children. It is made even more complex when learners have minimal command of English. This requires that testing opportunities, pacing, and groupings be modified so that children can demonstrate what they have learned without suffering interference from a native language and from misunderstanding directions.

The **MCP Phonics ESL Teacher Resource Guides** provide general strategies for modifying formal assessment tools, such as the unit Pretest and Posttest that appear at the beginning of each unit in the *MCP Phonics Teacher Resource Guides*. In addition, suggestions are offered to adapt Review pages, Unit Checkups, Take-Home Books, Portfolio collections, and end-of-lesson Assessment activities to provide the following.

☑ **Simplify directions.** If tasks are too language dense, break them down and eliminate the non-essential information or activities. Focus on assessing ESL learners' mastery of the specific phonics skills.

☑ **Test orally.** Many beginning ESL learners have insufficient language skills to successfully read directions, follow them, and write in a new language. Allow children to follow your lead. Read directions aloud, provide group practice with the first few items as examples, then work one-on-one with children to complete the task orally.

☑ **Test in multiple sittings.** Many ESL learners experience test anxiety because they feel that they cannot compete with more English-proficient peers. If so, allow ESL learners to take the tests separately from their classmates, possibly breaking up the tests into two or more sittings.

☑ **Use props to illustrate or cue key points.** Children may more easily recall specific information that used visuals and realia, or culturally authentic props, to prompt language.

☑ **Substitute tests.** Allow informal, oral assessments to substitute for written, independent evaluations. The end goals are the same—to record children's mastery of target skills and to remediate if performance does not reach a target level of proficiency.

☑ **Include, don't exclude.** Where possible, include ESL learners in your classroom activities, including assessment. Take care to alleviate anxiety and not add to an already heavy load by inadvertently excluding ESL learners from opportunities and activities for which they are ready, if done with some modification.

Focus on Various Languages

ESL STRATEGIES FOR THE ENGLISH-SPEAKING CLASSROOM

The following language acquisition strategies are recommended to assist elementary-school classroom teachers in presenting and teaching lessons from the *MCP Phonics* program to ESL learners.

- **Gestures** Limit unconscious, random hand movements in your presentations. For example, a hand gesture or symbol such as the "V" (peace sign) can be confusing to some ESL learners and, in some cultures, may have different linguistic or cultural connotations. But do use gestures to act out what you are trying to communicate.

- **Repetition and consistency** Applying the same activity and teaching formats throughout the program may appear repetitive to you. However, children at the pre-production and early production stages of language acquisition thrive on repetition to familiarize themselves with the rhythms of your classroom. When comprehension fails, language learners depend on familiarity with class routines and activity formats for contextual clues on how to proceed.

- **Visuals** Use pictures, objects, and realia, or real-world clues, to convey meaning whenever possible to name an object; to indicate color, size, shape, and so on. Pantomime or bring videos to class to familiarize your children with more conceptualized vocabulary such as verbs and adjectives.

- **High-frequency vocabulary** ESL learners acquire everyday words before specialized or content vocabulary. Bring in familiar household objects and use items in the classroom to model lesson content. Also, take advantage of other high-frequency vocabulary, such as sight words and proper names. For example if you live in Texas, incorporate the state's name into your presentation of Lesson 3 (Sound of *t*). Your classroom, school community, and the children themselves are good sources of daily vocabulary that use the target sounds.

- **Encouraging input** Support all responses and oral input offered by ESL learners as you proceed through the lessons and activities. Model native pronunciation naturally and indirectly by repeating the target word(s) in context several times after the speaker has finished, rather than interrupting with a direct correction as children talk. If additional pronunciation practice is needed, set aside small group time to reinforce this area.

- **Adapting conceptual activities** Activities and worksheets that require completion of more abstract tasks, such as word searches, crossword puzzles, mazes, and so on might be difficult for some ESL learners who are beginning to learn English words in a left-to-right writing pattern. These types of activities that contain words printed in vertical or diagonal patterns confuse the letter-order patterns children are trying to establish. You may wish to incorporate these kinds of activities after children appear to have mastered the concepts to reinforce word recognition, reading comprehension, or pronunciation practice.

- **Peer practice** Having ESL learners work in pairs with more English-proficient children who exhibit mastery of the content affords them one-on-one learning experiences as you work with other children. Have ESL learners cooperate on worksheet activities, read stories aloud in small groups, and complete activities on the various modules of *AstroWord* CD-ROM. Monitor pair work for participation of both children.

LINGUISTIC DIFFERENCES OF VARIOUS HOME LANGUAGES

The following pages identify specific linguistic issues that native speakers of Spanish, Russian, Korean, Tagalog, Hmong, Vietnamese, Cantonese, and Khmer may face as they begin to speak and write English. More linguistic issues are presented at point of use in the Informal Assessment Objectives box in most Unit Lessons.

Use each Introduce section of the lessons to informally determine what knowledge of the target sounds and concepts ESL learners bring to class. Increase or decrease the amount of introduction, relating to known content, direct practice, and independent practice to meet the needs of your children.

Note that a person's level of language proficiency changes, depending on the context, familiarity with similar patterns or concepts, and prior experiences. So, children who are successful with a particular lesson may perform less successfully with a different concept.

★ Native Speakers of Spanish

◼ **Written language** ESL learners who are proficient in writing Spanish as their native language may transfer the use of diacritical marks such as dieresis, accents, and tildes to written English to indicate syllabic stress or altered pronunciation. Give gentle reminders that English words do not use such written marks.

◼ **Spelling final consonants** The Spanish language lacks many final consonant sounds found in English (except final *n*, *s*, and *l*, which are present in many Spanish words). ESL learners might not pronounce them and may omit them in written language. Reinforce the sound of final consonants, blends, and digraphs throughout these lessons.

◼ **Sound to letter** Because Spanish and English use the same alphabet, some Spanish-speaking children will need additional practice associating a "new sound" to letters they already know. Areas of difficulty include distinguishing short from long vowel sounds in English (Spanish has one sound for each); pronouncing *h*, which is silent in Spanish; a fricative pronunciation of *v*, which is pronounced like *b* in Spanish.

◼ **Oral/aural contrasts** The following vowel, consonant, blend, and digraph sounds (in boldface) may pose problems for children whose home language is Spanish. Practice listening and speaking with repeated use of minimal pairs and target words in context such as b**ea**t, b**i**t; m**e**t, m**a**te; h**a**t, h**o**t, h**u**t; p**u**ll, p**oo**l, p**o**le; **b**ase, **v**ase; **wh**ale, **h**ail; **w**ail; **w**ent, **Gw**en; **th**ank, **t**ank; **thr**ee, **fr**ee; **th**ere, **d**are; **z**oom, **s**oon; **sh**ows, **ch**ose, Joe'**s**; **th**in, **th**ing, thi**nk**; **j**elly, **y**ellow.

★ Native Speakers of Russian

◼ **Roman alphabet** Children who speak Russian at home might be learning the Roman alphabet for the first time. Several English letters may be problematic, since they resemble characters from the Russian (Cyrillic) alphabet: *B*, *C*, and *P* stand for the sounds of *v*, *s*, and *r*, respectively, in Russian. Provide additional written practice, emphasizing correct letter choice, size discrimination between uppercase and lowercase forms (such as *S* and *s*), and correct "height" of lowercase forms such as *h* vs. *n*.

◼ **Grammar and syntax** In Russian, nouns decline (change form according to grammatical function, such as subject, object, and genitive). Articles (*the, a, an*) do not exist. Thus, ESL learners might say *I go to storah* instead of *I go to the store*. Listen for possible problems with these sounds and naturally reinforce correct pronunciation.

◻ **Oral/aural contrasts** The following vowel, consonant, blend, and digraph sounds (in boldface) may pose problems for children whose home language is Russian. Practice listening and speaking with repeated use of minimal pairs and target words in context, such as b**ea**t, b**i**t; m**a**t, m**e**t; **h**at, **h**ot, **h**ut; **wh**ale, **h**ail, **w**ail; **w**in, **r**ain; **th**ree, **f**ree; thi**n**, ri**m**, ri**ng**; **th**is, **z**ip; **th**ere, **d**are; **j**ar, **ch**ar.

★ Native Speakers of Korean

◻ **Roman alphabet** Children who speak Korean at home might be learning the Roman alphabet for the first time. Emphasize written as well as oral practice, focusing on size discrimination between uppercase and lowercase forms (such as *S* and *s*), the correct "height" of lowercase forms (for example, *h* vs. *n*), and the correct placement of descending characters below the bottom line (*g, j, p, q,* and *y*).

◻ **Spelling final consonants** The Korean language lacks the final consonant sounds found in English. ESL learners might not pronounce them or may omit them in written language. Reinforce the sound of final consonants, blends, and digraphs at every opportunity.

◻ **Writing English** Korean is traditionally written in vertical columns, from the top right corner of the page to the bottom left. ESL learners who have learned to write Korean may require additional practice to orient themselves to the English system of horizontal writing from left to right on the page.

◻ **Oral/aural contrasts** The following vowel, consonant, blend, and digraph sounds (in boldface) may pose problems for children whose home language is Korean. Practice listening and speaking with repeated use of minimal pairs and target words in context such as b**ea**t, b**i**t; m**a**t, m**e**t, m**a**te; h**a**t, h**o**t; **p**it, **b**it; **p**an, **f**an; **wh**ale, **h**ail, **w**ail; li**f**e, li**v**e; **z**oo, **d**o; **z**oom, **s**oon; la**ck**, ra**ck**; col**d**, gol**d**; **t**ank, **th**ank, **d**ank; **th**ree, **f**ree; **sh**ows, **ch**ose, Joe'**s**.

★ Native Speakers of Tagalog (also called Pilipino)

◻ **Spelling final consonants** The Tagalog language lacks most of the final consonant sounds found in English. ESL learners may not pronounce them or will possibly omit them in writing. Reinforce the sound of final consonants, blends, and digraphs at every opportunity.

◻ **Vocabulary and cognates** Because of the history of the Philippines, many cognates and words have transferred between Chinese, Spanish, and English. Thus, speakers of Tagalog may comprehend meaning easily but will require additional practice with correct pronunciation of English loan words and cognates.

◻ **Oral/aural contrasts** The following vowel, consonant, blend, and digraph sounds (in boldface) may pose problems for children whose home language is Tagalog. Practice listening and speaking with repeated use of minimal pairs and target words in context such as b**ea**t, b**i**t, b**e**t; h**a**t, h**o**t, h**u**t; **p**an, **f**an; p**u**ll, p**oo**l, p**o**le; **wh**ale, **w**ail; li**f**e, li**v**e; **b**and, **v**an; **th**ough, **d**oe; **z**oom, **s**oon; **d**ate, **r**ate; **t**ank, **th**ank; **th**ree, **f**ree; **sh**ows, **ch**ose, Joe'**s**.

★ Native Speakers of Hmong

◻ **Roman alphabet** Children who speak Hmong at home might be learning the Roman alphabet for the first time. Emphasize written as well as oral practice, focusing on size discrimination between uppercase and lowercase forms (such as *S* and *s*), correct "height" of lowercase forms (for example, *h* vs. *n*), and the correct placement of descending characters below the bottom line (*g, j, p, q,* and *y*).

◻ **Intonation and syntax** Hmong is a tonal language in which changes in tone alter the meaning of individual words or phrases, and syntax is almost wholly determined by word (syllabic) order. Hmong is also a monosyllabic language. Thus each unit (word) consists of only one syllable. Native speakers of Hmong may therefore experience initial difficulty with the concept of inflectional endings (*-ed, -ing*), prefixes and suffixes, compound words, or the use of intonation to differentiate questions from statements. Provide frequent classroom opportunities to practice the target sounds.

◻ **Cultural literacy** Since Hmong was an oral language with no writing system until the second half of the 20th Century, your classroom may provide the first experience children from this culture have with reading and writing any language. While some Hmong speakers may have limited experience writing or reading their native language, this can be a plus for young ESL learners: They likely will have less difficulty adapting from one system of writing and spelling system to another.

◻ **Oral/aural contrasts** The following vowel, consonant, blend, and digraph sounds (in boldface) may pose problems for ESL learners whose home language is Hmong. Practice listening and speaking with repeated use of minimal pairs and target words in context such as b**ea**t, b**i**t; m**a**t, m**e**t, m**a**t**e**; h**a**t, h**o**t; **p**it, **b**it; **p**an, **f**an; **wh**ale, **h**ail, **w**ail; life, li**v**e; **z**oo, **d**o; **z**oom, **s**oon; lack, rack; **c**old, **g**old; **t**ank, **th**ank, **d**ank; **three**, **fr**ee; **s**uit, **sh**oe; **sh**ows, **ch**ose, Joe'**s**.

★ Native Speakers of Vietnamese

◻ **Written language** ESL learners who are proficient in writing Vietnamese may transfer diacritical marks, such as diereses, accents, circumflexes, and tildes to written English to indicate syllabic stress or changes in pronunciation. Give children who experience recurring difficulties gentle reminders that English does not use such written marks.

◻ **Intonation and syntax** Vietnamese is a tonal language in which changes in tone alter the meaning of individual words or phrases, and syntax is almost wholly determined by word (syllabic) order. It is also a monosyllabic language, thus each unit (word) consists of only one syllable. Native speakers of Vietnamese may therefore have trouble with the concept of inflectional endings (*-ed, -ing*), prefixes and suffixes, compound words, or the use of intonation to differentiate questions from statements.

◻ **Oral/aural contrasts** The following vowel, consonant, blend, and digraph sounds (in boldface) may pose problems for children whose home language is Vietnamese. Practice listening and speaking with repeated use of minimal pairs and target words in context such as b**ea**t, b**i**t, b**e**t; m**a**t, m**e**t, m**a**t**e**; h**a**t, h**o**t, h**u**t; c**ou**ld, c**oo**l, c**o**ld, c**u**ll; **p**it, **b**it; **p**an, **f**an; **wh**ale, **w**ail; life, li**v**e; **f**ine, **s**ign, **sh**ine; **t**ank, **th**ank, **d**ank; lack, rack; **c**old, **g**old; **r**ain, **r**ail; **z**oom, **s**oon; **sh**ows, **ch**ose, Joe'**s**; ra**g**, ra**ng**.

★ Native Speakers of Cantonese

◘ **Roman alphabet** Children who speak Cantonese at home might be learning the Roman alphabet for the first time. Emphasize written as well as oral practice, focusing on size discrimination between uppercase and lowercase forms (such as *S* and *s*), correct "height" of lowercase forms (for example, *h* vs. *n*), and the correct placement of descending characters below the bottom line (*g, j, p, q,* and *y*).

◘ **Spelling final consonants** The Cantonese language lacks many final consonant sounds found in English (except final *n* and *ng*). ESL learners might not pronounce them or may omit them in written language. Reinforce the sound of final consonants, blends, and digraphs as you pronounce words to your class.

◘ **Intonation and syntax** Cantonese is a tonal language in which changes in tone alter the meaning of individual words or phrases. It is also a monosyllabic language, thus each unit (word) consists of only one syllable. Children who speak Cantonese may therefore have trouble with the concept of inflectional endings (*-ed, -ing*), prefixes and suffixes, compound words, or the use of intonation to differentiate questions from statements.

◘ **Oral/aural contrasts** The following vowel, consonant, blend, and digraph sounds (in boldface) may pose problems for children whose home language is Cantonese. Practice listening and speaking with repeated use of minimal pairs and target words in context such as b**ea**t, b**i**t, b**e**t; m**a**t, m**e**t, m**a**te; h**a**t, h**o**t, h**u**t; c**ou**ld, c**oo**l, c**o**ld, c**u**ll; **p**it, **b**it; **p**an, **f**an; **wh**ale, **w**ail; li**f**e, li**v**e; **f**ine, **s**ign, **sh**ine; **t**ank, **th**ank, **d**ank; la**ck**, ra**ck**; **c**old, **g**old; rai**n**, rai**l**; **z**oom, **s**oon; **sh**ows, **ch**ose, Joe'**s**; ra**g**, ra**ng**.

★ Native Speakers of Khmer (also known as Cambodian)

◘ **Roman alphabet** Children who speak Khmer at home may be learning the Roman alphabet for the first time. Emphasize written as well as oral practice, focusing on size discrimination between uppercase and lowercase forms (such as *S* and *s*), correct "height" of lowercase forms (for example, *h* vs. *n*), and the correct placement of descending characters below the bottom line (*g, j, p, q,* and *y*).

◘ **Spelling final consonants** Khmer lacks most final consonant sounds found in English. ESL learners might not pronounce them or they may omit them when writing in English. Reinforce the sound of final consonants, blends, and digraphs as you model pronunciation to your ESL learners.

◘ **Oral/aural contrasts** The following vowel, consonant, blend, and digraph sounds (in boldface) may pose problems for children whose home language is Khmer. Practice listening and speaking with repeated use of minimal pairs and target words in context such as b**ea**t, b**i**t; m**a**t, m**e**t, m**a**te; h**a**t, h**o**t, h**u**t; f**igh**t, f**a**t; **p**it, **b**it; **p**an, **f**an; **wh**ale, **h**ail, **w**ail; li**f**e, li**v**e; **z**oo, **d**o; **z**oom, **s**oon; la**ck**, ra**ck**; **c**old, **g**old; **t**ank, **th**ank, **d**ank; **th**ree, **f**ree; **s**uit, **sh**oe; **sh**ows, **ch**ose, Joe'**s**.

Suggestions for Communicating with Parents of ESL Learners

Motivation is key to learning a foreign language. To maximize your ESL learners' opportunities to acquire English, it is important to develop a knowledge and understanding of the culture and heritage of the children in your classroom. Likewise, conveying this understanding to the parents of your young learners transfers interest to the home. Following are strategies for enlisting your ESL family members' support for learning English.

▶ **Visit the home.** Many cultures shy away from direct contact, in deference to teachers' respect and authority. Make the first contact. Show appreciation and respect for your ESL learners' cultures, customs, and convey to family members your interest in helping their children succeed in your class.

▶ **Acknowledge that acquiring English may be difficult for adult family members.** Many families of ESL learners have less fluency in English than do your children. Use gestures, a soft tone of voice, and interpreters to convey your genuine interest and support.

▶ **Identify a support group at home.** If parents do not speak or read English, try to identify a family friend, extended family member, or neighbor who speaks sufficient English to mentor your ESL learners. These individuals can model and support out-of-class assignments, help with reading practice, and engage your children in producing English naturally for personal communication.

▶ **Enlist the community.** Community leaders who speak the home language of your ESL learners may offer resources and support.

▶ **Invite family into your class.** Encourage family members to visit your class and observe or work with their children. Ask them to provide models of clothing, foods, culture, and customs for you and all your class to share.

▶ **Present language naturally.** In a "natural" approach to language acquisition, drills and practice are secondary to using language to communicate personal messages. As with many skills, people "learn by doing." Allow your ESL learners, in and out of class, to use English as best they can, without formal interruptions to correct errors. Repetition of the desired pronunciation of a word, clarification of a statement, and gestures all convey meaning and present oral correction.

▶ **Practice "parent-eze."** When using language with their own children, many parents unconsciously adopt a language pattern known as "parent-eze." Parents intuitively add meaning to short utterances and phrases and often respond with more complete repetition and elaboration. For example, if a child points to a blue ball and says, "Blue", a parent may respond, "Yes, that is a ball. It is round. What color is the ball? Do you want to play with it now?" Listening to a language spoken by native speakers in natural contexts is one of the best ways to acquire pronunciation, speed, and fluency—in any language.

Assessment Strategy Overview

Throughout Unit 1, you have opportunities to assess English as a Second Language (ESL) learners' ability to identify and write consonants that represent beginning and ending sounds. Some of your ESL learners may require additional assessment strategies to meet their special language needs.

FORMAL ASSESSMENT

Before you start Unit 1, administer the Unit 1 Pretest, on pages 3e–3f of *MCP Phonics Teacher Resource Guide*. Children's scores will help you assess their knowledge base before beginning the unit and alert you to areas for further support. Complete the Student Progress Checklist on page 3i. Note which consonants children are struggling with and whether confusion is with beginning or ending sounds.

◆ Some children may understand a concept but have difficulty with directions. Read the directions aloud and model how to complete the worksheets.

◆ Before administering the Pretest, gather in a paper bag items that match the visuals on pages 3e–3f. Have volunteers select an item, then name it. Ask other children to tell you what sound the beginning letter of that word name makes.

INFORMAL ASSESSMENT

Review pages, Unit Checkups, and Take-Home Books are effective ways to evaluate children's progress. Following are other suggestions for ways to assess children's understanding of the concepts.

◆ Gather realia or pictures of objects that reflect children's areas of difficulty. Allow them to select a visual and name it. Have children match each item to its counterpart letter on an alphabet chart.

◆ Bring to class props that use the target sounds. Use them to create make-believe scenarios in which small groups have a context in which to produce the target sounds. Record responses as an informal assessment grade.

PORTFOLIO ASSESSMENT

Portfolio

Portfolio Assessment opportunities are identified by the logo shown here. In addition to collecting the pages mentioned on page 3c, gather other examples of children's work for comparison and evaluation at critical periods in the unit, as indicated below.

◆ **Initial practice** Add to children's portfolios completed Student Edition page 5, in which they shaded partner letters *s, t, b, h, m,* and *k*. This will allow you to evaluate their initial level of comprehension.

◆ **Midunit classwork** On a sheet of paper, make a copy for each child of the chalkboard chart from the *Teach* activity on page 22 of this Guide. Review the activity, this time noting performance.

◆ **Final products or projects** Encourage children to select their favorite book(s) from the unit and summarize it in their own words. Have them draw a picture of the story and write the words that begin (or end) with the target letters.

STUDENT PROGRESS CHECKLIST

Photocopy and attach the checklist on page 3i of *MCP Phonics Teacher Resource Guide* to each child's portfolio. Evaluate growth and areas of weakness from your assessment tools. Then use the strategies and activities suggested in this Guide to build a strong phonics foundation for your ESL learners.

Administering and Evaluating the
Pretest and Posttest

➤ Read the information on page 3d of *MCP Phonics Teacher Resource Guide*. Answers for the Pretest and Posttest are provided on page 3d.
➤ Record test results on the Student Progress Checklist on page 3i after children complete the Pretest.
➤ Record results again after children take the Posttest.
➤ Compare the results of the two tests.
➤ Use the Performance Assessment Profile at the bottom of page 3d to help you draw conclusions about children's performance. Opportunities to reteach each specific skill in the unit are identified by page number.

TEST OBJECTIVES

Note that the objective of both the Unit 1 Pretest and Posttest of *MCP Phonics Teacher Resource Guide* is sound identification, not vocabulary recognition, with which children may be unfamiliar. To ensure that vocabulary comprehension does not interfere with sound recognition, say each of the items aloud as children move from item to item in the tests.

UNIT 1 PRETEST, pages 3e–3f

Page 3e of *MCP Phonics Teacher Resource Guide* focuses on visual identification of picture clues and the consonants that represent the beginning sound of those picture names. Note that some children may be able to discriminate the sound of the consonant but might not recognize the picture. Some may recognize the picture but may be unable to name it in English. You may wish to support these beginning language learners by implementing any of the following suggestions prior to administering the Pretest to ESL learners.

♦ **Practice test-taking skills.** Test-taking skills such as filling in bubbles may be new to some children. Ask a child peer-mentor, teacher aide, or faculty co-worker to work one-on-one to relieve test anxiety.

♦ **Provide models.** Read the direction line aloud. Model how to mark the correct response. On the chalkboard, using an overhead projector, or on a sheet of paper at a child's desk, provide one or more practice opportunities to model test-taking procedures.

♦ **Use props.** Provide a variety of additional visuals, such as photographs, to ensure children recognize—and can name—the picture clues. Allow children to complete the pages. Many of these activities are dependent upon children's comprehension of key terms prior to their ability to discrim-inate the initial consonant sounds.

♦ **Confirm Comprehension.** Before the test, ensure that children recognize the words in spoken English and do not respond in their native language. For example, item 5 is a bug, but some native speakers of Spanish may immediately think of *bicho* which, while correct, would indicate native language interference.

♦ **Assign partners.** In pairs, have the more proficient reader read the picture names aloud. This moves the focus to correctly identifying the initial consonant sound. Ask the reader to speak slowly, clearly, and model realistic pronunciation.

Page 3f focuses on recognizing the beginning or ending consonant sound of the 12 picture clues shown. In addition to the suggestions provided for adapting page 3e for English Language Learners, you may wish to incorporate these strategies.

♦ **Simplify tasks.** If this activity is too complex for certain children, break down the tasks into individual steps. Create a rebus to illustrate each task in the proper sequence. Next, ask children to identify the picture in each exercise and pronounce its name. Have children focus on the letter in the box and repeat it. Then have children determine if the word begins or ends with that sound and print it on the appropriate line.

♦ **Seek alternatives.** Children who are uncomfortable speaking in English can complete the activity by having you or a partner identify and pronounce the word clearly and slowly. This eliminates having to identify the picture name correctly as well as speaking in English—a situation that may be difficult for them.

The Unit 1 Posttest of Level A, *MCP Phonics Teacher Resource Guide* again requires children to correctly name picture clues in English and identify beginning consonant sounds on page 3g or beginning and ending consonant sounds on page 3h. If some ESL learners continue to demonstrate significant anxiety over assessment opportunities, you may wish to use any of the strategies suggested for taking the Pretest, or you may wish to work one-on-one or with small groups to give the test.

You also may wish to follow these suggestions for ESL learners as they complete pages 3g–3h:

♦ **Confirm children understand directions.** Read aloud the directions for each page and confirm whether children know how to proceed with the pages. If not, refer to the strategies suggested for taking the Pretest.

♦ **Emphasize important directions.** Point out that the arrow at the bottom right corner of the page indicates that children are to continue to the next page.

♦ **Model test-taking skills.** Model correct answer-marking procedures on the chalkboard or one-on-one with children. Pantomime desired outcomes through gestures and by marking answers together on sample sheets.

Unit 1
Phonics Games, Activities, and Technology

Pages 3j–3m of *MCP Phonics Teacher Resource Guide* provide a collection of ideas and opportunities to actively engage children as they develop or reinforce phonics strategies. Many of the activities provided on these pages can be implemented with little or no modification for children whose native language is not English. However, be alert to pictures that are unfamiliar in context or in their names. Multistep directions may also be difficult for some ESL learners to understand or follow.

To ensure comprehension of activity directions and allow time to think, speak in simple, complete sentences and at a slow, but not exaggerated, pace. Incorporating visuals and props (realia), audiotapes, and CDs provides additional contexts and clues for new learners of English. For activities that require written response, determine whether children have sufficient command of written print to complete the activity. Be aware that some children might write in cursive letters.

- ● **Pick a Match** (page 3j) requires that children understand the English alphabet and recognize capital and lowercase letters. Have children practice using the letter cards before they begin to play.

- ▲ **Consonant Concentration** and **Pile Up** (page 3j) can be simplified by reducing the number of letter cards or objects used to play the games. When children become more familiar with the game, increase the number of items to be identified.

- ◆ **Mystery Sound Boxes** (page 3j) increase children's sound-letter discrimination when you provide more, not fewer, items in each box.

- ■ **Quick Draw** (page 3j) is easily modified if you supply notecards with both the uppercase and lowercase letters already printed on them and a corresponding alphabet chart for visual reference. Children can discriminate between uppercase and lowercase letters without the pressure of writing them.

- ● **Beginning, Middle, or End?** and **Wonder Wheel** (page 3k) can be simplified for ESL learners by allowing them to observe or work with a partner until comfort level increases. Encourage children to "jump in" at any time they are comfortable doing so.

- ▲ **Target Toss** (page 3k) can be played in teams rather than individually. To adapt this activity, allow the team the opportunity to brainstorm their responses, then allow one child to respond on the group's behalf.

◆ **Slide It Down** and **Sorting Sounds** (page 3k) and **Consonant Catch** (page 3l) rely on natural pronunciation. Be sure to say each word clearly and distinctly, but be aware of overexaggeration or a heavy regional accent, which can distort the sound of a letter or word.

■ **Move Along** (page 3l), **Go for Three**, and **Listen for Sounds** (page 3m) are individual activities that can be modified by dividing the class into teams of three or more children. This allows children to participate when they can as well as eliminates peer pressure focusing on one person.

● **First or Last** (page 3l) relies on comprehension of the words *first* and *last*. If children have difficulty understanding the meaning of these words in the chart, use the numerals 1 and 2 to show sequence.

▲ **Who Is It?** and **My Favorite Letter** (page 3l) assume your children know, can pronounce, and can spell their classmates' names. Boost self-concept by asking children to decorate their own name tags and attach them to their desks with clear tape before you conduct these activities.

◆ **Secret Consonant** (page 3l) and **Consonant Caterpillars** (page 3m) can be simplified by posting a few letter cards or clues in special places in your classroom. Tell children that the secret consonant or special objects begin (or end) with one of these letters.

Technology

Use children's interest in technology to their advantage in learning English. If possible, allow English Language Learners to work in small groups at the computer before or after class or during center time, using the specific *AstroWord* Modules suggested in each lesson. Preview skill levels and supervise the groups directly to eliminate frustration and to target specific phonics development. You may wish to add your observations to the Student Progress Checklist, found on page 3i, Level A, *MCP Phonics Teacher Resource Guide*, as well as use the software suggested on page 3m to provide additional phonics practice for ESL learners.

Lesson 1
Partner Letters Ss, Tt, Bb, Hh, Mm, Kk

INFORMAL ASSESSMENT OBJECTIVE

Can children

✔ identify by name the uppercase and lowercase forms of the letters *s, t, b, h, m,* and *k*?

★ *Some ESL learners may be learning the Roman alphabet for the first time, so discriminate form from size between uppercase and lowercase letters.*

1 INTRODUCE

Materials:
Alphabet chart;
Student Edition,
page 5

Find out if children are familiar with the Roman alphabet in general and the six target partner letters, specifically.

➤ Using an alphabet chart, verify whether children can point to the uppercase and lowercase forms of the target letters presented on page 5 of the Student Edition as you say them aloud.

➤ Ask children to repeat each letter after you, several times if necessary. Offer a lot of encouragement and positive reinforcement for correct responses.

2 TEACH

Materials:
Pick a Match
activity, *MCP
Phonics Teacher
Resource Guide,*
page 3j; 12 sheets
of construction
paper, marker

This activity is a variation of the Pick a Match activity.

➤ Write the uppercase and lowercase forms of *s, t, b, h, m,* and *k* on the sheets of construction paper, one letter form per sheet.

➤ Randomly distribute the papers to 12 children and ask them to stand in the front of the class.

➤ Ask an English Language Learner to name the letter held by the first child. Then ask, "Who is [child's] partner?" The volunteer must pair the child holding the uppercase *B* with the child who has the lowercase *b*.

➤ Call on another volunteer to pair letter forms. Continue until all children have been paired up correctly.

➤ Redistribute the papers and repeat the activity.

★ *For specific notes on various home languages, see pages xiii–xvii of this Guide.*

3 PRACTICE

Materials:
Letter Cards *Ss, Tt, Bb, Hh, Mm, Kk*; Student Edition, page 5; crayons

Complete the activity on Student Edition page 5 in a more structured format with English Language Learners.

➤ Draw the eight balls on the chalkboard exactly as they appear on page 5.

➤ Model the first one by holding up a Letter Card.

➤ Have children shade the appropriate ball on the board.

➤ Repeat this process with the remaining five cards.

4 APPLY

Materials:
12 sheets of tagboard, 12 index cards, marker, tape

Continue recognition of the uppercase and lowercase forms of the target letters by playing a variation of Twister.

➤ Write the uppercase and lowercase forms of *s, t, b, h, m,* and *k* on each of 12 sheets of tagboard and 12 index cards.

➤ Tape the sheets of tagboard to the floor in a 3-x-4 grid.

➤ Select and read a card, asking a child to place his or her right hand (or foot, and so on) on the corresponding block on the letterboard. Continue for all letters.

➤ Work with individual ESL learners who have difficulty making the partner connections.

5 ASSESS

Materials:
Blackline Master 6, page 3n; card stock; Student Edition, page 6

Begin to assess each child's progress in this lesson by making letter cards. Sort the uppercase from the lowercase cards. Place the uppercase letters face up in a grid and the others face down. Have a child turn over a lowercase card, name it aloud, then match it with its uppercase partner. Repeat with all cards.

Book Corner

MORE PHONICS PRACTICE

Set aside class time to read trade books with ESL learners. Preview these books and do a first reading to children.

SCHOOL LUNCH by Polly Peterson. Ready Readers, Stage 0 (Modern Curriculum Press, 1997)

ZELDA'S ZIPPER by Cass Hollander. Discovery Phonics (Modern Curriculum Press, 1994)

Technology

AstroWord
Some children will benefit from additional individualized feedback, such as that provided by the CD-ROMs *AstroWord Consonant Letters and Sounds* and *Phonemic Awareness* (Modules 1 and 2). Encourage groups of children to work together to explore the activities. Model how to manipulate the computer mouse. Then assist children in maneuvering through the *AstroWord* program for the first time.

Lesson 2
The Sound of s

INFORMAL ASSESSMENT OBJECTIVES

Can children

✔ identify pictures whose names begin with the sound of *s*?

✔ identify and print the uppercase and lowercase forms of the letter *s*?

★ *Native speakers of Spanish may introduce an* e *sound when pronouncing English words that begin with* s *blends, like* snow, student; *provide oral practice with English words if this is an issue.*

1 INTRODUCE

Materials:
Alphabet chart;
Rhyme Poster 2;
Phonics Picture
Cards (numbers 33,
34, 35, 60, 67);
Student Edition,
pages 7–8

Using an alphabet chart, verify whether ESL learners can identify the uppercase and lowercase forms of the letter *s*.

➤ Model the sound of *s* by reviewing the appropriate words on pages 7–8 of the Student Edition and/or those found on the Phonics Picture Cards listed on the left.

➤ Ask volunteers whose first or last names begin with *s* to write their names on the chalkboard. Point out *Suzy* as an example in the rhyme on page 7 and model the sound.

➤ Continue reviewing words that begin with the sound of *s*, encouraging children to respond individually as their mastery and confidence build.

2 TEACH

Materials:
Pictures of
household objects
or realia that model
the sound of *s*, two
or three other
"non-*s*" objects,
crayons and paper
for each child,
chart paper, paper
bag

Build everyday vocabulary with "*S* around the house."

➤ On the chalkboard or on chart paper, draw an outline of a house large enough to contain several words. Have children each draw a house on their papers.

➤ Put objects (or pictures) inside a paper bag and invite volunteers, one at a time, to reach inside the bag without looking. Encourage each volunteer to say what object is.

➤ Ask, "Does [*object*] begin with the sound of *s*?" If it does, model writing the word inside your *s* house and have children add the word(s) to their drawings. You may wish to draw a quick sketch next to each word to assist ESL learners to learn new vocabulary.

➤ After writing four or five *s* words, review them chorally with the class.

★ *For specific notes on various home languages, see pages xiii–xvii of this Guide.*

3 PRACTICE · · * · · · · · · · · * · · · · · · * · · · · · · · · · ·

Materials:
Student Edition,
page 7; Rhyme
Poster 2 (optional);
index cards

Continue practicing the sound of *s* with the rhyme on page 7.

➤ Write *sand*, *sun*, and *sea* on index cards (one word per card, one card per child) and on the chalkboard.

➤ Have children stand up as you read the rhyme aloud and point to the target word. Children sit down when they hear you say their word.

➤ Collect the index cards, redistribute them. Tell children that this time they will stand up when they hear you say their new word.

4 APPLY · · * · · · · · · · · · * · · · · · · * · · · · · · · · · * · · · · · ·

Materials:
Consonant
Caterpillars activity,
*MCP Phonics Teacher
Resource Guide*, page
3m; two squares of
white construction
paper shaped like
sandwich bread and
three circles of
colored construction
paper per child,
crayons, old
magazines, scissors,
glue

"*S* Sandwich" is a variation of Consonant Caterpillars on page 3m. Bring a sandwich to class to explain what it is.

➤ Hand out two squares of white paper to each child in the group; this is the "bread" of the sandwich. Assist those children who need support to write *S sandwich* on the top "slice."

➤ Distribute three additional sheets of paper to each child. Have children draw or clip pictures of items that begin with the sound of *s* and paste one on each piece of paper. Help children write the name of the object below each picture.

➤ Assemble each sandwich by stacking the bread and "fixings" in order and clipping them together.

➤ Pair children to take apart and read their sandwiches to each other.

5 ASSESS · · * · · · · · · · · · * · · · · · · * · · · · · · · · · * · · · · ·

Materials:
Student Edition,
page 8

Read the direction line for the activity on page 8 of the Student Edition. Complete items 1–3 aloud together. Ask children to work in pairs to complete items 4–12. Review answers.

Book Corner

MORE PHONICS PRACTICE

Set aside class time to read trade books with ESL learners. Preview these books and do a first reading to children.

A PICNIC IN THE SAND by Maryann Dobeck. Ready Readers, Stage 0 (Modern Curriculum Press, 1996)

PACO'S POCKETS by Barbara Reeves. Beginning Discovery Phonics (Modern Curriculum Press, 1994)

Technology

AstroWord
Some children will benefit from additional individualized feedback, such as that provided by the CD-ROMs *AstroWord Consonant Letters and Sounds* and *Phonemic Awareness* (Modules 1 and 2). Encourage groups of children (native speakers of English and ESL learners) to work together to complete activities that interest them using the sound of *s*. Monitor the groups' progress.

Lesson 3
The Sound of *t*

INFORMAL ASSESSMENT OBJECTIVES

Can children

✔ identify pictures whose names begin with the sound of *t*?

✔ identify and print the uppercase and lowercase forms of the letter *t*?

★ *Children who speak Spanish, French, Russian, or Haitian Creole may pronounce the* t *softly. Tapping your tongue against your teeth offers an accurate aproximation of the sound.*

---

1 INTRODUCE

Materials:
Alphabet chart; Phonics Picture Cards (numbers 36, 37, 68, 75); Student Edition, pages 9–10

Using an alphabet chart, have children identify the uppercase and lowercase forms of the letter *t* and write them on the chalkboard.

➤ Model the sound of *t* by reviewing the words and picture cues on pages 9–10 and/or those found on the Phonics Picture Cards listed to the left.

➤ Ask volunteers whose names begin with *t* to write their names on the chalkboard. Point out *Teddy* as an example in the rhyme on page 9 and model the sound.

➤ Continue reviewing words that begin with the sound of *t*, encouraging children to respond individually.

2 TEACH

Materials:
Four or five pictures of objects or realia that make the sound of *t*, three or four "non-*t*" objects, two large index cards per child, markers

In this activity, children vote on whether each object begins with the sound of *t*.

➤ Complete and review the worksheet on page 9.

➤ Hand out two index cards to each child. Instruct children to write uppercase and lowercase *t* on one of the cards; model writing *Tt* on the board. Write the word *no* on the board and tell them to write *no* on the other card. Prepare a set of cards for your use in modeling the activity.

➤ Hold up a picture or an object. Ask, "Does the name of this object begin with the sound of *t*?"

➤ Instruct children to hold up their *Tt* card if the picture clue begins with the sound of *t* or the *no* card if it does not.

➤ Once all children "vote," have a volunteer name the object aloud. Ask, "Does [word] begin with the sound of *t*?" Hold up the correct card to verify children's answers. Repeat the procedure.

★ *For specific notes on various home languages, see pages xiii–xvii of this Guide.*

3 PRACTICE

Materials:
Student Edition, page 9; Rhyme Poster 3; teddy bear (optional)

Continue practicing the sound of *t* with the rhyme on page 9.

➤ Write the word *tap* on the board. Say the word and act it out by tapping on the board as children tap on their desks with their fingers. Repeat the procedure with *nose* and *toes*.

➤ Read the rhyme aloud. Have volunteers use a teddy bear to point to target words while you read.

➤ Have children act out the rhyme as they say it. You may wish to have ESL learners tap other body parts and include them in the rhyme in order to increase vocabulary.

4 APPLY

Materials:
Five pictures of everyday objects or realia that model the sound of *t*, five other "non-*t*" objects, ten paper lunch bags, colored markers, pencil and paper, chart paper

The Mystery *T* Bag activity is an adaptation of the Mystery Sound Boxes activity on page 3j of the *MCP Phonics Teacher Resource Guide*.

➤ Number lunch bags from 1 to 10 using colored markers. Place one picture or object inside each bag and close. Place the bags at different stations around the room.

➤ Ask a group of children to go to Mystery Bag 1. Instruct them to open the bag. Then ask, "What is inside the bag?" One child removes the picture or object and names it.

➤ Create a list on the chart paper of the objects that begin with *t* for children to review and copy.

5 ASSESS

Materials:
Student Edition, page 10.

Read aloud the direction line for the activity on page 10. Verify that children understand what they are to do by completing items 1–3 together. Have your ESL learners work in pairs to complete items 4–12. Review the answers aloud to ensure comprehension.

MORE PHONICS PRACTICE

Set aside class time to read trade books with ESL learners. Preview these books and do a first reading to children.

TWO TURTLES by Carly Easton. Ready Readers, Stage 0 (Modern Curriculum Press, 1997)

COUNT TO TEN by Amy Anderson. Winners' Circle (Modern Curriculum Press, 1995)

AstroWord

Some children will benefit from additional individualized feedback, such as that provided by the CD-ROMs *AstroWord Consonant Letters and Sounds* and *Phonemic Awareness* (Modules 1 and 2). Encourage native speakers of English and ESL learners to work together to complete activities that interest them using the sound of *t*. Monitor each group's progress.

Lesson 4
The Sound of *b*

INFORMAL ASSESSMENT OBJECTIVES

Can children

✔ identify pictures whose names begin with the sound of *b*?

✔ identify and print the uppercase and lowercase forms of the letter *b*?

★ *Some ESL learners may have trouble with initial /b/ and /p/ or /d/. Model the different pronunciation of the sounds with* bay, pay, *and* day; big, pig, *and* dig; *and so on.*

1 INTRODUCE

Materials:
Alphabet chart; Phonics Picture Cards (numbers 1, 2, 3, 47, 61, 62, 76); Student Edition, pages 11–12

Using an alphabet chart, verify whether ESL learners can identify the uppercase and lowercase forms of the letter *b*. Ask volunteers to point to the letter *b* and to write it on the chalkboard.

➤ Model the sound of *b* by reviewing the appropriate words and picture clues on pages 11–12 of the Student Edition and/or those found on the Phonics Picture Cards listed to the left.

➤ Continue reviewing words that begin with the sound of *b*, modeling how to position the lips when pronouncing *b*. Encourage children to respond individually. Ask children to supply other words with initial *b* sound as their mastery and confidence build.

2 TEACH

Materials:
Shopping bag or grocery bag, shoebox, basket, rubber ball, bell, large index cards

Teach the sound of *b* using the familiar objects listed to the left and others that your ESL learners know.

➤ Write the name of each object you will be using in the activity on the top few lines of an index card, one word per card. Leave enough space for children to write the same word below.

➤ Display the items, with the corresponding index card face down next to each item.

➤ As each child correctly identifies an object, have him or her take the card and write the word below the printed model. Encourage the child to draw a picture of the object on the card.

➤ After all of the objects have been identified, collect the cards.

★ *For specific notes on various home languages, see pages xiii–xvii of this Guide.*

3 PRACTICE

Materials:
Student Edition, page 11; Rhyme Poster 4 (optional)

Use the repetitive rhyme on page 11 to practice *b* and *high, low, fast,* and *slow.*

➤ Write the words *bounce* and *ball* on the chalkboard.

➤ Demonstrate and verbalize an action, such as "I can (like to, want to) bounce the ball." Ask, "Can you (Do you want to) bounce the ball?" Encourage responses.

➤ Add the words *high, low, fast,* and *slow* to the board. Model meaning through words and actions.

➤ Read Rhyme Poster 4 aloud several times as you point to each word. Ask confident volunteers to read the lines.

4 APPLY

Materials:
Consonant Concentration activity, *MCP Phonics Teacher Resource Guide,* page 3j; 16–24 index cards, colored markers, pictures of objects beginning with the letter *b,* tape or glue

This activity is a variation of the Consonant Concentration activity.

➤ Select 8 to 12 objects that begin with the sound of *b.* On index cards, glue pictures of the objects. On the remaining cards, write the name of the objects. Prepare 8 to 12 sets.

➤ Hold up each word card and ask volunteers to read the words aloud. Have children pronounce the words.

➤ Place the cards face down in a grid. Have children take turns matching picture and word cards. Matched cards are picked up by the child saying the word or naming the object.

5 ASSESS

Materials:
Student Edition, page 12

Read aloud the direction line for the activity on page 12. Verify that children understand what they are to do by completing items 1–3 aloud together. Have children complete items 4–12 in pairs.

Book Corner

MORE PHONICS PRACTICE

Set aside class time to read trade books with ESL learners. Preview these books and do a first reading to children.

THE BATH by Judy Nayer. Ready Readers, Stage 0 (Modern Curriculum Press, 1997)

GRANDPA'S HOUSE by Robin Clyne. Winners' Circle (Modern Curriculum Press, 1994)

Technology

AstroWord

Some children will benefit from additional individualized feedback, such as that provided by the CD-ROMs *AstroWord Consonant Letters and Sounds and Phonemic Awareness* (Modules 1 and 2). Encourage native speakers of English and ESL learners to work together to complete activities that interest them using the sound of *b.* Monitor each group's progress.

Lesson 5
Reviewing Consonants s, t, b

INFORMAL ASSESSMENT OBJECTIVE

Can children

✔ identify pictures whose names begin or end with the sounds of s, t, and b?

1 INTRODUCE

Materials:
Phonics Picture Cards (numbers 1–3, 33–37, 47, 60–62, 67, 68, 75, 76) or realia of items whose names begin with the sounds of s, t, and b; colored chalk

Use the Phonics Picture Cards or realia to review the name of each picture clue and the sounds of initial s, t, and b.

➤ Invite volunteers to name the objects and say which letter stands for the beginning sound.

➤ Have children write each word on the chalkboard, using colored chalk to highlight the first letter. Provide help with writing if necessary.

2 TEACH

Materials:
Pictures of objects or realia whose names end with the sounds of s, t, and b; colored chalk

In Lesson 5, along with reviewing the initial sounds of s, t, and b, demonstrate words ending with the three target sounds. Select items that English Language Learners likely have encountered in daily life and objects from previous lessons.

➤ Write s, t, and b two times on the chalkboard—once in the initial sound position and once in the end sound position.

➤ Write sun, toy, and ball under the beginning letters. Use brightly colored chalk to write the first letter of each word.

➤ Ask each child to identify the first letter and the sound it stands for.

➤ Hold up a visual and have a volunteer name it.

➤ In the column for ending sounds, write bus, using colored chalk to write the s.

➤ Model the pronunciation of initial s in sun and of final s in bus. Explain that the letter s stands for the same sound at the beginning or the end of a word.

➤ Continue, covering at least two objects that end with each sound. Encourage children who demonstrate sufficient ability to write the words on the board.

★ *For specific notes on various home languages, see pages xiii–xvii of this Guide.*

3 PRACTICE

Materials:
Student Edition, page 13

Use the worksheet on page 13 to practice reading, writing, speaking, and listening skills with your ESL learners.

➤ As a warm-up, practice with children words that begin or end with each of the target sounds.

➤ Read the directions aloud, and complete item 1 as a group. Ask a volunteer to name the letter in the box in item 1 and the picture below it. Ask, "Is the sound of *b* at the beginning or the end of the word *ball*?" When a volunteer has responded correctly, model writing the lowercase *b* on the first set of lines.

➤ Have children complete items 2–12 with you.

4 APPLY

Materials:
Consonant Catch activity, *MCP Phonics Teacher Resource Guide,* page 3l; foam ball; Phonics Picture Cards (numbers 1–3, 33–37, 47, 60–62, 67, 68, 75, 76)

Adapt the Consonant Catch activity as follows for your ESL learners.

➤ Select one of the Phonics Picture Cards listed to the left.

➤ Hold the card up so children can see it. Write the picture name on the chalkboard.

➤ Toss the ball to one of the children.

➤ That child is to name the object on the card and identify the beginning consonant. Have the child toss the ball to another child.

➤ Repeat this procedure for the additional phonics picture cards.

5 ASSESS

Materials:
Student Edition, page 14

Tic-tac-toe is not known in all cultures and may be confusing to your English Language Learners. Use the worksheet on page 14 of the Student Edition to provide oral practice for ESL learners by having them identify the picture clues and the beginning or ending sound of each word from the activity.

Book Corner

MORE PHONICS PRACTICE

Set aside class time to read trade books with ESL learners. Preview these books and do a first reading to children.

A BIG, BIG BOX by Rebecca Haber. Ready Readers, Stage 0 (Modern Curriculum Press, 1997)

A MESS by Bob Allen. Ready Readers, Stage 1 (Modern Curriculum Press, 1996)

Technology

AstroWord
Some children will benefit from additional individualized feedback, such as that provided by the CD-ROMs *AstroWord Consonant Letters and Sounds* and *Phonemic Awareness* (Modules 1 and 2). Encourage native speakers of English and ESL learners to work together to complete activities that interest them using the sounds of *s, t,* and *b*. Monitor activities.

Lesson 6
The Sound of *h*

INFORMAL ASSESSMENT OBJECTIVES

Can children

✔ identify pictures whose names begin with the sound of *h*?

✔ identify and print the uppercase and lowercase forms of the letter *h*?

★ *Some ESL learners who speak Middle Eastern languages or Russian may pronounce the* h *with a throaty sound. In Spanish, French, Hmong, and Haitian Creole, the* h *is silent.*

1 INTRODUCE

Materials:
Alphabet chart;
Phonics Picture
Cards (numbers 16,
17, 18, 50, 51, 52);
Student Edition,
pages 15–16;
feathers

Using the alphabet chart, ask volunteers to point to the letter *h* and then write the uppercase and lowercase letters.

➤ Model the sound of *h* by holding a feather in front of your mouth. Call children's attention to how the feather moves when you say /h/.

➤ Review the words and picture clues on pages 15–16 of the Student Edition or the Phonics Picture Cards listed to the left.

➤ Give ESL learners a feather; have them follow along and repeat after you: "/h/, hat," "/h/, heart," and so on. Add familiar parts of the body (head, hand, hair).

➤ Continue reviewing words that begin with the sound of *h*.

2 TEACH

Materials:
Student Edition,
page 15; Rhyme
Poster 5 (optional);
chalkboard or
posterboard,
marker

The rhyme on page 15 of the Student Edition lends itself to kinesthetic learning and acting out.

➤ Write the word *hop* on the board. Say the word and hop on one foot to reinforce the meaning. Ask children to stand up and hop as they repeat the word.

➤ Model the words *high* and *low*. Integrate the two elements.

➤ Have children line up and hop along behind you, follow-the-leader style, as you model pronunciation of "hop in a row."

➤ Have children help you read the rhyme on page 15. Read the first line aloud as children follow along. Have them repeat chorally, and then ask volunteers to read the line aloud individually. Reinforce good pronunciation.

➤ Continue with the remaining three lines of the rhyme.

★ *For specific notes on various home languages, see pages xiii–xvii of this Guide.*

3 PRACTICE

Materials:
Student Edition, page 15-16; safety mirrors from a science kit

Involve children in forming the correct sounds of English as they use small safety mirrors (from a science kit) to check their pronunciation.

➤ Write on the board the words from pages 15–16 that begin with the sound of *h: hat, heart, hand, hill hot, horse, hose, hen, heel.*

➤ Using the mirrors, call on children to form the name of each picture clue on these pages.

➤ Reinforce pronunciation and meaning by asking such questions as, "How many fingers are on your hand?"

4 APPLY

Materials:
Six familiar objects (or pictures) that model the sound of *h*, six objects (or pictures) that model a different initial consonant sound, two shoeboxes, two index cards, red marker, tape

This variation of the Sorting Sounds activity on page 3k of the *MCP Phonics Teacher Resource Guide* helps children identify and sort familiar objects beginning with the sound of *h*.

➤ Write *Hh* on one index card and a red circle with a slash through it (the international symbol for no) on the other. Tape one card to the front of each box.

➤ Display the objects/pictures, then have children name and sort them into the appropriate boxes.

➤ Verify that each item in the *Hh* box begins with the sound of *h*.

5 ASSESS

Materials:
Student Edition, page 16

Read aloud the direction line for the activity on page 16. Together, review the sound of *h*, and complete items 1–3. Have ESL learners of varying levels of proficiency work in pairs to complete items 4–12. Review the answers aloud to ensure comprehension.

Book Corner

MORE PHONICS PRACTICE

Set aside class time to read trade books with ESL learners. Preview these books and do a first reading to children.

HOW TO MAKE A HEN HOUSE by Bill Holly. Ready Readers, Stage 0 (Modern Curriculum Press, 1997)

UP THEY GO by Stanley Francis. Ready Readers, Stage 0 (Modern Curriculum Press, 1997)

Technology

AstroWord
Some children will benefit from additional individualized feedback, such as that provided by the CD-ROMs *AstroWord Consonant Letters and Sounds* and *Phonemic Awareness* (Modules 1 and 2). Encourage native speakers of English and ESL learners to work together to complete activities that interest them using the sound of *h*. Monitor each group's progress.

Lesson 7
The Sound of *m*

INFORMAL ASSESSMENT OBJECTIVES

Can children

✔ identify pictures whose names begin with the sound of *m*?

✔ identify and print the uppercase and lowercase forms of the letter *m*?

★ *Some ESL learners may be learning the Roman alphabet for the first time, so discriminate form from size between uppercase and lowercase m.*

---

1 INTRODUCE

Materials:
Alphabet chart; Phonics Picture Cards (numbers 23, 24, 25, 73); Student Edition, pages 17–18

Using an alphabet chart, identify whether ESL learners can identify the uppercase and lowercase forms of the letter *m*. Then encourage volunteers to point to the letter *m* and then to practice writing it on the chalkboard.

➤ Explain that the letter *m* stands for /m/ in English. Model the sound of *m* by showing ESL learners how to position the lips and by reviewing the appropriate words and picture clues on pages 17–18 and/or those found on the Phonics Picture Cards listed to the left.

➤ Further engage children by asking volunteers whose names begin with *m* to write their names on the chalkboard.

➤ Continue reviewing words that begin with the sound of *m*.

2 TEACH

Materials:
Pictures of household objects or realia that make the sound of *m*, two or three other "non-*m*" objects, crayons, paper, chart paper

Build upon everyday vocabulary and the sound of *m* with "*M* around the house."

➤ On the chart paper, draw an outline of a house large enough to contain several words. Have children each draw a house on their papers.

➤ Mix up objects (or pictures) and display them one at a time. Invite a volunteer to say what each object is.

➤ Ask, "Does [object] begin with the sound of *m*?" If it does, model writing the word inside your *m* house and have children add the word to their drawings. You may wish to draw a quick sketch by the word to enhance comprehension.

★ *For specific notes on various home languages, see pages xiii–xvii of this Guide.*

3 PRACTICE

Materials:
Student Edition, page 17; Rhyme Poster 6 (optional); muffins

Continue practicing the sound of *m* by bringing muffins to class. This food may be unfamiliar to some children, and there is no picture clue on page 17 of the Student Edition.

➤ Write the words *muffin*, *munch*, and *Mom* on the chalkboard. Share the muffins. Have ESL learners work in pairs to create oral sentences with the words on the chalkboard.

➤ Read the rhyme aloud, pointing to each word as you read it.

➤ Model the verb *give*. Check for comprehension by asking questions such as "Who gave me a muffin?" and "What did Mom give me?"

4 APPLY

Materials:
Pick a Match activity, *MCP Phonics Teacher Resource Guide*, page 3j; Index cards, pictures of objects beginning with the target letter *m*, tape or glue

This activity is a variation of the Pick a Match activity.

➤ Select objects that begin with the sound of *m*. On index cards, affix pictures of the objects. On the remaining cards, write the name of the objects. Prepare 8 to 12 sets.

➤ Hold up the picture cards. Have ESL learners identify the pictures.

➤ Then, hold up each word card and ask volunteers to read the words aloud. Have children pronounce them.

➤ Place the cards face down in a grid. Explain to children that they will match picture and word cards. Matched cards are picked up by the child naming the object correctly.

5 ASSESS

Materials:
Student Edition, page 18

Read aloud the direction line for the activity on page 18. Verify that children understand what they are to do by completing items 1–3 aloud together. In small groups, have children complete items 4–12. Answer questions as needed.

MORE PHONICS PRACTICE

Set aside class time to read trade books with ESL learners. Preview these books and do a first reading to children.

MONSTER MOP by Aimee Mark. Ready Readers, Stage 0 (Modern Curriculum Press, 1997)

THE ANIMAL PARADE by Barb Jansen. Winners' Circle (Modern Curriculum Press, 1995)

AstroWord
Some children will benefit from additional individualized feedback, such as that provided by the CD-ROMs *AstroWord Consonant Letters and Sounds* and *Phonemic Awareness* (Modules 1 and 2). Encourage native speakers of English and ESL learners to work together to complete activities that interest them using the sound of *m*. Monitor each group's progress.

Lesson 8
The Sound of *k*

INFORMAL ASSESSMENT OBJECTIVES

Can children

✔ identify pictures whose names begin with the sound of *k*?

✔ identify and print the uppercase and lowercase forms of the letter *k*?

★ *Native speakers of Spanish may be familiar with the sound of* k *(which is the same as the sounds of soft* c, que, *and* qui) *but not recognize the written letter, which is not used as commonly in Spanish. Model with* king, key, *and* kite.

1 INTRODUCE

Materials:
Alphabet chart; Phonics Picture Cards (numbers 20, 56, 98); Student Edition, pages 19–20

Using an alphabet chart, verify ESL learners previous knowledge of the uppercase and lowercase of the letter *k*. Then explain that the letter *k* stands for the sound of *k* in English.

➤ Model the sound of *k* by reviewing the appropriate words and picture clues on pages 19–20 and/or those found on the Phonics Picture Cards listed to the left.

➤ Further engage children by asking volunteers whose names begin with *k* to write their names on the chalkboard. Point out *Katy* as an example in the rhyme on page 19 and model the initial *k* sound. You might want to have cards with names that start with *k* ready in case there aren't any children with names that start with *k*.

➤ Continue reviewing words that begin with the sound of *k*, encouraging children to respond individually as their mastery and confidence build.

2 TEACH

Materials:
Realia or pictures of the objects that model the sound of *k*, three or four "non-*k*" objects from previous lessons

In small groups, play a chalkboard game to help children discriminate words that begin with the sound of *k* from others they have learned in recent lessons.

➤ Have children, individually or in groups, go to the chalkboard.

➤ Explain that you are going to hold up a picture or an object for children to name when called upon. When the object has been named aloud, ask them to decide if the name begins with the sound of the letter *k*.

➤ If they believe the word begins with /k/, have them write it on the chalkboard. Provide help with writing if necessary.

★ *For specific notes on various home languages, see pages xiii–xvii of this Guide.*

3 PRACTICE

Materials:
Student Edition, page 19; Rhyme Poster 7 (optional)

Using the picture clues on page 19, encourage ESL learners to name objects they see in Katy's room.

➤ As children respond, ask them to point to the items in their books. Write the names of the target objects (*kite, key*, and *kitten*) on the chalkboard. Model pronunciation and have children repeat first as a group, then individually.

➤ Read the rhyme aloud as children follow along. Ask volunteers to read each line as their confidence and competence build.

4 APPLY

Materials:
Listen for Sounds activity, *MCP Phonics Teacher Resource Guide*, page 3m; paper, pencils, and crayons (all optional)

This activity is a variation of the Listen for Sounds activity.

➤ Prepare a list of 10 to 12 words, some beginning with *k* and others with an initial hard *g* sound /g/, since some ESL learners need practice discriminating between these two sounds.

➤ Tell children to hop up and down like a kangaroo if they hear the sound /k/ at the beginning of the word. If they do not, they should stay seated. Model the activity.

➤ Then read the list of words and invite children to join in.

➤ List the *k* words on the chalkboard for children to copy.

5 ASSESS

Materials:
Student Edition, page 20

Confirm vocabulary recognition by having ESL learners take turns naming the pictures. Then read aloud the direction line for the activity as children follow along. Complete items 1–3 as a group. Monitor progress, then have children complete items 4–12.

MORE PHONICS PRACTICE

Set aside class time to read trade books with ESL learners. Preview these books and do a first reading to children.

KEEP OUT by Will Hardy. Ready Readers, Stage 0 (Modern Curriculum Press, 1997)

KANGAROO IN THE KITCHEN by Maryann Dobeck. Ready Readers, Stage 1 (Modern Curriculum Press, 1996)

AstroWord

Some children will benefit from additional individualized feedback, such as that provided by the CD-ROMs *AstroWord Consonant Letters and Sounds* and *Phonemic Awareness*. (Modules 1 and 2). Encourage native speakers of English and ESL learners to work together to complete activities that interest them using the sound of *k*. Monitor each group's progress.

Lessons 9–10
Reviewing Consonants s, *t, b, h, m, k*

INFORMAL ASSESSMENT OBJECTIVE

Can children

✔ identify and print the initial or final consonant for pictures whose names begin or end with the sounds of *s, t, b, h, m,* and *k*?

★ *Native speakers of Spanish and Hmong may have difficulty pronouncing t, m, b, or k at the end of words, since words ending in these consonants are not a common occurrence in these languages.*

1 INTRODUCE

Materials:
Letter Cards *Ss, Tt, Bb, Hh, Mm, Kk*

Using the Letter Cards, assess whether ESL learners have learned the sounds of each letter. Then review with children the name and sound of each of the target consonants.

➤ Hold up one card and ask a volunteer to name the letter and say what sound the letter stands for.

➤ Ask children to differentiate between beginning and ending sounds of target consonants, with words from previous lessons.

2 TEACH

Materials:
Pictures of objects or realia whose names begin or end with the sounds of *s, t, b, h, m,* and *k* (optional), colored chalk

Review the six target consonants in initial and final position, using familiar words from the previous lessons.

➤ Write *s, t, b, h, m,* and *k* on the chalkboard. Divide the space under each letter to create a two-column list. Shade in the right column under *h*, and explain to children that in English no words end with the sound of *h*.

➤ Say *sit, tap, bounce, hop, muffin,* and *kite* aloud. Invite volunteers to say in what column each word goes. After correcting misconceptions, write the words in the left column under the corresponding letters. Use colored chalk for first letter of each word.

➤ Review these words aloud. Encourage volunteers to read the words and name the first letter.

➤ Continue this activity with additional words that end in the target sounds.

➤ Use realia or picture cards for those not able to read the words.

➤ Invite children who have demonstrated sufficient ability to supply additional words and write the words in the correct location on the chalkboard.

★ *For specific notes on various home languages, see pages xiii–xvii of this Guide.*

3 PRACTICE

Materials:
Student Edition,
pages 21–22

Continue practicing the target consonants and sounds in initial and final positions by using the worksheets on pages 21–22.

➤ Read the directions aloud and review the picture clues.

➤ Model each activity by working through items 1–3 aloud with children.

➤ Assess whether children are able to complete the activities individually. Encourage those who can to do so. If not, pair ESL learners of varying levels of proficiency to complete the page.

➤ Do an oral review of items 1–12, to reinforce results and correct any misconceptions.

4 APPLY

Materials:
Wonder Wheel
activity, *MCP Phonics
Teacher Resource
Guide,* page 3k;
Phonics Picture
Cards with objects
whose names begin
or end with *s, t, b,
h, m, k*

This activity is a variation of the Wonder Wheel activity.

➤ Construct a Wonder Wheel following directions on page 3k. Divide paper plate in 6 sections. Write one letter (*s, t, b, m, h, k*) in each.

➤ In the first round, children spin the wheel and name a word that begins with the sound of the consonant indicated by the arrow. In the second round, they name words that end with that sound. (If the wheel stops on *h*, spin again.) Some ESL learners will need support with ending sounds.

➤ Tape picture cards around the wheel for ESL learners to point to instead of having to remember a word just by looking at a letter.

5 ASSESS

Materials:
Student Edition,
page 23

Read the directions on page 23 aloud and review the picture clues. Model the activity with ESL learners by completing items 1–2 aloud. Have children work in pairs to complete items 3–12. Monitor progress and offer support as needed. Correct any misconceptions.

Book Corner

MORE PHONICS PRACTICE

Set aside class time to read trade books with ESL learners. Preview these books and do a first reading to children.

A MESS by Bob Allen. Ready Readers, Stage 1 (Modern Curriculum Press, 1996)

MY BIG BUDDY by Jill M. Moffit. Winners' Circle (Modern Curriculum Press, 1996)

Technology

AstroWord

Some children will benefit from additional individualized feedback, provided by the CD-ROMs *AstroWord Consonant Letters and Sounds and Phonemic Awareness* (Modules 1 and 2). Encourage native speakers of English and ESL learners to complete a variety of activities that interest them using the six target sounds being reviewed. Monitor each group's progress.

Lesson 11
Partner Letters *Jj, Ff, Gg, Ll, Dd, Nn*

INFORMAL ASSESSMENT OBJECTIVE

Can children

✔ identify by name the uppercase and lowercase forms of the letters *j, f, g, l, d,* and *n*?

★ *Some English Language Learners may be learning the Roman alphabet for the first time, so discriminate form from size between uppercase and lowercase letters.*

1 INTRODUCE

Materials:
Alphabet chart;
Student Edition,
pages 25–26

Work one-on-one with your ESL learners or with pairs of children to find out if each child is familiar with the six target partner letters and can identify the uppercase and lowercase forms as you say them aloud.

➤ Using an alphabet chart, point to one of the target letters. Have the child say the name of the letter. Reinforce correct responses.

➤ Repeat this activity. As competence and confidence build, expand and review the consonants presented in Lessons 1–10 (*s, t, b, h, m, k*) along with the new ones.

➤ Have children who need additional support practice writing the uppercase and lowercase forms of the six target consonants as you say the name of the word pictured.

2 TEACH

Materials:
*MCP Phonics Teacher
Resource Guide:*
Pick a Match
activity, page 3j;
Blackline Master 6,
page 3n; tagboard

Continue teaching this lesson by employing a variation of the Pick a Match game.

➤ Duplicate Blackline Master 6 on tagboard and cut it apart to make letter cards with blank backs. Use the cards for the six target partner letters presented in the lesson.

➤ Sort the uppercase letter cards from the lowercase ones. Place the uppercase letter cards face up in a grid of three cards by two cards. Place the lowercase letter cards face down in a pile.

➤ Have a child turn over one of the face-down lowercase letter cards and name the letter. Then have the child match the lowercase letter with its uppercase partner.

➤ Repeat the procedure, this time placing the uppercase letter cards face down.

★ *For specific notes on various home languages, see pages xiii–xvii of this Guide.*

3 PRACTICE

Materials:
Letter Cards *Jj, Ff, Gg, Ll, Dd, Nn*; Student Edition, page 25; crayons

Complete the worksheet on page 25 in a more structured format with English Language Learners.

➤ Review the target partner letters aloud with the group. Hold up a Letter Card and ask a child to name it. Have the group repeat chorally. Review all the Letter Cards several times.

➤ Explain to children that they will color the ducks on page 25.

➤ Say, "Let's color the duck that has these partner letters in it" as you hold the card. Monitor children's work. Repeat with the remaining five cards.

4 APPLY

Materials:
Consonant Concentration activity, *MCP Phonics Teacher Resource Guide,* page 3j; 12 sheets of construction paper (same color); colored markers; tacks; tape

This activity is a variation of Consonant Concentration activity.

➤ Write the uppercase and lowercase forms of the target consonants on separate construction paper "cards." Number them randomly on the back from 1 to 12.

➤ Hang the cards around the room, numbered side showing.

➤ Have one child call out a number. Turn the card over to reveal the letter form. Have the child name the letter and choose another numbered card. If a match is found, take the cards down. If not, hang them back up.

➤ Continue playing until all partner letters are matched.

5 ASSESS

Materials:
Student Edition, page 26

Read the direction line aloud. Clarify as necessary. Copy worksheet items 1–3 on the chalkboard. Model the activity by circling each pair of partner letters. Have children complete items 4–12 individually. Review to ensure comprehension.

MORE PHONICS PRACTICE

Set aside class time to read trade books with ESL learners. Preview these books and do a first reading to children.

WHAT RHYMES WITH CAT? by Kathleen Wilson. Ready Readers, Stage 1 (Modern Curriculum Press, 1996)

FRIENDS OF ALL COLORS by Susan Dixon. Winners' Circle (Modern Curriculum Press, 1995)

AstroWord

Some children will benefit from additional individualized feedback, such as that provided by the CD-ROM *AstroWord Consonant Letters and Sounds* (Module 2). Encourage groups of native speakers of English and ESL learners to work together to complete a variety of activities, such as the Easy level of *Word Sort*, in which children help alien creatures sort picture clues by specific consonants.

Lesson 12
The Sound of *j*

INFORMAL ASSESSMENT OBJECTIVES

Can children

✔ identify pictures whose names begin with the sound of *j*?

✔ identify and print the uppercase and lowercase forms of the letter *j*?

★ *Native speakers of Spanish may pronounce the sound of j as y, and say "Yimmy" instead of "Jimmy." Practice with jack, jet, jacket, and other picture clues on pages 27–28.*

1 INTRODUCE

Materials:
Alphabet chart;
Student Edition,
pages 27–28

Use an alphabet chart to verify whether children can identify the uppercase and lowercase forms of the letter *j*. Have volunteers write *Jj* on the chalkboard. Reinforce correct responses.

➤ Explain that the letter *j* stands for /j/ in English. Model the sound of *j* and review the words and picture cues on pages 27–28.

➤ Have children practice saying /j/ with their hands in front of their mouths, so they can feel the air being expelled.

➤ Point out and practice the words *Janie, Jack,* and *jump* in the rhyme on page 27.

➤ Continue reviewing words that begin with /j/, encouraging children to respond individually as their confidence builds.

2 TEACH

Materials:
Pictures of
household objects
or realia that model
the sound of *j*;
three other "non-*j*"
objects; crayons
and paper for each
child; chart paper;
scissors

Continue teaching the sound of *j* with "J around the house."

➤ On chart paper, draw an outline of a house large enough to contain several words. Have children each draw an outline of a house on their papers, and cut the papers in a shape of a house.

➤ Mix up objects (or pictures) and display them one at a time. Invite volunteers to say what the objects are.

➤ Ask, "Does [object] begin with the sound of *j*?" If it does, model writing the word inside your *j* house and have children add the word to their drawings.

➤ Draw a quick sketch next to each word to aid ESL learners with learning new vocabulary.

➤ After writing four or five *j* words, review them chorally with the class. Have children use words in oral sentences.

★ *For specific notes on various home languages, see pages xiii–xvii of this Guide.*

3 PRACTICE

Materials:
Student Edition, page 27; Rhyme Poster 8 (optional)

Practice the sound of *j* by incorporating kinesthetic learning into your presentation of the rhyme on page 27.

➤ Write the word *jump* on the board. Say the word and act it out. Ask the children to stand up, say the word, and then jump.

➤ Ask children to listen carefully as you read the rhyme. Have each child read one line of the rhyme after you model pronunciation again. Repeat the rhyme several times.

➤ Complete the worksheet on page 27.

4 APPLY

Materials:
Listen for Sounds activity, *MCP Phonics Teacher Resource Guide*, page 3m

Vary the Listen for Sounds activity for your ESL learners.

➤ Use the following words: *jack, chip, jeep, jet, sugar, jar, hump, jump, chin,* and *Jim.*

➤ Have children stand up. Explain that you are going to say a word. If they hear the sound of *j* at the beginning of the word, they jump forward. If they do not hear the sound *j*, they sit down.

➤ Model the activity by participating in the first two words.

➤ Write *Jumping for Jj* on the board along with the *j* words used. Have children copy the final list and read the list chorally. Encourage ESL learners to draw a picture next to the words to help them remember the vocabulary.

5 ASSESS

Materials:
Student Edition, page 28

Have ESL learners complete the worksheet on page 28. Read the directions aloud, clarifying as necessary. Model the activity by completing items 1–2 aloud. Review the picture clues in items 3–12, if needed. Have children complete items 3–12 in pairs. Review answers.

Book Corner

MORE PHONICS PRACTICE

Set aside class time to read trade books with ESL learners. Preview these books and do a first reading to children.

JAN CAN JUGGLE by Kate McGovern. Ready Readers, Stage 0 (Modern Curriculum Press, 1997)

LITTLE KITTENS by Mary Solins. Ready Readers, Stage 0 (Modern Curriculum Press, 1997)

Technology

AstroWord

Some children will benefit from additional individualized feedback on the CD-ROM *AstroWord Consonant Letters and Sounds* (Module 2). Encourage native speakers of English and ESL learners to work on the easy level of *Make-a-Word*, where children help alien creatures create words, based on a picture clue, by joining the initial consonant to the appropriate word ending. Monitor each group's progress.

Lesson 13
The Sound of *f*

INFORMAL ASSESSMENT OBJECTIVES

Can children

✔ identify pictures whose names begin with the sound of *f*?

✔ identify and print the uppercase and lowercase forms of the letter *f*?

★ *Native speakers of Spanish may have trouble distinguishing between /f/ and /v/ or /p/. Practice with words like* fan, van, *and* pan; face, vase, *and* pace.

---

1 INTRODUCE

Materials:
Alphabet chart;
Student Edition,
pages 29–30;
Phonics Picture
Cards (numbers 10,
11, 12, 94)

Use an alphabet chart to verify whether children can identify the uppercase and lowercase forms of the letter *f*.

➤ Have volunteers write *Ff* on the chalkboard. Reinforce correct responses.

➤ Explain that the letter *f* stands for /f/ in English. Model the sound of *f* and review the appropriate words and picture clues on pages 29–30, as well as those found on the Phonics Picture Cards listed to the left.

➤ Point out and practice the words *five, furry, foxes, fanning,* and *feet* in the rhyme on page 29. Have children respond individually as their confidence builds.

2 TEACH

Materials:
Pictures cards or
realia of words that
begin with the
sound of *f*; Twister-
style, floor-size
game board; word
cards

Continue practicing the sound of *f* with your ESL learners.

➤ Arrange picture cards on the floor, Twister-style.

➤ You might want to bring in real objects that represent the objects in the picture cards to better illustrate the words.

➤ Select a corresponding word card; call out the name of the picture clue.

➤ Have ESL learners stand on (or touch) that card. Ensure children's safety as they are asked to touch several cards at the same time.

➤ Continue with other words as children select and touch the words named.

★ *For specific notes on various home languages, see pages xiii–xvii of this Guide.*

3 PRACTICE

Materials:
Student Edition, page 29; Rhyme Poster 9 (optional)

Practice the sound of *f* by reading the rhyme on page 29.

➤ Review the target words *five, furry, foxes, fanning,* and *feet.*

➤ Ask children to listen carefully as you model pronunciation of the rhyme. Have each child read one line after you. Repeat reading the rhyme individually or chorally several times.

➤ Complete the worksheet on page 29 orally as a group.

4 APPLY

Materials:
Consonant Caterpillars activity, *MCP Phonics Teacher Resource Guide*, page 3m; 9" × 12" sheets of construction paper; one wooden dowel per child; glue; scissors; magazines

This variation of the Consonant Caterpillars activity is called the *F* Flag.

➤ Hand out one sheet of construction paper to each child. Assist children in writing "*F* Flag" in the center of the papers.

➤ Have children draw pictures of 4 to 5 items that begin with the sound of *f*. They can also clip and paste pictures of *f* items on their flags. Have children work in pairs to write the name of the objects beneath each picture.

➤ Assemble each flag by gluing the dowel to the flag's left side.

➤ Create a special area in which to display the flags.

5 ASSESS

Materials:
Student Edition, page 30

Read the direction line aloud. Clarify as necessary. Model the activity by working closely with children to complete items 1–2. Review the picture clues in the remaining worksheet items. Have children complete items 3–12 individually or in pairs. Review all items aloud to ensure comprehension and correct any misconceptions.

Book Corner

MORE PHONICS PRACTICE

Set aside class time to read trade books with ESL learners. Preview these books and do a first reading to children.

TIME FOR LUNCH by Kathryn E. Lewis. Ready Readers, Stage 0 (Modern Curriculum Press, 1997)

IF I WERE A FISH by Susan Caver. Winners' Circle (Modern Curriculum Press, 1995)

Technology

AstroWord

Some children will benefit from additional individualized feedback, such as that provided by the CD-ROM *AstroWord Consonant Letters and Sounds* (Module 2). Encourage native speakers of English and ESL learners to work together to write some of the words with the sound of *f* they have learned, using the Word Board and Notepad in the *AstroWord* Free Play room. Monitor each group's progress.

Lesson 14
The Sound of *g*

INFORMAL ASSESSMENT OBJECTIVES

Can children

✔ identify pictures whose names begin with the sound of *g*?

✔ identify and print the uppercase and lowercase forms of the letter *g*?

★ *Some ESL learners may have difficulty distinguishing between the voiced /g/ and the unvoiced /k/. Clearly model the different initial sounds in* good, go, *and* get *versus* king, key, *and* kite.

1 INTRODUCE

Materials:
Alphabet chart; Student Edition, pages 31–32; Phonics Picture Cards (numbers 13, 14, 15, 89, 112, 129, 138)

Use an alphabet chart to verify whether children can identify the uppercase and lowercase forms of the letter *g*. Have volunteers write *Gg* on the chalkboard. Reinforce responses.

➤ Explain that the letter *g* stands for /g/ in English. Model the sound of *g* and review the appropriate words and picture clues on pages 31–32, as well as those found on the Phonics Picture Cards listed to the left.

➤ Point out and practice the words *good, goose, goat, garden,* and *give* in the rhyme on page 31.

➤ Continue reviewing words that begin with the sound of *g*. Have children respond individually as their confidence builds.

2 TEACH

Materials:
Colored construction paper; pictures of objects beginning with the target letter *g* clipped from magazines; hangers; string; scissors

This activity focuses ESL learners on identifying picture clues that begin with the sound of *g*.

➤ Hand out sheets of construction paper onto which uppercase and lowercase *g* have been traced, in the shape of balloons. Have children cut them out.

➤ Ask ESL learners to find magazine pictures that begin with the sound of *g*, clip them, and paste them to their partner letters.

➤ Attach letter displays to hangers with string.

➤ Display the *g* mobiles in class. Review as a warm-up activity.

★ *For specific notes on various home languages, see pages xiii–xvii of this Guide.*

3 PRACTICE

Materials:
Student Edition, page 31; Rhyme Poster 10 (optional)

Practice the sound of *g* by reading the rhyme on page 31.

➤ Review the words *good, goose, goat, grapes,* and *give* from the rhyme.

➤ Ask children to listen carefully as you read the rhyme aloud. Have each child read one line of the rhyme after you again. Model pronunciation. Reread the rhyme several times.

➤ Complete the worksheet activity on page 31 aloud as a group.

4 APPLY

Materials:
Mystery Sound Boxes activity, *MCP Phonics Teacher Resource Guide*, page 3j; six small boxes or gift bags; six small objects (or pictures) whose names begin with the sound of *g*

This Mystery Gift activity is a variation of the Mystery Sound Boxes activity.

➤ Place one small object in each box. Number each box 1 to 6.

➤ Have each child select a box, open it, and look at what's inside. Ask, "What is inside Mystery Gift Box 1?"

➤ When the child responds, model writing the name of the object on the chalkboard.

➤ After all the mystery gifts have been opened, have the group write a mystery gift list, listing all the names of the objects you wrote on the board. Have children read the name of the objects chorally.

5 ASSESS

Materials:
Student Edition, page 32; eight paper cutouts of partner letters *Gg* per child; glue

Have children say the names of the picture clues aloud as a group. Correct pronunciation and misconceptions. Hand out eight cutouts to each child. Direct children to glue the letters on the line of each item that begins with the sound of *g*. Complete the first item together and review. Complete items 2–12 in pairs.

Book Corner

MORE PHONICS PRACTICE

Set aside class time to read trade books with ESL learners. Preview these books and do a first reading to children.

GOOD GIRL! by Seth Jacobs. Ready Readers, Stage 0 (Modern Curriculum Press, 1997)

WHERE DO WE GO? by Kara James. Ready Readers, Stage 0 (Modern Curriculum Press, 1997)

Technology

AstroWord
Some children will benefit from additional individualized feedback, such as that provided by the CD-ROM *AstroWord Consonant Letters and Sounds* (Module 2). Encourage children to work in groups to complete the Easy level of *Make-a-Word*, in which children help alien creatures create words based on a picture clue by joining the initial consonant to the appropriate word ending. Monitor each group's progress.

Lesson 15
Reviewing Consonants *j, f, g*

INFORMAL ASSESSMENT OBJECTIVES

Can children

✔ identify the initial consonants of pictures whose names begin with the sounds of *j, f,* and *g*?

✔ identify and print the initial or final consonant for pictures whose names begin or end with the sounds of *j, f,* and *g*?

★ *Native speakers of Spanish and Hmong may have difficulty pronouncing words that end with* j, f, *and* g, *since words ending with these consonants are not a common occurrence in these languages.*

1 INTRODUCE

Materials:
Letter Cards *Jj, Ff, Gg;* Student Edition, page 33

Using the Letter Cards, assess whether ESL learners have learned the sounds of each letter. Then review the target letter names, the sound each stands for, and words that begin with each target sound.

➤ Hold up a Letter Card. Ask a volunteer to name the letter, model the sound, and say a word that begins with the target sound. Review cards several times.

➤ Pronounce each word beginning with the sounds of *j, f,* and *g* in the worksheet on page 33. Have ESL learners repeat.

➤ Working one-on-one, point to a picture clue from the worksheet. Have the child name the object.

➤ Have children close their books and say a picture name. Encourage individuals to say what beginning sound they hear.

2 TEACH

Materials:
Pictures of objects or realia whose names begin or end with the sounds of *j, f,* and *g;* colored chalk

Review the sounds of *j, f,* and *g* in initial position while teaching words with the target sounds in final position.

➤ Write *f* and *g* on board twice, once in initial sound column and once in end sound column. Write *j* in initial sound column only.

➤ Write *jump, fox,* and *good* to model initial sound position, using colored chalk to write the first letter.

➤ Point out that *f* and *g* stand for the same sound in either word position: *fox, leaf; good, log.*

➤ Hold up a visual and have a volunteer name it. Write the word in the appropriate column (beginning or ending sound). Once you have two words in each column, review them all.

★ *For specific notes on various home languages, see pages xiii–xvii of this Guide.*

3 PRACTICE

Materials:
Student Edition,
page 33

Use the worksheet on page 33 to practice the sounds of *j*, *f*, and *g* in initial and final positions.

➤ Read the direction line for the activity aloud.

➤ Complete items 1–3 together with ESL learners.

➤ Ask children to work in pairs to complete items 4–12. Review.

4 APPLY

Materials:
Mystery Sound
Boxes, *MCP Phonics
Teacher Resource
Guide*, page 3j; ten
paper lunch bags;
ten small objects (or
pictures) that model
the sounds of *j*, *f*,
and *g*; markers;
pencil and paper

Adapt the Mystery Sound Boxes activity for use with ESL learners.

➤ Number the bags from 1 to 10. Place one object or picture inside each bag and close. Place the bags at different stations around the room.

➤ Ask one pair or one group of children to go to Mystery Bag 1. Instruct them to open the bag. Then ask, "What is inside?"

➤ A child removes the picture or object and names it aloud.

➤ As children continue, create a list on the chalkboard of the objects that begin with *j*, *f*, and *g* for them to review and copy.

5 ASSESS

Materials:
Student Edition,
page 34

Read the directions on page 34 aloud. Ask children to name the objects shown in the pictures. Have them decide which letter is missing and write it in the correct position. When finished, have children rewrite all words for items 1 to 8.

MORE PHONICS PRACTICE

Set aside class time to read trade books with ESL learners. Preview these books and do a first reading to children.

WHERE DO WE GO? by Kara James.
Ready Readers, Stage 0 (Modern Curriculum Press, 1997)

TIME FOR LUNCH by Kathryn E. Lewis.
Ready Readers, Stage 0 (Modern Curriculum Press, 1997)

AstroWord
Some children will benefit from additional individualized feedback, such as that provided by the CD-ROM *AstroWord Consonant Letters and Sounds* (Module 2). Encourage native speakers of English and ESL learners to work together to write some of the words with the sounds of *j*, *f*, and *g* they have learned, using the Word Board and Notepad in the *AstroWord* Free Play room. Monitor each group's progress.

Lesson 16
The Sound of *l*

INFORMAL ASSESSMENT OBJECTIVES

Can children

✔ identify pictures whose names begin with the sound of *l*?

✔ identify and print the uppercase and lowercase forms of the letter *l*?

★ *Native speakers of Vietnamese, Hmong, Korean, and Cantonese may confuse /l/ and /r/. Help them distinguish the difference between these sounds by practicing with* **lock, rock; lid, red; light, right;** *and so on.*

1 INTRODUCE

Materials:
Alphabet chart; Rhyme Poster 11 (optional); Student Edition, pages 35–36

Using an alphabet chart, invite volunteers to point to the uppercase and lowercase forms of the letter *l*. Ask a volunteer to say the letter aloud. Then model the sound of *l* for children.

➤ Assist ESL learners in naming the picture clues and reviewing target words on pages 35–36 of the Student Edition. Model correct pronunciation.

➤ Review the words *lick, lollipop, last,* and *long* from the rhyme on page 35. Have children repeat the words.

➤ Review by pointing to a picture clue and having ESL learners name the object.

2 TEACH

Materials:
Phonics Picture Cards (numbers 16, 22, 27, 31, 32); photos or realia of a lamp, a leaf, a lid, lips, and a lollipop; Student Edition, page 35

Teach the sound of *l*, focusing on oral/aural discrimination.

➤ Say the following words one at a time as you show the picture card or the photo for each: *lamp, horse, lion, leaf, rooster, lid, ladder, nurse, lips, ribbon, lollipop.*

➤ Have ESL learners clap when they hear a word that begins with the sound of *l*. Then ask them to repeat/say the word. Again model pronunciation, as needed.

➤ Review *l* words with children as you write them on the chalkboard (*lamp, lion, leaf, lid, ladder, lips, lollipop*). Tape the picture cards or draw a quick sketch next to each written word to ensure comprehension.

➤ Help children complete the worksheet on page 35.

★ *For specific notes on various home languages, see pages xiii–xvii of this Guide.*

3 PRACTICE

Materials:
Student Edition, page 35; Rhyme Poster 11 (optional); lollipops (optional)

Apply the sound of *l* as you act out the rhyme at the top of page 35. Demonstrate licking a lollipop as you act it out.

➤ Write *lick, lollipop, last,* and *long* on the chalkboard. Have volunteers read the words aloud.

➤ Read the rhyme aloud, using a lollipop to point to target words on the board as you say them. Model natural pronunciation. Have children repeat after you.

➤ Have ESL learners act out the rhyme as they take turns reading a line. Repeat until all children who wish to do so have taken a turn.

➤ Share lollipops with the group. Encourage children to talk about the experience.

4 APPLY

Materials:
Six familiar objects (or pictures of objects) that model the sound of *l* and six that model a different sound (*n* and *r*), two shoeboxes, two index cards, red marker; tape

Adapt the Sorting Sounds activity on page 3k of the *MCP Phonics Teacher Resource Guide* to help children identify and sort familiar objects by initial consonant sounds.

➤ Write *Ll* on one index card and a red circle with a slash through it (international symbol for no) on the other.

➤ Tape one card to the front of each box.

➤ Display the objects/pictures; then have children name and sort them into the appropriate boxes.

➤ Verify that each item in the *Ll* box begins with the sound of *l*.

5 ASSESS

Materials:
Student Edition, page 36

Have children work in pairs according to level of mastery to complete page 36. Together, review the sound of *l* and the picture clues from the activity. Read directions aloud and complete items 1–3 together. Have pairs complete items 4–12. Review the answers.

MORE PHONICS PRACTICE

Set aside class time to read trade books with ESL learners. Preview these books and do a first reading to children.

LOOK CLOSER by Claudia Logan. Ready Readers, Stage 0 (Modern Curriculum Press, 1997)

WHERE DO THEY LIVE? by Stanley Francis. Ready Readers, Stage 1 (Modern Curriculum Press, 1996)

AstroWord

Some learners will benefit from additional practice and individualized feedback, such as that provided by the CD-ROM *AstroWord Consonant Sounds and Letters* (Module 2). Encourage native speakers of English and ESL learners to work together to complete activities that interest them using the sound of *l*. Monitor each group's progress.

Lesson 17
The Sound of *d*

1 INTRODUCE

Materials:
Alphabet chart;
Rhyme Poster 12
(optional); Phonics
Picture Cards
(numbers 7, 8, 9,
71, 72, 79)
(optional); Student
Edition, pages
37–38

Using the Rhyme Poster or the alphabet chart, have ESL learners point to the uppercase or lowercase forms of the letter *d*. Then model the sound of *d* for children.

➤ Clearly pronounce each word beginning with the sound of *d* on pages 37–38 of the Student Edition. Have children repeat. Model the words from the appropriate Phonics Picture Cards as well.

➤ Ask children whose names begin with *d* to write them on the chalkboard. Point out Denny and Dorie in the rhyme on page 37.

➤ Quickly review words beginning with the target sound.

➤ Encourage children to respond individually.

2 TEACH

Materials:
Four or five objects
(pictures or realia)
that model the
sound of *d*; three
or four "non-*d*"
objects; two large
index cards per
child; markers;
Student Edition,
page 37

In this activity, children vote on whether each object begins with the target sound.

➤ Complete and review the worksheet on page 37.

➤ Hand out two index cards to each child. Instruct children to write *Dd* on one of the cards. Tell them to write *no* on the other card; model writing *no* on the chalkboard. Prepare a set of cards to model the activity, if necessary.

➤ Hold up one object or picture (for example, a duck). Ask, "Does the name of this object begin with the sound of *d*?"

➤ Tell children to hold up the *Dd* card if the object does or the *no* card if it does not.

➤ Once all children have voted, have a volunteer name the object aloud. Check for correct voting and hold up your *Dd* card. Repeat with other objects and pictures.

★ *For specific notes on various home languages, see pages xiii–xvii of this Guide.*

3 PRACTICE

Materials:
Student Edition, page 37; Rhyme Poster 12 (optional); play dishes and toy dog (optional)

Use the rhyme on page 37 to further practice the sound of *d*.

➤ Write *does, dishes, Dad,* and *dog* on the chalkboard. Review target words aloud.

➤ Read the rhyme aloud, pointing to the target letter as you say words that begin with the *d* sound.

➤ Make play dishes and a toy dog available to ESL learners. Have them act out the rhyme as they take turns reading a line.

➤ Repeat reading the rhyme.

4 APPLY

Materials:
Mystery Sound Boxes activity, *MCP Phonics Teacher Resource Guide,* page 3j; Ten paper lunch bags, five small objects (or pictures) that model the sound of *d* and five that do not, marker, pencil and paper

Adapt the Mystery Sound Boxes activity for use with ESL learners.

➤ Number the bags from 1 to 10. Place one object inside each bag and close. Place the bags at different stations around the room.

➤ Ask a volunteer to go to Mystery Bag 1. Instruct him or her to open the bag. Ask, "What is inside bag number 1?"

➤ The child removes the picture or object and names it aloud.

➤ As children continue, create a list on the chalkboard of the objects that begin with *d* for children to review and copy. Add a quick sketch next to the written word to ensure ESL learners understand what the written word means.

5 ASSESS

Materials:
Student Edition, page 38

Read the direction line for the activity on page 38 of the Student Edition. Complete items 1–3 aloud together. Have children of different levels of proficiency work in pairs to complete items 4–12. Review answers.

Book Corner

MORE PHONICS PRACTICE

Set aside class time to read trade books with ESL learners. Preview these books and do a first reding to children.

STORY TIME by Polly Peterson. Ready Readers, Stage 0 (Modern Curriculum Press, 1997)

WHO MADE THAT? by Melissa Nicholas. Ready Readers, Stage 1 (Modern Curriculum Press, 1996)

Technology

AstroWord

Some children will benefit from additional practice and individualized feedback on the CD-ROM *AstroWord Consonant Sounds and Letters* (Module 2). Encourage native speakers of English and ESL learners to work on the Easy level of *Make-a-Word,* where children help alien creatures create words by joining the initial consonant with the correct word ending. Monitor each group's progress.

Lesson 18
The Sound of *n*

INFORMAL ASSESSMENT OBJECTIVES

Can children

✔ identify pictures whose names begin with the sound of *n*?

✔ identify and print the uppercase and lowercase forms of the letter *n*?

★ *Some ESL learners may have difficulty discriminating between the English sounds of n and l. Help children differentiate between these sounds by practicing* nine, line; night, light; net, let; *and so forth.*

1 INTRODUCE

Materials:
Rhyme Poster 13;
Student Edition,
pages 39–40

Use the Rhyme Poster to determine if ESL learners can identify the letter *n*. Then model the sound of *n* by reading the rhyme on page 39.

➤ Point to each word beginning with /n/ on Rhyme Poster 13 as you model pronunciation. Have children repeat chorally.

➤ Have a volunteer randomly point to any words beginning with *n* while you and the rest of the children read the word chorally.

➤ Assist ESL learners in naming the picture clues and reviewing words beginning with the sound of *n* on pages 39–40 of the Student Edition. Model correct pronunciation.

2 TEACH

Materials:
Large paper bag or
pillowcase, realia
(or pictures of
objects) beginning
with the sound of
n, chart paper

Prepare a "sound of *n*" grab bag activity by bringing to class several objects whose names begin with the sound of *n*, such as a newspaper, a numeral 9, a nut, a net, a nickel, and so on.

➤ Display items for ESL learners one at a time, modeling correct pronunciation of each. Ask children to repeat chorally.

➤ Put the objects in the bag.

➤ Have volunteers pick one item from the bag and name it aloud. Write the name of the object on the board.

➤ When all objects have been identified, review the list of *n* words on the board. Have children repeat each word.

➤ Ask children to copy the list of words onto chart paper.

➤ Invite them to draw pictures of one or two of the items and use the words in oral sentences.

★ *For specific notes on various home languages, see pages xiii–xvii of this Guide.*

3 PRACTICE

Materials:
Student Edition,
page 39

Practice the sound of *n* by completing the worksheet on page 39 of the Student Edition.

➤ Invite volunteers to name the picture clues one at a time.

➤ Read the directions aloud. Verify comprehension by completing items 1–3 together with ESL learners.

➤ Have children work in pairs to complete items 4–12. Review answers aloud as one group. Correct misconceptions.

4 APPLY

Materials:
Listen for Sounds
activity, *MCP Phonics
Teacher Resource
Guide,* page 3m;
Paper, pencils,
crayons

This activity is a variation of the Listen for Sounds activity for use with ESL learners.

➤ Prepare a list of 10 to 12 words, some beginning with *n* and others with initial /l/ since some ESL learners may need practice discriminating between these two sounds.

➤ Tell children to stand up if they hear the sound of *n* at the beginning of the word. If they do not, they should remain seated. Model the activity.

➤ List the *n* words on the chalkboard for children to copy. You may wish to have ESL learners begin to compile their own picture dictionaries of the new English vocabulary they have learned.

5 ASSESS

Materials:
Student Edition,
page 40

Quickly assess children's level of mastery of the letter *n* by completing the worksheet on page 40. Read the directions aloud. Ask children to work individually to complete the task. Model items 1–3, if necessary, to ensure comprehension.

MORE PHONICS PRACTICE

Set aside class time to read trade books with ESL learners. Preview these books and do a first reading to children.

SOCKS by Mary Solins. Ready Readers, Stage 0 (Modern Curriculum Press, 1997)

NANNY GOAT'S NAP by Ashley Dennis. Ready Readers, Stage 1 (Modern Curriculum Press, 1996)

AstroWord
Some learners will benefit from additional practice and individualized feedback, such as that provided by the CD-ROM *AstroWord Consonant Sounds and Letters* (Module 2). Encourage groups of native speakers of English and ESL learners to work together to complete the Easy level of *Word Sort,* in which children help alien creatures sort picture clues by initial consonant sound.

Lessons 19–20
Reviewing Consonants *s, t, b, h, m, k, j, f, g, l, d, n*

INFORMAL ASSESSMENT OBJECTIVE

Can children

✔ identify and print the initial or final consonant for pictures whose names begin or end with the sounds of *s, t, b, h, m, k, j, f, g, l, d,* and *n*?

★ *For ESL learners who are overwhelmed by this comprehensive a review, focus first on reviewing l, d, n, and areas of recurring difficulty. Add more sounds as children's confidence builds. For more help, refer to this section in Lessons 2–18.*

1 INTRODUCE

Materials:
Student Edition, page 41; Phonics Picture Cards (numbers 1–37); Letter Cards *Ll, Dd, Nn*

Review *l, d, n* to assess ESL learners' ability to identify, pronounce, and print these consonants. Gradually include the remaining nine target consonants.

➤ Have children model the sounds of *l, d,* and *n* as you hold up Letter Cards *Ll, Dd, Nn* one at a time.

➤ Ask volunteers to name each picture clue on page 41 and say if the target sound is at the beginning or end of each word.

➤ Flip through Phonics Picture Cards 1–37, having children name each object and identify the beginning and ending sounds (*s, t, b, h, m, k, j, f, g, l, d,* and *n*).

2 TEACH

Materials:
Student Edition, pages 41–42; *MCP Phonics TRG*, pages 41–42

The Picture search portion of the activity on page 42 may confuse some ESL learners.

➤ Assist children in completing the activity on page 41 in writing. Review answers.

➤ Have children review the picture clues in items 1–6 of the worksheet on page 42.

➤ Tell children they are to write the letter that stands for the beginning sound of each object. Have them complete items 1–6. If children have difficulty, allow them to work in pairs.

➤ Explain the Picture search portion of the activity to children. Assist them in finding and circling one of the hidden picture clues. If a child cannot grasp this concept, simply have him or her talk about the illustration or point to items as you name them.

★ *For specific notes on various home languages, see pages xiii–xvii of this Guide.*

3 PRACTICE

Materials:
Student Edition,
pages 43–44

Expand the review to include all 12 target consonants in initial and final positions.

➤ Read the direction line aloud. Make sure children understand they are to supply both the beginning and the ending sound for each picture clue.

➤ Complete items 1–3 on page 43 aloud with the group.

➤ Have children work individually to complete items 4–12.

➤ Have them work in pairs to complete the activity on page 44.

➤ Review answers orally.

4 APPLY

Materials:
Foam ball, Phonics
Picture Cards
(numbers 1–37)

Adapt the Consonant Catch activity on page 31 of the *MCP Phonics TRG* as follows for ESL learners.

➤ Select one of the Phonics Picture Cards listed to the left.

➤ Hold up the card so children can see it.

➤ Toss the ball to one of the children. Pair a limited English speaker with a more fluent speaker to respond together.

➤ Ask the child to name the object shown on the card and identify the consonant at the beginning of the word.

➤ Repeat, having children name the consonant at the end of each word on the cards.

5 ASSESS

Materials:
Student Edition
pages 43–44; paper
and pencil for each
child

Using the picture names on pages 43–44 of the Student Edition, dictate a list of words beginning or ending with the target sounds. Have children write each word as you say it. Allow less confident writers to only write the beginning and ending letters if writing the word is too challenging. Review answers chorally.

Book Corner

MORE PHONICS PRACTICE

Set aside class time to read trade books with ESL learners. Preview these books and do a first reading to children.

LITTLE KITTENS by Mary Solins. Ready Readers, Stage 0 (Modern Curriculum Press, 1997)

BY THE TREE by Marilyn Minkoff. Ready Readers, Stage 1 (Modern Curriculum Press, 1996)

Technology

AstroWord

ESL learners will benefit from additional individualized feedback provided by the *CD-ROM AstroWord Consonant Sounds and Letters* (Module 2). Encourage native speakers of English and ESL learners to work together to write some of the words with the 12 review consonants, using the Word Board and Notepad in the *AstroWord* Free Play room. Monitor each group's progress.

Lesson 21
Partner Letters *Ww, Cc, Rr, Pp, Qq, Vv*

INFORMAL ASSESSMENT OBJECTIVE

Can children

✔ identify by name the uppercase and lowercase forms of the letters *w, c, r, p, q,* and *v?*

★ *Some English Language Learners may be learning the Roman alphabet for the first time, so discriminate form from size between uppercase and lowercase letters.*

1 INTRODUCE

Materials:
Alphabet chart;
Student Edition,
pages 45–46

Work one-on-one with your ESL learners to evaluate how familiar each child is with the six target partner letters to see if he or she can identify the uppercase and lowercase forms as you say them aloud.

➤ Using an alphabet chart, point to one of the target letters and have the child name the letter. Reinforce correct responses.

➤ Repeat this activity. As competence builds, expand and review the consonants presented in Lessons 1–20 along with the new ones from this lesson.

➤ Have children who need additional support practice writing the uppercase and lowercase forms of the new target consonants.

2 TEACH

Materials:
Student Edition,
page 45; colored
chalk

Review the forms of the new partner letters while introducing words beginning with the target sounds.

➤ Write lowercase *w, c, r, p, q,* and *v* on the board. Ask ESL learner volunteers to write the uppercase form of each. Erase.

➤ Repeat by writing uppercase *W, C, R, P, Q,* and *V* on the chalkboard and having children write the lowercase forms.

➤ Read aloud the directions for the worksheet on page 45.

➤ Work with ESL learners to complete item 1. Write *Pig* on the chalkboard, using colored chalk for the uppercase *P*.

➤ Model the pronunciation; have children repeat several times.

➤ Ask a volunteer to name the first letter in *pig*. Tell children they must now color all the pigs that contain the partner of the uppercase letter *P* shown in the box.

➤ Repeat with items 2 (*wagon*) and 3 (*robot*).

★ *For specific notes on various home languages, see pages xiii–xvii of this Guide.*

3 PRACTICE

Materials:
12 index cards, marker, five or six familiar classroom objects

Practice visual recognition of the target partner letters while reinforcing general language comprehension.

➤ Write one letter form of the target letters on each index card.

➤ Randomly display cards face up in a grid on a desk or ledge, along with a variety of classroom objects.

➤ Direct each ESL learner to perform a task, such as "Pick up both *p* cards and put them under the book (in the box, and so on)." Ask focused comprehension questions: "Where are the *p* cards?"

➤ Shuffle cards. Repeat, varying letters and questions.

4 APPLY

Materials:
Student Edition, page 46; red and blue crayons

Have children complete this activity to demonstrate comprehension of the target partner letters.

➤ Read aloud to the group the direction line for the activity on page 46 of the Student Edition.

➤ Model the task by completing item 1 with children. Check work.

➤ Ask children to work in pairs to complete the worksheet.

5 ASSESS

Materials:
Blackline Master 6, *MCP Phonics Teacher Resource Guide*, page 3n; tagboard; scissors

Copy Blackline Master 6 onto one side of the tagboard. Cut apart to make cards with blank backs. Place the uppercase target letters face up in a grid and the lowercase letters face down in a pile. Have children turn over one lowercase card, name the letter, and match it with its uppercase partner. Repeat, using letters from previous lessons as a review.

MORE PHONICS PRACTICE

Set aside class time to read trade books with ESL learners. Preview these books and do a first reading to children.

A MESS by Bob Allen. Ready Readers, Stage 1 (Modern Curriculum Press, 1996)

LET'S GO MARCHING! by Judy Spevak. Ready Readers, Stage 1 (Modern Curriculum Press, 1996)

AstroWord

Some learners will benefit from additional practice and individualized feedback, such as that provided by the CD-ROM *AstroWord Consonant Sounds and Letters* (Module 2). Encourage ESL learners to work together with more English-proficient children to complete activities that interest them. Monitor each group's progress.

Lesson 22
The Sound of *w*

INFORMAL ASSESSMENT OBJECTIVES

Can children

✔ identify pictures whose names begin with the sound of *w*?

✔ identify and print the uppercase and lowercase forms of the letter *w*?

★ *Many ESL learners will confuse both the sound and the form of* w *with those of* v *because* w *may be an uncommon letter and sound in their native language. Practice* wet, vet; well, veil; west, vest; *and so on.*

---

1 INTRODUCE

Materials:
Student Edition, page 47; Rhyme Poster 14 (optional); Alphabet chart

Using an alphabet chart, assess ESL learners' prior knowledge of the sound of *w*. Then model the sound of *w* and review the appropriate words and picture clues on page 47 of the Student Edition.

➤ Review the words *we*, *watch*, *window*, *winter*, *wind*, and *wish* from the rhyme on page 47. Have children repeat these words.

➤ Working with individual children, point to a picture clue in the book. Have the child name the object and model for you the sound of *w*. Practice until children are successful.

2 TEACH

Materials:
Four or five objects (pictures or realia) that make the sound of *w*; three or four "non-*w*" objects; two large index cards per child; markers; Student Edition, page 47

In this activity, children will vote on whether each object they see begins with the sound of *w*.

➤ Complete and review the worksheet on page 47.

➤ Hand out two index cards to each child. Have children write *Ww* on one of the cards and *no* on the other. Model writing *no* on the chalkboard. Prepare a set of cards for you to use as you model the activity.

➤ Hold up one object or picture (for example, a watch). Ask, "Does the name of this object begin with the sound of *w*?"

➤ Tell children to hold up the *Ww* card if it does or the *no* card if it does not.

➤ Once all children have voted, ask a volunteer to name the object aloud. Model how to vote correctly by holding up your *Ww* card. Verify children's comprehension by asking additional questions.

➤ Repeat with other objects and pictures.

★ *For specific notes on various home languages, see pages xiii–xvii of this Guide.*

3 PRACTICE

Materials:
Student Edition, page 47; Rhyme Poster 14 (optional)

Use the rhyme on page 47 to further practice the sound of *w*.

➤ Write *we*, *watch*, *window*, *winter*, *wind*, and *wish* on the chalkboard. Review the words aloud. Have children repeat chorally at first, then individually.

➤ Read the rhyme aloud, pointing to target words on the chalkboard or on Rhyme Poster 14 as you say them.

➤ Have ESL learners take turns reading a line. Ask reinforcing comprehension questions such as "What can we watch from our window?" and "Is the wind blowing today?"

➤ Assign turns as children continue reading the rhyme.

4 APPLY

Materials:
Student Edition, page 47

Have children of varying English language proficiency levels work in pairs to complete the worksheet on page 47.

➤ Review the sound of *w* and the picture clues.

➤ Read the directions aloud and complete items 1 and 2 together.

➤ Ask ESL learners to complete items 3–9 in pairs. Review the answers together as a class.

5 ASSESS

Materials:
Student Edition, page 48

Adapt the worksheet on Student Edition page 48 for individualized assessment with ESL learners. Read the directions orally. Have each child complete the worksheet aloud with you. Offer support as needed.

Book Corner

MORE PHONICS PRACTICE

Set aside class time to read trade books with ESL learners. Preview these books and do a first reading to children.

ALL WET by Judy Nayer. Ready Readers, Stage 0 (Modern Curriculum Press, 1997)

WILMA'S WAGON by John Hudson. Ready Readers, Stage 1 (Modern Curriculum Press, 1996)

Technology

AstroWord

Some children will benefit from additional audiovisual feedback, such as that provided by the CD-ROM *AstroWord Consonant Sounds and Letters* (Module 2). Encourage native speakers of English and ESL learners to work together to complete the Easy level of *Word Sort*, in which children help alien creatures sort picture clues by initial consonant sound.

Lesson 23
The Sound of c

INFORMAL ASSESSMENT OBJECTIVES

Can children

✔ identify pictures whose names begin with the sound of *c*?

✔ identify and print the uppercase and lowercase forms of the letter *c*?

★ *Native speakers of Asian languages, especially Korean, may not discriminate /k/ from /g/, and so on. So practice* coat, goat; cold, gold; *and so on. In Russian, the written* Cc *is equivalent to the English* Ss. *Reinforce the* k *sound of* c *with* cat, sat; can, sand; *and so on.*

1 INTRODUCE

Materials:
Alphabet chart;
Student Edition, page
49; Rhyme Poster 15
(optional); Phonics
Picture Cards
(numbers 5, 6, 48,
49, 63, 86)

Using an alphabet chart, verify whether ESL learners can identify the uppercase and lowercase forms of the letter *c*.

➤ Pronounce each word beginning with the sound of *c* in the activities on pages 49–50 of the Student Edition. Have children repeat each word after you.

➤ Ask children whose names begin with *c* to write them on the chalkboard. Point out Carla and Cory in the rhyme on page 49.

➤ Review the sound of *c* using Phonics Picture Cards.

2 TEACH

Materials:
Pictures of
household objects
or realia that make
the sound of *c*, two
or three "non-*c*"
objects, crayons
and paper for each
child

Build everyday vocabulary with "*c* around the house."

➤ Draw an outline of a house on the chalkboard; make it large enough to contain several words. Have children draw a house shape on their papers.

➤ Use household items with the sound of *c*, such as *cup, coat, comb, candle, cat, can, cookie,* and *carrot*.

➤ Mix up the objects and display them one at a time. Invite volunteers to name aloud each object.

➤ Ask children to determine if the object name begins with the sound of *c*. If it does, write the word inside your house; instruct children to add the word to their drawing. Encourage children to draw a quick sketch beside each word to remind them of the meaning.

➤ After writing four or five *c* words, review them chorally. Correct misconceptions.

★ *For specific notes on various home languages, see pages xiii–xvii of this Guide.*

3 PRACTICE

Materials:
Student Edition, page 49; six index cards; markers, such as buttons, bingo chips, or pennies

Adapt the worksheet on page 49 of the Student Edition to provide additional practice with the sound of *c*.

➤ Write the words *cat, cone, can, cup, cake,* and *coat* on index cards, one word per card. Review the word cards one at a time, orally, with the group.

➤ Hold up a word card. Instruct ESL learners to cover the matching picture clue on their papers with a marker.

➤ When finished, remove the markers. Read the directions aloud. Have individuals complete the worksheet.

4 APPLY

Materials:
Student Edition, page 49; Rhyme Poster 15 (optional); props from the rhyme

Apply kinesthetic learning while having children read and act out the rhyme on page 49.

➤ Ask children to talk about the drawing that accompanies the rhyme.

➤ Read the rhyme aloud. Have each ESL learner read or repeat one line at a time.

➤ Invite children to role-play what Carla and Cory do next.

5 ASSESS

Materials:
Student Edition, page 50

As a group, review the sound of *c* and the picture clues. Read directions aloud and complete items 1 and 2 on page 50 together. Then have children of varying English language proficiency levels work in pairs to complete items 3–12. Review answers together as a class.

MORE PHONICS PRACTICE

Set aside class time to read trade books with ESL learners. Preview these books and do a first reading to children.

THE CAT CAME BACK by Carly Easton. Ready Readers, Stage 0 (Modern Curriculum Press, 1997)

I LIKE TO COUNT by Cynthia Rothman. Ready Readers, Stage 1 (Modern Curriculum Press, 1996)

AstroWord
Some children will benefit from additional practice and individualized feedback on the CD-ROM *AstroWord Consonant Sounds and Letters* (Module 2). Encourage native speakers of English and ESL language Learners to work on the Easy level of *Make-a-Word*, where children help alien creatures create words based on a picture clue by joining the initial consonant with the correct word ending. Monitor each group's progress.

Lesson 24
The Sound of *r*

INFORMAL ASSESSMENT OBJECTIVES

Can children

✔ identify pictures whose names begin with the sound of *r*?

✔ identify and print the uppercase and lowercase forms of the letter *r*?

★ *Spanish and Tagalog speakers might trill initial* r *or pronounce "tap* r*" (similar to* tt *in* better*). Native speakers of languages such as Vietnamese, Hmong, Korean, and Cantonese may confuse /r/ and /l/; practice* rock, lock; right, light; red, lid; *and so forth.*

---

1 INTRODUCE

Materials:
Student Edition, pages 51–52; *MCP Phonics TRG*, pages 51–52; Phonics Picture Cards (numbers 31, 32, 66, 91, 104) (optional); hand mirrors

The sound of *r* is one of the more difficult sounds for many ESL learners to master. Emphasize oral practice at all phases of teaching this lesson.

➤ Model the sound of *r* and review the appropriate words and picture clues on pages 51–52 of the Student Edition and/or the Phonics Picture Cards listed to the left.

➤ Introduce the words *row* and *red* from the rhyme on page 51.

➤ Have children repeat. Have them look at how your mouth looks while producing the /r/. Provide mirrors so that they can watch their own mouths.

➤ Working with individual children point to a picture clue in the Student Edition. Have the child name the object and model the sound of *r*. Repeat several times. Tape-record responses so that children can hear their improvement.

2 TEACH

Materials:
Pencils and paper

Teach the sound of *r*, focusing on oral/aural discrimination.

➤ Say the following words one at a time: *row, red, lake, rake, radio, rat, wet, rabbit, wing, ring, rain, star, ribbon, let,* and *rug*.

➤ Ask ESL learners to stand up when they hear you say a word that begins with the sound of *r*.

➤ Review the *r* words with children; have them repeat each word chorally, then individually.

➤ Write the words beginning with the sound of *r* on the chalkboard; have children copy the list. Encourage children to draw a quick sketch next to the word if they need a reminder of what it means.

★ *For specific notes on various home languages, see pages xiii–xvii of this Guide.*

3 PRACTICE

Materials:
Student Edition, page 51; Rhyme Poster 16 (optional); pencils

Use the rhyme and the worksheet on page 51 to further practice the sound of *r*.

➤ Write *row, red, rake, robot, rat, rain, radio,* and *ring* on the board. Review target words aloud.

➤ Read the rhyme aloud. Have ESL learners take turns reading a line. Repeat reading the rhyme.

➤ As you point to target words on the chalkboard, have children circle the matching picture on the worksheet.

4 APPLY

Materials:
4–6 familiar objects (or pictures of items) that make the sound of *r* and 4–6 that make a different consonant sound, two shoe-boxes, two index cards, red marker, tape

This activity is an adaptation of Sorting Sounds on page 3k of the *MCP Phonics Teacher Resource Guide.*

➤ Write *Rr* on one index card and a red circle with a slash through it (the international symbol for no) on another.

➤ Tape one card to the front of each box.

➤ Display the objects/pictures and have children name and sort them into the appropriate containers.

➤ Verify that each item in the *Rr* box begins with the sound of *r*.

5 ASSESS

Materials:
Student Edition, page 52

Read the directions and explain the task to ESL learners as needed. Ask children to name each picture; assist with less familiar objects. Complete the worksheet as a group and review answers. Ask children what sound they hear at the end of the words *four* and *star*.

MORE PHONICS PRACTICE

Set aside class time to read trade books with ESL learners. Preview these books and do a first reading to children

RED OR BLUE? by Jenni Stevens. Ready Readers, Stage 0 (Modern Curriculum Press, 1997)

WHO IS READY? by Katherine E. Lewis. Ready Readers, Stage 1 (Modern Curriculum Press, 1996)

AstroWord

Some ESL learners will benefit from additional practice and individualized feedback, such as that provided by the CD-ROM *AstroWord Consonant Sounds and Letters* (Module 2). Encourage native speakers of English and ESL learners to work together to complete activities that interest them using the sound of *r*. Monitor each group's progress.

Lesson 25
Reviewing Consonants *l, d, n, w, c, r*

INFORMAL ASSESSMENT OBJECTIVE

Can children

✔ identify and print the initial or final consonants for pictures whose names begin or end with the sounds of *l, d, n, w, c,* and *r?*

★ *If ESL learners are overwhelmed by this comprehensive a review, focus first on areas of specific trouble and gradually expand the review to include all six target letters and their sounds.*

1 INTRODUCE

Materials:
Letter Cards *Ll, Dd, Nn, Ww, Cc,* and *Rr*; Phonics Picture Cards (numbers 5–8, 21, 22, 26, 27, 31, 32, 40, 41)

Review the six target consonants by checking visual recognition and reviewing familiar words that begin with the target sounds.

➤ Hold up a Letter Card and have a volunteer name the letter.

➤ Display Phonics Picture Cards face up in a grid. Ask each ESL learner to choose a card, name the object on that card, and identify the letter that stands for the beginning sound. Pair less confident ESL learners with partners to do the activity.

➤ Have the child locate the Phonics Picture Card that has an object beginning with the same sound. Continue until all six matches have been made. Shuffle the cards and repeat.

2 TEACH

Materials:
Chalkboard, colored chalk

Review the six target sounds in initial position while teaching words with the target sounds in final position.

➤ Write lowercase *l, d, n, w, c,* and *r* on the chalkboard. Ask ESL learners to write the uppercase form of each.

➤ Write *lick, dish, not, wet, can,* and *rug,* using colored chalk to write the first letter of each. Orally model the beginning sounds, and have children say the words aloud. Encourage children to offer other words that begin with the six target sounds and add them to the chalkboard.

➤ Write *l, d, n, w,* and *r* on the chalkboard in final sound position (preceded by blank rule: ____l, ____d, and so on).

➤ Have children suggest words that end in these sounds.

➤ Provide support by pointing to objects in the classroom (such as a bell, a wall, a pencil, a board, a pad, a pen, a crayon, a chair, a window, a ruler, and paper).

★ *For specific notes on various home languages, see pages xiii–xvii of this Guide.*

3 PRACTICE

Materials:
Student Edition, page 53; Letter Cards *Ll, Dd, Nn, Ww, Cc,* and *Rr*

Adapt the worksheet on page 53 to practice letter and vocabulary recognition.

➤ Tell children you are going to hold up a letter card. Instruct them to find a picture on page 53 whose name begins with the sound of the letter you display.

➤ When volunteers match correctly, have children write the letter in the correct initial position. Repeat.

4 APPLY

Materials:
Ten paper lunch bags, ten small objects (or pictures) that make the target sounds in initial or final position, pencil and paper

Adapt the Mystery Sound Boxes activity from page 3j of *the MCP Phonics Teacher Resource Guide* to support your ESL learners.

➤ Number the bags from 1 to 10. Place one object or picture inside each bag and close. Display bags on a table or a desk.

➤ Have a volunteer open Mystery Bag 1 and name the object or picture inside. Then ask the child, "What letter stands for the beginning (or ending) sound you hear in the word [*object name*]?"

➤ As children continue, create a list of the objects on the chalkboard for children to copy and review.

5 ASSESS

Materials:
Student Edition, page 54

Read the direction line for the activity on page 54 of the Student Edition. Ask ESL learners to name the 12 picture clues. Have children write the initial letter next to each picture, if they need the references. Model the activity by helping the group complete item 1. Ask children to work together to complete items 2–6. Review responses orally.

Book Corner

MORE PHONICS PRACTICE

Set aside class time to read trade books with ESL learners. Preview these books and do a first reading to children.

KEYS by Mark Adams. Ready Readers, Stage 0 (Modern Curriculum Press, 1997)

NIGHT ANIMALS by Gale Clifford. Ready Readers, Stage 1 (Modern Curriculum Press, 1996)

VAN'S SANDWICH by Dina Anastasio. Beginning Discovery Phonics (Modern Curriculum Press, 1994)

Technology

AstroWord
Some ESL learners will benefit from additional individualized feedback such as that provided by the CD-ROM *AstroWord Consonant Sounds and Letters* (Module 2). Encourage native speakers of English and ESL learners to work together to write some of the words with the sounds of *l, d, n, w, c,* and *r,* using the Word Board and Notepad in the *AstroWord* Free Play room. Monitor each group's progress.

Lesson 26
The Sound of *p*

INFORMAL ASSESSMENT OBJECTIVES

Can children

✔ identify pictures whose names begin with the sound of *p*?

✔ identify and print the uppercase and lowercase forms of the letter *p*?

★ *To distinguish initial /p/ from /f/ or /v/, practice* pine, fine, vine; pan, fan, van. *Speakers of Korean may confuse initial /p/ with /b/; practice* pig, big; pie, bye; *and* pat, bat.

1 INTRODUCE

Materials:
Rhyme Poster 17;
Alphabet chart;
Student Edition,
pages 55–56;
Phonics Picture
Cards (numbers
28, 29)

Using the Rhyme Poster or alphabet chart, have ESL learners point to the uppercase or lowercase forms of the letter *p* to verify ESL learners' prior knowledge of the distinction. Model the difference between the sound of *p* and that of *v, f, b*, or others your ESL learners confuse. Provide independent practice as needed.

▶ Model the sound of *p* and review the appropriate words and picture clues on pages 55–56 of the Student Edition and/or those from the Picture Cards listed. Have children practice pronouncing the *p* while looking at how you position your lips when you model.

▶ Review the words *Penny, passed, peach,* and *piece* from the rhyme on page 55. Have children repeat.

▶ Point to a picture clue. Have a child name the object and make the initial consonant sound.

2 TEACH

Materials:
One large index
card per child;
markers; pencils
and paper; Student
Edition, page 55

Teach the sound of *p*, focusing on oral/aural discrimination.

▶ Assist ESL learners in writing *Pp* on their index cards. Check their work.

▶ Say the following words one at a time: *pig, big, fan, pan, pie, vine, puppet, bird, purse,* and *pot.*

▶ Have ESL learners hold up their *Pp* cards when they hear a word that begins with the sound of *p*.

▶ Create a list of words that begin with *p* (*pig, pan, pie, puppet, purse, pot*) on the chalkboard. Review orally and have children copy the list. Encourage children to draw a quick sketch for words they need to learn. Have children use the words in oral sentences.

▶ Complete the worksheet on page 55 aloud as a group.

★ *For specific notes on various home languages, see pages xiii–xvii of this Guide.*

3 PRACTICE

Materials:
Student Edition,
page 55; Rhyme
Poster 17 (optional)

Use the rhyme on page 55 to practice words that begin with the sound of *p*.

➤ Write *Penny, peach, pie,* and *piece* on the chalkboard. Review target words aloud.

➤ Act out *passed the pie* to clarify meaning, if necessary.

➤ Read the rhyme aloud, pointing to target words as you say them.

➤ Have ESL learners act out the rhyme as they take turns reading a line.

➤ Repeat reading the rhyme.

4 APPLY

Materials:
Consonant
Caterpillars activity,
*MCP Phonics Teacher
Resource Guide,* page
3m; Construction
paper circles,
markers or crayons,
old magazines,
scissors, glue or
tape, pipe cleaners

Have ESL learners create Consonant Caterpillars for the sound of *p*.

➤ Hand out five or six paper circles to each child. Assist those ESL learners who need support in writing *Pp* on one circle.

➤ Ask children to draw a smiling face on one circle. On the others, have them draw or cut and paste pictures of objects that begin with the sound of *p*. Have, or help, them write the name of each object beneath the picture.

➤ Assemble the caterpillars by pasting or taping circles together. Add pipe cleaner antennae and feet.

➤ Have children read their caterpillars to a partner.

5 ASSESS

Materials:
Student Edition,
page 56; peanuts or
pennies

Hand out several pennies or peanuts to each ESL learner. Say the name of one of the objects on worksheet page 56 whose name begins with the sound of *p*. Instruct children to cover the pictures with a penny. After practicing five or six words, collect the pennies. Read the worksheet directions aloud. Have individuals complete the worksheet.

Book Corner

MORE PHONICS PRACTICE

Set aside class time to read trade books with ESL learners. Preview these books and do a first reading to children.

PINK PIG by Tim Anton. Ready Readers, Stage 0 (Modern Curriculum Press, 1997)

PAT'S PERFECT PIZZA by F. R. Robinson. Ready Readers, Stage 1 (Modern Curriculum Press, 1996)

Technology

AstroWord

Some ESL learners will benefit from additional audiovisual feedback, such as that provided by the CD-ROM *AstroWord Consonant Sounds and Letters* (Module 2). Encourage children to work together to complete the Easy level of *Word Sort,* in which children help alien creatures sort picture clues by specific consonant. Monitor each group's progress.

Lesson 27
The Sound of *qu* and the Sound of *v*

INFORMAL ASSESSMENT OBJECTIVES

Can children

✔ identify pictures whose names begin with the sounds of *qu* and *v*?

✔ identify and print the uppercase and lowercase forms of the letters *qu* and *v*?

★ *Native speakers of Spanish may pronounce* qu *like the sound of* k *instead of* kw. *Practice with* queen, key; quarter, kangaroo; *and* quiet, kite. *Spanish speakers will also pronounce /v/ as /b/.*

---

1 INTRODUCE

Materials:
Student Edition, pages 57–58; Valentine's Day realia

Introduce the sounds of *qu* and *v* to ESL learners by reviewing the picture clues in the Student Edition. Assess ESL learners' prior knowledge of the sounds and reinforce individually, as needed.

➤ Model the sounds of *qu* and *v* for children. Emphasize that *q* is never used without *u* in English, with words like *quiet* and *quack*.

➤ Assist ESL learners in naming the picture clues. Model correct pronunciation.

➤ Review the words *quack*, *quiet*, and *valentine* from the rhymes on pages 57–58. Have children repeat. Note that some ESL learners may not have experienced Valentine's Day in their own cultures and may need some background information about the holiday. Bring in Valentine's Day realia to help illustrate this concept.

➤ Point to a picture clue and have a volunteer name the object.

2 TEACH

Materials:
Three index cards per child, markers

Teach the sounds of *qu* and *v*, focusing on oral/aural discrimination.

➤ Have ESL learners prepare a set of three cards; write *Qq*, *Vv*, and a red circle with a slash through it (international symbol for no) on cards.

➤ Say the following words one at a time: *valentine*, *quiet*, *wet*, *face*, *vase*, *question*, *vegetable*, *quarter*, *water*, and *vest*.

➤ Have children hold up the card containing the letter that stands for the sound they hear at the beginning of each word.

➤ Review all words with children. Repeat the activity.

★ *For specific notes on various home languages, see pages xiii–xvii of this Guide.*

3 PRACTICE

Materials:
Student Edition, pages 57–58; Rhyme Posters 18 and 19 (optional); props from each rhyme (optional)

Use the rhymes to further practice the sounds of *qu* and *v*.

➤ Write *Quinn, quiet, quack, Viv, Val, Van,* and *valentine* on the chalkboard. Review target words aloud.

➤ Read the first rhyme aloud, encouraging ESL learners to read with the intonation of a dialogue.

➤ Have ESL learners take turns reading a line.

➤ Repeat with the second rhyme. Emphasize rhythm and intonation associated with this kind of poem.

4 APPLY

Materials:
Mystery Sound Boxes activity, *MCP Phonics Teacher Resource Guide,* page 3j; ten paper lunch bags, five small objects (or pictures) that make the sound of *qu* and five that make the sound of *v,* markers, pencil and paper

Adapt the Mystery Sound Boxes activity for your ESL learners.

➤ Number the bags from 1 to 10. Place one object or picture inside each bag and close. Place the bags in different locations around the room.

➤ Ask an ESL learner volunteer to go to and open Mystery Bag 1. Ask, "What is inside bag number 1?"

➤ Tell the child to remove the picture/object and say the name.

➤ Write *Q* and *V* on the chalkboard. Keep a list of the words that begin with each for children to review and copy. Children may wish to draw a quick sketch to remind them what the words mean. Have children use the words in oral sentences.

5 ASSESS

Materials:
Student Edition, pages 57–58

Read the directions on page 57 and review the picture clues on pages 57–58. Clarify as necessary. Complete items 1 and 2 aloud with the group. Have pairs work together to finish the activity, then do the activity on page 58. Review answers as a group.

Book Corner

MORE PHONICS PRACTICE

Set aside class time to read trade books with ESL learners. Preview these books and do a first reading to children.

QUEEN ON A QUILT by Maryann Dobeck. Ready Readers, Stage 0 (Modern Curriculum Press, 1997)

VERY BIG by Cherie Horn. Ready Readers, Stage 1 (Modern Curriculum Press, 1996)

Technology

AstroWord

Some children will benefit from additional practice and individualized feedback on the CD-ROM *AstroWord Consonant Sounds and Letters* (Module 2). Encourage children to work on the Easy level of *Make-a-Word,* where they will help alien creatures create words based on picture clues by joining the initial consonant with the correct word ending. Monitor each group's progress.

Lesson 28
Reviewing Consonants *w, c, r, p, q, v*

INFORMAL ASSESSMENT OBJECTIVE

Can children

✔ identify and print the initial or final consonant for pictures whose names begin or end with the sounds of *w, c, r, p, q,* and *v*?

1 INTRODUCE

Materials:
Letter Cards *Ww, Cc, Rr, Pp, Qq, Vv;*
Phonics Picture Cards (numbers 4, 5, 28–32, 38–41)

Using the Letter Cards, assess whether ESL learners have learned the sounds of each target letter. Then review aloud the letter names, the sound each stands for, and words that begin with each target sound.

➤ Have available Phonics Picture Cards for those ESL learners who may need a picture clue to help them retrieve a word that begins with the target letter. Children can also refer to any word wall you have created together with the class with words beginning or ending with those sounds.

➤ Hold up a Letter Card. Ask an ESL learner to name the letter, model the sound, and say a word that begins with the target sound. Review cards several times.

➤ Pronounce each word beginning with the sounds of *w, c, r, p, q,* and *v* on the worksheet on page 59 of the Student Edition. Have ESL learners repeat each word after you.

➤ Point to picture clues from the worksheet. Ask a volunteer to name the objects.

2 TEACH

Materials:
Pictures of objects or realia whose names begin or end with the sounds of *w, c, r, p, q,* and *v;* colored chalk; Phonics Picture Cards (numbers 4, 5, 28–32, 38–41)

Review the sounds of *w, c, r, p, q,* and *v* in initial position while teaching words with the sounds of final consonants *r* and *p.*

➤ Write the six letters on the chalkboard in colored chalk. Write *r* and *p* twice (in two columns): once as an initial consonant and once in the final position.

➤ Have volunteers suggest aloud the names of objects that begin or end with each sound and write each word in the correct column.

➤ Underline *r* and *p* to show that they stand for the same sound in either word position: *rake, car, pig, top.*

➤ Hold up a picture or object and have a volunteer name the object and its beginning or ending sound.

➤ Add the word to the appropriate column. Review the list orally.

★ *For specific notes on various home languages, see pages xiii–xvii of this Guide.*

3 PRACTICE

Materials:
Student Edition, page 59

Use the worksheet on page 59 to practice the target sounds in initial and final positions.

➤ Read the directions aloud.

➤ Assist ESL learners in completing items 1–3 as a small group.

➤ Ask children to work in pairs to complete items 4–12. Review answers together as a class.

4 APPLY

Materials:
10–12 familiar objects (or pictures of objects) that make the sounds of *w, c, r, p, q,* and *v;* Letter Cards *Ww, Cc, Rr, Pp, Qq, Vv*

This activity is an adaptation of Sorting Sounds from page 3k of the *MCP Phonics TRG.*

➤ Display the objects or pictures on a table. Have ESL learners name the objects or pictures aloud one at a time.

➤ Place the Letter Cards in a row on the table.

➤ Tell children to sort the objects by initial sound, placing them with the corresponding Letter Card. Model with one object if necessary.

➤ Repeat the procedure, this time sorting the objects by final sound.

5 ASSESS

Materials:
Student Edition, page 60

Read the directions aloud. Ask children to name the picture clues. Have them decide which letter is missing and write it in the correct position. When finished, assist them with the "secret message." If children have difficulty reading vertically, rewrite the message for them from left to right.

Book Corner

MORE PHONICS PRACTICE

Set aside class time to read trade books with ESL learners. Preview these books and do a first reading to children.

MAMA HEN, COME QUICK by Janet Fisher. Ready Readers, Stage 0 (Modern Curriculum Press, 1997)

NIGHT ANIMALS by Gale Clifford. Ready Readers, Stage 1 (Modern Curriculum Press, 1996)

Technology

AstroWord

Some learners will benefit from additional practice and individualized feedback, such as that provided by the CD-ROM *AstroWord Consonant Sounds and Letters* (Module 2). Encourage ESL learners and native speakers of English to work together to write some of the words with the sounds of *w, c, r, p, q,* and *v* they have learned, using the Word Board and Notepad in the *AstroWord* Free Play room. Monitor each group's progress.

Lesson 29
Partner Letters *Xx, Yy, Zz*

INFORMAL ASSESSMENT OBJECTIVE

Can children

✔ identify by name the uppercase and lowercase forms of the letters *x*, *y*, and *z*?

★ *Native speakers of Spanish may need extra pronunciation practice with the sounds of* x *and* z, *which sometimes sound like* ss.

---

1 INTRODUCE

Materials:
Alphabet chart, set of Letter Cards for each child

Introduce ESL learners to the letters *x*, *y*, and *z* by telling them these are the last three letters of the English alphabet. Use an alphabet chart and point to *x* to verify children's ability to name the letter. Repeat with *y* and *z*.

➤ Give each ESL learner a shuffled set of Letter Cards. Call out one of the three letters and have children find the correct card. When all three cards are found, ask children to sequence them in alphabetical order.

➤ Have children who need additional support practice writing the uppercase and lowercase forms of the target consonants.

2 TEACH

Materials:
Student Edition, page 61; crayons

Review the forms of the new partner letters and reinforce visual recognition.

➤ Write lowercase *x*, *y*, and *z* on the chalkboard. Ask ESL learner volunteers to write the uppercase form of each.

➤ Discuss the picture clues on the worksheet on page 61. Assess whether children can name any of the animals shown. Encourage all verbal input.

➤ Read the directions for the worksheet aloud to the group.

➤ Structure the activity by having children use a specific color for each target letter: "Let's color the animals with matching *y* partners yellow."

★ *For specific notes on various home languages, see pages xiii–xvii of this Guide.*

3 PRACTICE

Materials:
Letter Cards *Xx, Yy, Zz*; five or six familiar classroom objects

Practice visual recognition of the new partner letters as you reinforce general language comprehension.

➤ Display the Letter Cards face up in a grid on a desk along with the objects. Include items that model the new consonant sounds, such as numerals six and zero, yarn, and yellow paper.

➤ Give each ESL learner a task to perform, such as: "Put the yarn on top of the card with the letter *y*."

➤ Ask directed questions to assess comprehension such as, "David, can you point to the yellow card?" Where ESL learners can respond orally, ask questions that prompt word answers. Repeat.

4 APPLY

Materials:
Blackline Master 6, *MCP Phonics Teacher Resource Guide,* page 3n; tagboard; scissors

Have children discriminate between the new target letters and others learned previously that look similar by playing Consonant Concentration.

➤ Copy Blackline Master 6 onto tagboard. Cut apart to make cards with blank backs.

➤ Select uppercase and lowercase cards for *x, y, z, w, v,* and *k*.

➤ Place the cards face down in a grid.

➤ Have children turn over one card, name the letter, and match it with its uppercase partner. Paired partner letter cards are picked up.

5 ASSESS

Materials:
Student Edition, page 62; crayons

Assess children comprehension of the sounds presented in this lesson by completing the worksheet on page 62. Read aloud the directions for the activity on page 62. Further clarify if necessary. Help ESL learners to complete items 1 and 2. Have children work together in pairs to complete items 3–9. Review answers.

Book Corner

MORE PHONICS PRACTICE

Set aside class time to read trade books with ESL learners. Preview these books and do a first reading to children.

A BIG, BIG BOX by Bob Allen. Ready Readers, Stage 0 (Modern Curriculum Press, 1997)

GOOD-BYE, ZOO by Bob Egan. Ready Readers, Stage 1 (Modern Curriculum Press, 1996)

Technology

AstroWord

Some learners will benefit from additional practice and individualized feedback, such as that provided by the CD-ROM *AstroWord Consonant Sounds and Letters* (Module 2). Encourage ESL learners to work together with more English-proficient children to complete activities that interest them. Monitor each group's progress.

Lesson 30
The Sound of *x* and the Sound of *y*

INFORMAL ASSESSMENT OBJECTIVES

Can children

✔ identify pictures whose names end with the sound of *x*?

✔ identify pictures whose names begin with the sound of *y*?

★ *Children who speak Spanish or Tagalog may pronounce initial /y/ like* g *in* genre *or like* j *in* joy. *Those who speak Cambodian or Vietnamese may pronounce it like* ny *in* canyon.

1 INTRODUCE

Materials:
Letter Cards *Xx, Yy;* colored chalk

Review Pretest questions 11 and 21 to determine ESL learners' prior knowledge of the sounds of *x* and *y*. Hold up Letter Card *Xx*. Have children name the letter. Tell them that *x* usually comes at the end of words in English.

➤ Write the words *box, fox, six,* and *ax* on the board, highlighting the final *x* in colored chalk. Review the words orally.

➤ Hold up Letter Card *Yy*. Have children name the letter. Explain that *y* will appear at the beginning of the words in this lesson.

➤ Write the words *yarn, you, yellow,* and *yo-yo* on the board; write initial *y* in color. Review the words orally.

➤ Encourage ESL learners to name objects they know that begin with *y* and objects that end with *x*.

➤ Help children create an illustrated word wall with these names.

2 TEACH

Materials:
Worksheets on pages 63–64 of the Student Edition, nine index cards

Use the worksheets to help you teach and review the target letters.

➤ Write numbers 1–9 on index cards, one number per card. Shuffle.

➤ Have a volunteer pick a card and say the name of the corresponding picture clue on page 63. Ask the volunteer, "Does [object] end with the sound of *x*?" Model correct pronunciation by saying the picture name after the child has said it.

➤ Repeat for *y*, using only cards 1–6 and the worksheet on page 64.

➤ Review words with ESL learners. Challenge them to supply additional words. Display them in class as a reference and/or have children add them to their individual picture dictionaries.

★ *For specific notes on various home languages, see pages xiii–xvii of this Guide.*

3 PRACTICE

Materials:
Student Edition, pages 63–64; Rhyme Posters 20 and 21 (optional); index cards

Continue to practice the sounds of *x* and *y* by reading the rhymes on pages 63–64 aloud to the group as children read along after you.

➤ Have ESL learners find and point to words ending with *x* in the rhyme on page 63. Assist children with pronouncing the words as needed.

➤ Again read the rhyme aloud, adding gestures to demonstrate the actions described. Tell children to clap each time they hear a word ending in the sound of *x*.

➤ Have ESL learners read each line of the rhyme aloud, one line at a time. Check comprehension with directed questions after each line.

➤ Repeat for the sound of *y*, using the rhyme on page 64.

4 APPLY

Materials:
Consonant Catch activity, *MCP Phonics Teacher Resource Guide,* page 3l; foam ball, chalkboard

Adapt the Consonant Catch activity as follows for ESL learners.

➤ Toss the ball to one of the children. As you do, say "X" or "Y."

➤ The child who catches the ball must say a word beginning or ending with the sound of the target letter.

➤ Have children print their words on the chalkboard. Review all words orally with children.

5 ASSESS

Materials:
Worksheets on pages 63–64 of the Student Edition

Assess children's mastery and comprehension of the lesson content by completing in writing the worksheets on pages 63–64. Read aloud the direction line for each activity. Complete items 1 and 2 on page 63 together. Ask children to work in pairs to complete items 3–9. Repeat with page 64. Review answers.

MORE PHONICS PRACTICE

Set aside class time to read trade books with ESL learners. Preview these books and do a first reading to children.

FIX IT, FOX by Patricia Ann Lynch. Ready Readers, Stage 1 (Modern Curriculum Press, 1996)

DON'T SCRATCH, MAX! by Judy Nayer. Beginning Discovery Phonics (Modern Curriculum Press, 1994)

AstroWord

Some learners will benefit from additional practice and individualized feedback, such as that provided by the CD-ROM *AstroWord Consonant Sounds and Letters* (Module 2). Encourage native speakers of English and ESL learners to work together to complete activities that interest them using the sounds of *x* and *y*. Monitor each group's progress.

Lesson 31
The Sound of z; Reviewing Consonants x, y, z

INFORMAL ASSESSMENT OBJECTIVES

Can children

✔ identify pictures whose names begin with the sound of z?

✔ identify and print the initial or final consonant for pictures whose names begin or end with the sounds of x, y, and z?

★ *Speakers of Spanish, Tagalog, Korean, or Hmong may not distinguish /z/ from /s/. Practice zip, sip; zoo, soon; zigzag, sag.*

1 INTRODUCE

Materials:
Student Edition, page 65; Phonics Picture Cards (numbers 43, 44)

Begin your introduction of the sound of z by writing Zz on the chalkboard. Verify ESL learners' prior knowledge of the sound by writing zoo, zebra, zero, and zipper on the chalkboard. Have children pronounce the words individually.

➤ Model the sound of z, contrasting it with the sound of s. Using the picture clues on page 65 of the Student Edition and/or those from the Phonics Picture Cards listed to the left, review words beginning with /z/.

➤ Review the words Zelda, Zena, zoo, and zebra from the rhyme on page 65. Have children repeat.

2 TEACH

Materials:
Large paper bag or pillowcase, realia (or pictures of objects) beginning with z and s, chart paper, markers

Prepare a "Sound of Z" grab bag activity by bringing to class several objects that begin with the sounds of z and s.

➤ Display objects or pictures of these for ESL learners one at a time, modeling correct pronunciation.

➤ Put the objects or pictures in the bag.

➤ Have volunteers pick one item from the bag, name it aloud, and write the name of the object or picture on the chalkboard if it begins with the sound of z. Assist ESL learners who need support writing the word.

➤ When all objects have been identified, review the list of z words. Have children repeat each word.

➤ Ask children to copy the list of words onto chart paper. Invite them to draw pictures of one or two of the items.

★ *For specific notes on various home languages, see pages xiii–xvii of this Guide.*

3 PRACTICE

Materials:
Student Edition, page 65; Rhyme Poster 22 (optional)

Use the rhyme and worksheet on page 65 to practice words with the sound of *z*.

➤ Orally review *Zelda, Zena, zebra,* and *zoo* from the rhyme.

➤ Assist ESL learners in reading each line of the rhyme. Model natural pronunciation and rhythm, if necessary.

➤ Read the directions for the worksheet aloud. Work with children to complete item 1. Have children complete the remaining items individually as you closely monitor their efforts.

4 APPLY

Materials:
Letter Cards *Xx, Yy, Zz;* Phonics Picture Cards (numbers 42–43, 44, 46, 60, 70)

Apply children's comprehension of the target consonants by adapting the Listen for Sounds activity on page 3m of the *MCP Phonics TRG.*

➤ Place the Letter Cards face up in front of children.

➤ Say a word and have a volunteer identify with which letter sound the word begins or ends.

➤ Further challenge ESL learners who exhibit mastery by pointing to a Letter Card and asking them to name a word that begins or ends with that letter. Have available Phonics Picture Cards so that ESL learners have an additional reference to use to come up with words.

5 ASSESS

Materials:
Student Edition, page 66

Verify children's understanding of the consonants *x, y,* and *z* by having them complete the worksheet on page 66 in pairs, according to level of mastery. Together, review the picture clues, read the directions aloud, and complete items 1–3. Have pairs complete items 4–12. Review children's responses together.

Book Corner

MORE PHONICS PRACTICE

Set aside class time to read trade books with ESL learners. Preview these books and do a first reading to children.

ZEBRA'S YELLOW VAN by Diane Phillips. Ready Readers, Stage 0 (Modern Curriculum Press, 1997)

ZELDA'S ZIPPER by Cass Hollander. Beginning Discover Phonics (Modern Curriculum Press, 1994)

Technology

AstroWord
Some ESL learners will benefit from additional linguistic interaction, such as that provided by the CD-ROM *AstroWord Consonant Sounds and Letters* (Module 2). Encourage children to work together to write some of the words with the sounds of *x, y,* and *z* they have learned, using the Word Board and Notepad in the *AstroWord* Free Play room. Monitor each group's progress.

Lesson 32
Reviewing Medial Consonants

INFORMAL ASSESSMENT OBJECTIVE

Can children

✔ identify and print the consonant that stands for the sound heard in the middle of a picture's name?

★ *Words in Hmong, Vietnamese, Cantonese, Korean, and Khmer are monosyllabic. Prolonging the medial consonant sound may cause children to say each word as two.*

---

1 INTRODUCE

Materials:
Flip chart, realia (or pictures) objects on Student Edition pages 67–68

Make ESL learners aware of medial consonants by reviewing everyday words with which they are familiar in addition to those on pages 67–68. Assess their ability to identify, pronounce, and print the names of the realia or pictures you display before continuing.

➤ Preview the worksheets on pages 67–68 and gather as many objects (or pictures) as possible to share with the group.

➤ One by one, assist children as they say the names of the objects, then write them on the flip chart.

➤ Have volunteers orally identify the medial sound for each word, then underline it on the flip chart.

2 TEACH

Materials:
Letter Cards *Bb, Hh, Ll, Mm, Nn, Rr, Tt*; mitten, hammer, lemon, bottle (or pictures); realia or pictures from pages 67–68; colored chalk

Repeat the consonants *Mm, Tt,* and *Nn.* Have children pronounce words (and visuals) with these letters as the middle sounds.

➤ Hold up Letter Cards *Mm, Tt,* and *Nn.* Ask ESL learners to pronounce the sound each letter stands for.

➤ Display a mitten (or a picture of one) and ask a volunteer to name the object. Write *mitten* on the chalkboard, using colored chalk to highlight the medial letters *tt*.

➤ Repeat with a hammer, a lemon, and a bottle. Continue with additional words from the picture clues on pages 67–68 of the Student Edition.

★ *For specific notes on various home languages, see pages xiii–xvii of this Guide.*

3 PRACTICE

Materials:
Student Edition, page 67; Letter Cards *Bb, Dd, Gg, Kk, Ll, Mm, Nn, Pp, Tt*

Practice the concept of medial consonants by assisting children in completing the worksheet on page 67.

➤ Review the Letter Cards (which correspond to activity answers) and have children pronounce the sound of each. Preview the names of picture clues 1–12.

➤ Read the directions aloud and model them for the group.

➤ Complete items 1–3 together.

➤ Have ESL learners work in pairs with more English-proficient peers to complete items 4–12. Monitor pairs for equal input.

➤ Review answers. Write each on the chalkboard, underscoring the medial consonant heard in the middle of the picture's name.

4 APPLY

Materials:
2–3 familiar objects (or pictures) that make the medial consonant sounds of *l, m, n,* and *t*; four shoeboxes; four index cards; red marker; tape

Have pairs of ESL learners participate in this adaptation of Sorting Sounds from page 3k of the *MCP Phonics Teacher Resource Guide*.

➤ Write *Ll, Mm, Nn, Tt* on each of the four index cards.

➤ Tape one card to the front of each box.

➤ Display the objects or pictures and have children name them. Tell children to sort the objects into the appropriate boxes according to the sounds they hear in the middle of the words.

➤ Verify that each item is in the correct box.

5 ASSESS

Materials:
Student Edition, page 68

Read the directions to the group. Write *b a* [space] *y* on the chalkboard. Complete item 1 with children; model writing the medial *b* in *baby* as you repeat the directions. Assist children as they complete items 2–9 individually or in pairs. Review answers.

MORE PHONICS PRACTICE

Set aside class time to read trade books with ESL learners. Preview these books and do a first reading to children.

YES, I CAN by Irma Singer. Ready Readers, Stage 1 (Modern Curriculum Press, 1996)

PACO'S POCKET by Barbara Reeves. Beginning Discover Phonics (Modern Curriculum Press, 1994)

AstroWord

Encourage children to explore the CD–ROM *AstroWord Multisyllabic Words* (Module 16), which will provide additional practice and individualized feedback. Have native speakers of English and ESL learners work together to complete the Easy level of *Word Sort*, in which children help alien creatures sort picture clues by medial consonant sound.

Lesson 33
Consonants

1 INTRODUCE

Materials:
Consonant Letter Cards

Verify ESL learners' recognition and recall of consonants.

➤ Have ESL learners recite aloud the alphabet.

➤ Shuffle the Letter Cards. Ask a volunteer to pick a card and name the letter. Ask, "What is the sound of [*letter*]?"

➤ Challenge children of greater ability to say a word that begins with the sound of their letter and, if possible, to write the word.

2 TEACH

Materials:
Several objects or pictures with three- or four-letter names, such as *bat*, *pen*, or *nut*

Begin this review of consonants using short words (three or four letters) and expand into longer, multisyllabic words.

➤ Display an object or a picture of one (for example, a bat). Write ___ *a* ___ on the chalkboard.

➤ Have a volunteer say the name of the object. Ask, "What letter stands for the sound you hear at the beginning of *bat*?"

➤ After a correct response, write *b* as the initial consonant; continue with the final consonant and fill in the last blank.

➤ Review several objects or pictures and their names.

➤ Encourage ESL learners to do the same activity in pairs with words they have learned in this unit. Provide assistance with vowels.

★ *For specific notes on various home languages, see pages xiii–xvii of this Guide.*

3 PRACTICE

Materials:
Student Edition, page 69

Use the worksheet on page 69 to practice recognizing and writing initial and final consonants.

➤ Read the directions aloud to the group. Verify children's understanding of the task.

➤ Have volunteers read a word from the Word List. Review the picture clues as needed.

➤ Complete items 1 and 2 together with ESL learners. Have them work individually to complete items 3–12. Review responses.

4 APPLY

Materials:
Large paper bag or pillowcase, realia or pictures of familiar objects

Prepare a "Consonant Grab Bag" by bringing to class several objects that begin and end with consonant sounds.

➤ Display items one at a time. Model correct pronunciation.

➤ Put the objects in the bag.

➤ Have volunteers pick one object from the bag and name it aloud. Restate what children say by modeling correct pronunciation. Have them name the beginning and ending sounds and the consonants that stand for these sounds.

➤ Ask children to write the names of the objects on the chalkboard.

➤ For less proficient writers, write the middle sound(s) and encourage children to add the initial and final sounds.

5 ASSESS

Materials:
Student Edition, page 70

Be sensitive to the diversity of family units that are represented in your class. Listen carefully to what ESL learners try to say about their families. Assist children in writing a sentence that describes their artwork in words.

Book Corner

MORE PHONICS PRACTICE

Set aside class time to read trade books with ESL learners. Preview these books and do a first reading to children.

LET'S GO MARCHING by Judy Spevack. Ready Readers, Stage 1 (Modern Curriculum Press, 1996)

A DAY AT OUR DAIRY FARM by Barbara Reeves. Beginning Discover Phonics (Modern Curriculum Press, 1994)

Technology

AstroWord

Have children participate in the diverse activities found on the CD-ROM *AstroWord Multisyllabic Words* (Module 16), which provide additional practice and individualized feedback. Ask ESL learners and more English-proficient children to work together to complete various activities that interest them, focusing on the target consonant you suggest. Monitor each group's progress.

Lesson 34
Reviewing Consonants

> **INFORMAL ASSESSMENT OBJECTIVE**
>
> **Can children**
> ✔ recognize initial and final consonant sounds of words in the context of a story?

1 INTRODUCE

Materials:
Large cardboard box

Many of your ESL learners may have had personal experiences with moving. Introduce *Family Moving Day* by inviting ESL learners to share their experiences with moving and relating those experiences to the characters in the story.

➤ Display the box. Ask children what happens when a family moves, why they need boxes, and so on. Invite them to talk about a time they, or someone they know, moved.

➤ Write the words Socks, Jon, Kim, Mom, and Dad on the chalkboard. Have children read and pronounce each. Discuss the story pictures and assist children in identifying each character.

2 TEACH

Materials:
Consonant Letter Cards or alphabet chart, chart paper, crayons

Teach new words and review familiar ones before reading the story with English Language Learners.

➤ Place the Consonant Letter Cards or the alphabet chart on a desk.

➤ Review the familiar words *book, red, van, not, box, no, garden, yard, come,* and *quick.* As you say each, have children point to the letter that stands for the initial sound they hear. Repeat for final sounds.

➤ Present the words *family, moving, looks,* and *den.* Have children listen carefully and indicate all consonant sounds they hear in each new word. Write the new words on the board and review.

➤ You might want to create a word wall with children to include all the words related to the family, home, and moving themes mentioned in the book.

➤ Encourage children to add more words they know. Assist with the writing if necessary.

★ *For specific notes on various home languages, see pages xiii–xvii of this Guide.*

3 PRACTICE

Materials:
Family Moving Day story cards; red, yellow, and blue crayons; Consonant Letter Cards *Dd, Kk, Ll, Mm, Nn, Ss*

Practice consonant recognition and vocabulary recall by having ESL learners circle words according to initial, final, and medial consonant sounds.

➤ Say the name of a letter or hold up the Consonant Letter Cards, one at a time. Ask volunteers to name the letters they see.

➤ Read the story one page at a time. For each, assign children a task: "Listen for words that have the sound of *s* and circle them in blue." "Underline in red words that begin with the sound of *k*." Add tasks that focus on comprehension and build phonics skills.

➤ Read the story a second time. Have volunteers read aloud chorally.

➤ Check comprehension with directed questions, such as "Who is Socks?" and "Who looks in the den?"

4 APPLY

Materials:
Paper, crayons, markers

After reading *Family Moving Day*, have children work in groups to create an "end" to the story.

➤ Ask ESL learners to draw a picture of Socks, her family of kittens, and their new home and then write a sentence about the drawing. Support those ESL learners who need assistance with writing.

➤ Have children draw the family's new home. Assist them in writing sentences about it, such as *Mom likes the yard.*

5 ASSESS

Materials:
Photos from old magazines, paper, pencils

Supply photos from magazines as clues to words from Unit 1 (*bed, cup, dishes, mop,* and so on). Have children imagine they are moving. Ask them to think about what things they would need to bring to a new home. Brainstorm a list with all children, then instruct children to list the names of 8–10 things they want to pack. Review lists.

Book Corner

MORE PHONICS PRACTICE

Set aside class time to read trade books with ESL learners. Preview these books and do a first reading to children.

KANGAROO IN THE KITCHEN by Maryann Dobeck. Ready Readers, Stage 1 (Modern Curriculum Press, 1996)

HOP ON, HOP OFF by Janis Asad Raabe. Phonics Practice Readers (Modern Curriculum Press, 1986)

Technology

AstroWord

Some learners will benefit from additional practice and individualized feedback, such as that provided by the CD-ROMs *AstroWord Consonant Sounds and Letters* and *Multisyllabic Words* (Modules 2 and 16). Encourage native speakers of English and ESL learners to complete activities that interest them using consonant sounds. Monitor chidren's progress.

Lesson 35
Reviewing Consonants

INFORMAL ASSESSMENT OBJECTIVE

Can children

✔ identify and print the consonant that stands for the sound heard at the beginning or end of a picture name?

1 INTRODUCE

Materials:
Phonics Picture Cards (numbers 47, 48, 57, 59, 63, 76)

Reinforce recognition of consonants at the end of a word.

➤ Display Phonics Picture Cards face up on a desk or ledge.

➤ Together with the group, say the picture names, emphasizing the final sound.

➤ Ask ESL learners to name each picture. Then have them match the pictures whose names end with the same sound. (47 *bag*, 59 *pig*; 48 *cap*, 63 *cup*; 57 *lid*, 76 *bed*)

2 PRACTICE

Materials:
Student Edition, pages 73–74

Practice initial and final sounds and assess children's comprehension by completing the worksheets on pages 73–74 of the Student Edition.

➤ Read aloud the directions on page 73. Have children complete the worksheet individually. Review answers as a group.

➤ Have children work in pairs to complete page 74. Model the activity by completing items 1 and 2 orally with the group. Circulate to monitor progress and answer questions.

Book Corner

MORE PHONICS PRACTICE

Set aside class time to read trade books with ESL learners. Preview these books and do a first reading to children.

THE PARTY by Mary Evans. Ready Readers, Stage 1 (Modern Curriculum Press, 1996)

A MESS by Bob Allen. Ready Readers, Stage 1 (Modern Curriculum Press, 1996)

VULTURES ON VACATION by Kathleen Wilson. Ready Readers, Stage 1 (Modern Curriculum Press, 1996)

FUNNY FACES AND FUNNY PLACES Ready Readers, Stage 1 (Modern Curriculum Press, 1996)

Assessment Strategy Overview

Throughout Unit 2 you have opportunities to assess English as a Second Language (ESL) learners' ability to read and write words with short vowel sounds. Short vowel sounds may be especially problematic for your ESL learners. Note pronunciation difficulties, but assess based upon children's ability to distinguish short vowel sounds when pronounced by a native speaker.

FORMAL ASSESSMENT

Before you start Unit 2, administer the Unit 2 Pretest, found on pages 75e–75f of *MCP Phonics Teacher Resource Guide*. Children's scores will help you assess their knowledge base before beginning the unit and alert you to areas for further support. Complete the Student Progress Checklist on page 75i. Based on their responses to the Unit 2 Pretest, note which short vowel sounds children are struggling with. Monitor performance.

♦ Some children may understand a concept but have difficulty with direction. Read the directions aloud and model how to complete the worksheets.

♦ Before administering the Pretest, gather in a paper bag a variety of items (or pictures of them) that match the visuals on pages 75e–75f. Have volunteers select an item and then name it. Ask other children in the group to identify the vowel sound.

INFORMAL ASSESSMENT

Review pages, Unit Checkups, and Take-Home Books are effective ways to evaluate children's progress. Following are other suggestions for informal ways to assess children's understanding of the concepts.

♦ Gather realia or pictures of objects that reflect children's areas of difficulty. Allow them to select a visual and name it. Have children match each item to its counterpart letter on an alphabet chart.

♦ Bring to class props and pictures that use the target words and sounds. (Pets and some food items may be unfamiliar to ESL learners.) Record responses as an informal assessment grade.

PORTFOLIO ASSESSMENT

Portfolio Assessment opportunities are identified by the logo shown here. In addition to collecting the pages mentioned on page 75c, gather other examples of children's work for comparison and evaluation at critical periods in the unit, as indicated below.

♦ **Initial practice** Add to children's portfolios charts where they have independently added newly learned words that have short vowel sounds.

♦ **Midunit classwork** Have children work in small groups to make their own take-home storybooks to conclude study of each of the short vowels. Have children exchange work and share stories aloud.

♦ **Final products or projects** Read the Take-Home Book on pages 147–148 to children individually. Color a word card for each word in the story that has a short vowel the child identifies. Add the cards to the child's portfolio.

STUDENT PROGRESS CHECKLIST

Photocopy and attach the checklist on page 75i of *MCP Phonics Teacher Resource Guide* to each child's portfolio. Evaluate growth and areas of weakness from your assessment tools. Then, use the strategies and activities suggested in this Guide to build a strong phonics foundation for your ESL learners.

Administering and Evaluating the
Pretest and Posttest

➤ Read the information on page 75d of *MCP Phonics Teacher Resource Guide*. Answers for the Pretest and Posttest are provided on page 75d.

➤ Record test results on the Student Progress Checklist on page 75i after children complete the Pretest.

➤ Record results again after children take the Posttest.

➤ Compare the results of the two tests.

➤ Use the Performance Assessment Profile at the bottom of page 75d to help you draw conclusions about children's performance. Opportunities to reteach each specific skill in the unit are identified by page number.

TEST OBJECTIVES

Note that the objective of both the Unit 2 Pretest and Posttest of *MCP Phonics Teacher Resource Guide* is identification of short vowel sounds, not vocabulary recognition, with which children may be unfamiliar. To ensure that vocabulary comprehension does not interfere with sound recognition, name each of the items aloud as children move from item to item in the tests.

UNIT 2 PRETEST, pages 75e–75f

Page 75e of *MCP Phonics Teacher Resource Guide* focuses on visual identification of picture clues and the sound of the short vowels in those picture names. Some children may recognize the pictures but be unable to name them in English or produce the short vowel sounds comfortably. Support these ESL learners by implementing any of the following suggestions prior to beginning the Pretest.

◆ **Practice test-taking skills.** Skills such as filling in bubbles or printing letters in blank lines to finish a word may be new to some children. Work one-on-one with children who need extra practice.

◆ **Provide models.** Read the direction line aloud. Model how to mark the correct response. On the chalkboard, using an overhead projector, or on a sheet of paper at a child's desk, provide one or more practice opportunities to model test-taking procedures. Enhance meaning verbally or through pantomime.

◆ **Use props.** Provide realistic photographs to ensure children recognize—and can name—the picture clues. Then allow children to complete the pages.

◆ **Provide oral practice.** ESL learners may be hesitant to admit difficulty pronouncing some sounds in English. Provide frequent opportunities for children to practice in a non-threatening situation, such as choral repetition, before asking them to produce language on their own in front of their peers. Encourage, but don't force, oral participation if children hesitate.

♦ **Assign partners.** Pair a more proficient reader to read the picture names or take-home books aloud to an ESL learner. Ask the reader to speak slowly and clearly, and to model realistic pronunciation. For ESL learners this shifts the focus from speaking to comprehending.

Page 75f focuses on the short vowel sound of the 12 picture clues. For each, children are asked to say the name of the picture, match it to the correct word at right, then darken the bubble beside the picture name. You may wish to incorporate these strategies.

♦ **Simplify tasks.** Discriminating between vowel sounds is confusing for ESL learners. First ask children to identify the picture clue. Model correct pronunciation. Have children focus on the three words at right as you say them aloud and again say the name of the picture clue. Then have children determine which word is the correct picture name.

♦ **Work one-on-one.** Children who are uncomfortable speaking English can complete the activity directly with you or a partner to relieve test anxiety and build confidence in producing the new sounds.

<hr>

UNIT 2 POSTTEST, pages 75g–75h

The Unit 2 Posttest of *MCP Phonics Teacher Resource Guide* requires children to name picture clues and print the missing short vowel to complete each word. Use these suggestions for ESL learners as they complete pages 75g–75h:

♦ **Model correct pronunciation.** Distinguishing between vowels is

difficult for ESL learners. If children experience difficulty, say the name of each picture clue on page 75g. Display a chart showing the vowels. Point to each vowel as you repeat word choices, such as "Bed. Which sound did you hear? *Bad, Bid, Bud, Bod, Bed.*" Repeat. Help childen match the name of the picture clue to the sound of the word and print the missing letter of the sound they hear.

♦ **Review picture clues.** Children may be distracted by unfamiliar visuals. Introduce them in context. Some artwork may be unfamiliar to a specific cultural group; the spiral ham, the top, and the mop may be new. Have children look at the visuals as you "talk them through" the action. Then add the words to support meaning from the pictures.

♦ **Read items aloud to ESL learners.** ESL learners may more accurately identify the sound of short vowels when spoken by a native speaker. Read test items aloud as they follow along silently. Model the answer choices. Say, twice "The boy looks at a map. Did you hear *mop, map, mat*? Listen again." Repeat.

♦ **Check for understanding.** Determine if ESL learners feel that they are responding successfully by encouraging them to use language at their level to indicate if they understand what is required of them. For learners who have minimally developed verbal skills in English, a "thumbs up" or "thumbs down" may be sufficient for them to indicate their mastery of a skill. Encourage ESL learners to repeat what they hear and to interact with other learners during these periods.

Spelling Connections

Pages 75j–75k of *MCP Phonics Teacher Resource Guide* provide a collection of ideas and opportunities to actively incorporate spelling into your phonics program. It is recommended that ESL learners reach the intermediate fluency level of English proficiency before focusing on spelling.

✳ **Anticipate problem words.** Anticipated areas of difficulty for children who speak Spanish, Korean, Hmong, Khmer, Russian, or Vietnamese are noted by a star in the Informal Assessment Objectives box at the beginning of each lesson. You may wish to refer to these notes as you progress through specific lessons, especially as you make the link between oral and written forms.

✳ **Link sounds and print.** To ensure a link between oral speech and the written form of words, speak in simple, complete sentences and at a natural, slow, pace. Provide frequent opportunity for children to connect a visual, the sounds, and the printed (spelled) word by posting picture clues with the spelled words beneath them throughout your class. Use the picture clues to introduce, model, and prompt meaning. Then, cover up the printed words to assess spelling mastery and conduct an oral or written spelling test of new spelling words in the unit.

✳ **Develop personalized dictionaries.** Encourage children to add to their list of new words those with which they have difficulty or are unfamiliar. Accustom children to writing new words on their lists. Review regularly with ESL learners and have children sound them out and spell them for you, first by sight-reading, then from memory.

✳ **Provide frequent mini-lessons.** Repeated misspellings often indicate children do not understand how to spell words correctly. Provide ESL learners with customized mini-lessons in which they can catch up on misunderstood phonics skills. First, explain a rule that is a source of misspellings. Provide written, oral, and physical (gestures, pantomimes) reinforcement and examples. Supplement with practice in the form of short drills, writing charts, and opportunities to write independently in spelling dictionaries, journals, and so on.

✳ **Enhance meaning with visuals.** To ensure a link between oral speech and the written form of words, speak in simple, complete sentences and at a natural, not exaggerated, pace. Have children connect a visual, the sounds, and the spelling words by posting throughout your class picture clues with the spelled words beneath them. Use the picture clues to introduce, model, and prompt meaning. Then, cover up the printed words to assess spelling mastery and conduct an oral or written spelling test of new spelling words in the unit.

* **Read it, write it, remember it.** Encourage ESL learners to commit spelling to memory. Ask ESL learners to copy the words from the Unit Word List onto individual index cards. Have them study four or five words daily at frequent intervals—before recess and lunch, during center time, and at home, during other routine activities, such as during homework or bathing.

* **Conduct oral spelling drills.** Use oral repetition as a large group or in smaller groups, in a listening station. Provide quick drill opportunities to reinforce similarities, differences, or other word associations.

* **Make spelling fun.** Use fun writing mediums such as shaving cream, paints, clay, twine and sandpaper, and sand to practice spelling new or unfamiliar words. Children will have fun with the materials and enjoy writing the words you ask them to spell. Correct spelling before children "erase" their responses.

* **Enhance meaning with visuals.** Incorporating visuals and props, audiotapes and CDs provides additional modalities through which ESL learners can acquire English. For activities that require written response, determine whether children have sufficient command of written print to complete the activity. Be aware that some children might write in cursive letters.

* **Attach meaning to words.** Allow children to acquire meaning before they focus on spelling the word. As a group, introduce the short vowels *a, i, u, o,* and *e* separately, as they are grouped in the lessons. You may wish to focus on one vowel per day to minimize confusion for some ESL learners.

* **Incorporate games and flashcards into spelling practice.** Have ESL learners copy the words from the word list onto individual flashcards. Distribute words in specific letter patterns to small groups of children. Have children take turns playing "teacher" and quizzing the other group members orally on the words in their set. After all children have had a chance to spell each word in a set, exchange sets with another group.

* **Incorporate journal writing in your class.** Encourage ESL learners to freewrite in English and to use spelling words as a prompt for free expression. Have children review their journal writing with you one-on-one and decorate their pages with artwork, photos, pictures, or realia.

Blackline Master 14 (page 75k) requires that children have sufficient command of English and contextual background to sound out and spell the 30 words on the Unit Word List. For ESL learners, introduce 8–10 words at a time and their meanings through visuals or realia.

Unit 2

Phonics Games, Activities, and Technology

Pages 75l–75n of *MCP Phonics Teacher Resource Guide* provide a collection of ideas and opportunities to actively engage children as they develop or reinforce phonics strategies. Many of the activities provided on these pages can be implemented with little or no modification for children whose native language is not English. However, be alert to pictures that are unfamiliar in context or in their names. Multistep directions may also be difficult for some ESL learners to understand or follow.

To ensure comprehension of activity directions, speak in simple, complete sentences and at a natural, not exaggerated, pace. Incorporating visuals and props, audiotapes and CDs provides additional contexts and clues for new learners of English. For activities that require written response, determine whether children have sufficient command of written print to complete the activity. Be aware that some children might write in cursive letters.

● **Short Vowel Bingo, How Many Sounds** (page 75l) and **Isolating Vowel Sounds** (page 75m) may be overwhelming if ESL learners are asked to incorporate all five vowels. Adapt this activity so that children use individual vowels, in the order of the lessons, before they incorporate all five letters.

▲ **Animal Tic-tac-toe** (page 75l) and **Name a Word That Rhymes** (page 75m) can be simplified by reducing the size of the grid or the number of cards or objects used to play the games. When children become more familiar with the game, increase the number of items to be identified.

◆ **Oh, A-Hunting We Will Go** (page 75l) and **Word Finger-Puppets** (page 75n) work effectively by pairing ESL learners with more English-proficient peers. To ensure all children participate actively, assign tasks to each child.

■ **Word Slides** (page 75m), **Word Flip Books** (page 75m), **Word Wheels**, and **Change-a-Letter** (page 75n) are fun ways to introduce the Unit Word List on page 75j. Have children prepare their own word strips or wheels for each of the vowels you identify. Select phonograms representing each of the short vowels for the flip books or letter cards.

● **Musical Chairs and Words** (page 75m) is a variation of a familiar child's party game and may be intimidating to children of other cultures who do not recognize the activity or understand that each child asserts himself or herself to earn a seat. Model acceptable game behavior.

▲ **Circle Rhyme** (page 75m) can be played in two teams, rather than individually, to alleviate ESL learners insecurity over participating alone. Allow the teams the opportunity to brainstorm their responses, then respond chorally as a group, with all children participating in the response.

◆ **Follow the Path** (page 75n) has no written instructions for children and few clues for those confused as to how to proceed. On a flip chart, write the 16 words that make up the path, in random order. Allow children to use the chart to help them select choices to complete the words on the game board. Model how to play the game and fill up the game board. Allow children of similar ability levels to work together to complete the activity.

Technology

Use children's interest in technology to their advantage in learning English. If possible, allow ESL learners to work in small groups on the appropriate *AstroWord* CD-ROM Module before or after class or during center time. Preview skill levels and supervise the groups directly to eliminate frustration and to guide phonics development. You may wish to add your observations to the Student Progress Checklist, found on page 75i, *MCP Phonics Teacher Resource Guide*, as well as the software suggested on page 75n to provide additional phonics practice for ESL learners.

Lesson 36
Introduction to Vowels

INFORMAL ASSESSMENT OBJECTIVES

Can children

✔ identify vowels *a, i, u, o,* and *e*?

✔ recognize the vowels *a, i, u, o,* and e in words?

★ *The home languages spoken by ESL learners vary from five pure vowel sounds in Spanish to 35 syllabic vowels in Cantonese. ESL learners will need lots of opportunities to listen to English vowel sounds before being expected to produce them without error.*

1 INTRODUCE

Materials:
Letter Cards *Aa, Ee, Ii, Oo, Uu;* colored chalk

Familiarize ESL learners with the concept and sound of short vowels. Hold up each Letter Card, one at a time, and name the vowel.

➤ Have children repeat chorally, then individually.

➤ Model the short sound of each vowel saying a word, then isolating the vowel. Ask children to pronounce the sound.

➤ Write upper and lowercase vowels on the chalkboard in two columns, in random order. Have children match. Then, supply only uppercase forms and have children write their lowercase partners. Reverse and repeat.

2 TEACH

Materials:
Letter Cards *Aa, Ee, Ii, Oo, Uu;* Phonics Picture Cards (numbers 49, 59, 61, 71, 81); colored chalk

Begin teaching short vowel sounds using Picture Cards of familiar animals. You may select one vowel per day to avoid confusion. Begin reviewing previously introduced vowels, then focus on one vowel per day.

➤ Display the *Aa* Letter Card and Phonics Picture Card 49 (cat). Have ESL learners name the letter and the picture. Ask a volunteer to write *cat* on the chalkboard.

➤ Point out that the middle sound of *cat* is made by the vowel *a.* Ask children if they can say other words that rhyme with *cat.* Model changing the initial consonant sound and write *b, h, m,* and *r* on the board as clues. Write each word as children suggest them. Draw a sketch of each new word to ensure comprehension. Have each child go to the chalkboard and circle the *a.*

➤ Repeat for other vowels, substituting beginning or ending consonants. Suggestions: *hen: den, pen, ten, men; pig: pin, pit, pill; dog: log, fog, doll; bug: rug, mug, bun, bus.*

★ *For specific notes on various home languages, see pages xiii–xvii of this Guide.*

3 PRACTICE

Materials:
Student Edition, page 78; realia or pictures of objects shown on page 78

Practice vowel recognition and short vowel sounds.

▶ Have children name the pictures in the left column and the vowel in each box on page 78. Ask them to say the sound the vowel makes in each picture's name, after you have pronounced it clearly.

▶ Read the directions aloud. Model the activity by having children name *a, ant* (item 1) and tracing the circle around the *a* in *cap*. You may wish to show pictures of the objects listed in each item to make it easier for ESL learners to name the vowels. Have them complete the remaining *a* words in item 1.

▶ Repeat for items 2–5. Review answers.

4 APPLY

Materials:
Auditory/Kinesthetic Learners activity, *MCP Phonics Teacher Resource Guide,* page 78; Letter Cards *Aa, Ee, Ii, Oo, Uu;* colored chalk

Adapt the activity for Auditory/Kinesthetic Learners for use with ESL learners.

▶ Write *clap, sit, jump, hop,* and *bend* on the board; write each target vowel in color. Model each word and have ESL learners repeat. One at a time, have volunteers name the vowel sound in each word.

▶ Have children stand up. Act out each word, while others guess which word is being acted out.

▶ Hold up a vowel Letter Card. Tell children to act out the word that contains the vowel they see.

5 ASSESS

Materials:
Student Edition, page 77

Read the directions aloud for the worksheet activity on page 77. Ask a volunteer to name the vowel in the box in item 1. Have another volunteer name the first picture clue. Ask if *cat* contains the sound of *a* and have children circle the picture. Continue with *box, ax,* and *cub.* Repeat for items 2–5. Review answers.

MORE PHONICS PRACTICE

Set aside class time to read trade books with ESL learners. Preview these books and do a first reading to children.

WHAT IS UNDER THE HAT? by Judy Nayer. Ready Readers, Stage 0 (Modern Curriculum Press, 1997)

SANDY by Cynthia Rothman. Ready Readers, Stage 1 (Modern Curriculum Press, 1996)

AstroWord

Ask groups of children (ESL learners and native speakers of English) to explore the activities included on the CD-ROM *AstroWord Phonemic Awareness* (Module 1). Encourage children to work together to complete activities that interest them. Offer support, monitor group progress, and ask directed questions about short vowel sounds and vowel recognition.

Lesson 37
Short *a*

> ## INFORMAL ASSESSMENT OBJECTIVES
>
> **Can children**
>
> ✔ identify picture names and words that contain the sound of short *a*?
>
> ✔ sort short *a* words by word families?
>
> ★ *Speakers of Spanish, Tagalog, or Russian may pronounce* a */ah/ as in* father. *Speakers of Asian languages may make a tonal or nasal* a. *Koreans and Russians may say /ya/ after some consonant sounds, making* ga *of* gamble *sound like* gya *in* big yam.

1 INTRODUCE

Materials:
Letter Card *Aa*; Phonics Picture Cards (numbers 45, 47–52)

Introduce the sound of short *a* by reviewing and repeating familiar words that contain the sound. Assess by having children say the name of items shown on the Picture Cards.

➤ Display Letter Card *Aa*. Have children name the letter and pronounce the sound of short *a*.

➤ Holding up one Picture Card at a time, have a volunteer name the picture. Emphasize the sound of short *a* in each word.

➤ Ask children of greater English fluency to write some of the picture names on the chalkboard; have others read them and circle the *a*.

➤ Display Picture Cards 49 and 52 and write the rhyme *The fat cat sat on my hat* on the chalkboard. Use the visuals to ensure that children understand the sentence. Have children repeat.

2 TEACH

Materials:
Student Edition, page 79; Rhyme Poster 24; cane (optional)

Continue teaching the sound of short *a* by reading and acting out the rhyme on page 79 with ESL learners.

➤ Write *an ant can* on the chalkboard. Review the phrase aloud.

➤ Act out *dance* and *sing* to physically clarify meaning.

➤ Read the rhyme aloud to ESL learners, using a cane to point to target words on the chalkboard as you say them.

➤ Have them act out the rhyme as they take turns reading a line.

➤ Write on the chalkboard the rhyme: *An ant can clap, an ant can stand, an ant can sit and raise its hand.* Have children underline the short sound of *a* in each word as they recite each line.

★ *For specific notes on various home languages, see pages xiii–xvii of this Guide.*

3 PRACTICE

Materials:
Student Edition, page 79

Have ESL learners locate and name pictures containing the short *a*.

➤ Read aloud to the group the direction line for the activity.

➤ Randomly call out a number. Ask a volunteer to name the picture.

➤ Complete items 1–3 aloud together. Ask children to work in pairs to complete the remaining items. Review answers.

➤ Have children choose one picture and use it orally in a sentence.

4 APPLY

Materials:
MCP Phonics Teacher Resource Guide: Follow the Path game, page 75n; Blackline Master 15, page 75o; number cube; game markers

Use the Follow the Path game to practice words with the sound of short *a*.

➤ Reproduce Blackline Master 15. Play the game as a group. Give each pair a game board, and tell them they are playing against you.

➤ Tell children to make words with short *a* trying to fill the blank on each rock. If inserting *a* does not make a word, they cannot move.

➤ Tally your words with *a* and those of the children. When the game is finished, they copy the list and say the words aloud.

5 ASSESS

Materials:
Crayons; Student Edition, page 80

Some ESL learners may not know the concept of rhyming. Provide plenty of opportunities to practice rhyming before assessing. Point out that rhyming words sound alike, except for the beginning sound. Offer examples. Read activity directions aloud. Ask a volunteer to name the pictures in item 1. Assist children in determining which picture names rhyme and have them color those pictures. Have children complete items 2–5 in pairs. Review aloud as a group.

Book Corner

MORE PHONICS PRACTICE

Set aside class time to read trade books with ESL learners. Preview these books and do a first reading to children.

WHAT WILL YOU PACK? by Claudia Logan. Ready Readers, Stage 0 (Modern Curriculum Press, 1997)

WHEN THE ALLIGATOR CAME TO CLASS by Cass Hollander. Discovery Phonics (Modern Curriculum Press, 1992)

Technology

AstroWord

Some children will benefit from additional practice and feedback on the CD-ROM *AstroWord Short Vowels: a, i* (Module 3). Encourage native speakers of English and ESL learners to work on the Easy level of *Make-a-Word*, where children help alien creatures create words based on a picture clue by inserting the correct vowel. Monitor each group's progress.

Lessons 38–41
Short *a*

INFORMAL ASSESSMENT OBJECTIVES

Can children

✔ recognize the sound of short *a* in picture names?

✔ identify picture names and spell words that contain the sound of short *a*?

✔ write words that contain the sound of short *a* to complete sentences?

---

1 INTRODUCE

Materials:
4–6 realia items from home and class (bag, apple, pan, map, and so on); Student Edition, pages 81 and 83

Use everyday objects containing the sound of short *a* to identify children's comprehension of and ability to name objects containing the sound of short *a*.

▶ Display an object; ask a volunteer to name it and the vowel sound he or she hears. Provide assistance naming objects, if necessary.

▶ When all objects have been named, choose one and write its name plus two other words on the chalkboard. Have a volunteer underline the correct word and perhaps tell why a particular word was chosen.

▶ Have children complete the worksheets on pages 81 and 83.

2 TEACH

Materials:
Student Edition, pages 84 and 86

Teach children to spell words with the sound of short *a* by identifying initial and final consonant sounds.

▶ Read a rhyme to model what it is.

▶ Ask ESL learners to explain what rhyming words are. Offer support by giving examples of rhyming words from the rhyme.

▶ Read the directions for the worksheet on page 84. Work with children to complete item 1 and verify understanding of the task. Have them work in pairs to complete the activity.

▶ Build on children's ability to "sound out and spell" by completing the worksheet activity on page 86. Read the directions aloud and ask children to explain the task to you in their own words.

▶ Assist with items 1 and 2; have individuals work on items 3–16. Monitor children's work, offering assistance as needed.

▶ Review answers aloud with the group.

▶ Give a "sound of *a*" spelling quiz (5–8 words) to ESL learners.

★ *For specific notes on various home languages, see pages xiii–xvii of this Guide.*

3 PRACTICE

Materials:
Student Edition, page 88

Structure this worksheet to practice spelling, writing, and auditory comprehension.

➤ Have children silently look at the picture clues on the worksheet. Tell them to raise their hand if they need help naming them.

➤ Explain that you will name the first object. Children are to write the word you say under the picture. Repeat each word twice.

➤ Complete 5–6 of the target words. Then verify that ESL learners have correctly written the dictated words. Continue or review.

4 APPLY

Materials:
Student Edition, page 87; pictures of campsites and camping activities

Apply and expand children's ability to spell and recognize short *a* words by having them fill in missing words of a sentence.

➤ Display pictures of camping activities. Discuss camping or summer camp; make sure children from other cultures are familiar with this.

➤ Talk about the plot of the story told in the worksheet. Include vocabulary needed to complete the activity, such as talking about what a van is.

➤ Read the directions aloud and ask children to explain the activity to you in their own words. Model item 1 for the group.

➤ Have ESL learners work in pairs. Review answers aloud as a group.

5 ASSESS

Materials:
Student Edition, page 85

Help children to understand the vocabulary by asking them to identify the pertinent word for each picture. Say "What animal is that?" and "Where is the cat sitting?" Ask a volunteer to read the first part of item 1 aloud. Tell children to circle the word that will finish the sentence. Continue for items 2–6. Read the story. When finished, verify comprehension with questions.

MORE PHONICS PRACTICE

Set aside class time to read trade books with ESL learners. Preview these books and do a first reading to children.

EGGS! by F. R. Robinson. Ready Readers, Stage 0 (Modern Curriculum Press, 1997)

SANDY by Cynthia Rothman. Ready Readers, Stage 1 (Modern Curriculum Press, 1996)

AstroWord

Some ESL learners will benefit from additional practice and audiovisual feedback, such as that provided by the CD-ROM *AstroWord Short Vowels: a, i* (Module 3). Encourage native speakers of English and ESL learners to work together to complete the Easy level of *Word Sort,* in which children help alien creatures sort picture clues according to vowel sound. Offer assistance while monitoring progress.

Lesson 42
Short *a*

1 INTRODUCE

Materials:
Student Edition, page 89; ant farm (optional)

Allow ESL learners to observe ants at work; bring to class an ant farm, if possible.

➤ Ask children to talk about what ants do.

➤ Write on the chalkboard *Dan and Dad like to camp.* and *The ants ran fast.* Read the sentences aloud; have children repeat.

➤ Ask a volunteer to go to the chalkboard and circle all the *a*'s in the first sentence. Repeat for the second sentence.

➤ Have other volunteers go to the chalkboard and underline target words as you say them. Assist children who need support in making the sound of *a* to pronounce each word.

2 TEACH

Materials:
Student Edition, page 89; crayons or pencils; writing paper; large butcher paper; construction paper

Prepare ESL learners for the writing activity on page 89 by discussing and reading aloud *"Looking at Ants."*

➤ Read aloud to ESL learners *"Looking at Ants."* As you read the story a second time, tell children to underline all the words that contain short *a*.

➤ Read the story again, asking children to read one line at a time.

➤ Draw an anthill or ant farm on the butcher paper. Ask each child to read one of the underlined words from the story and write it inside the anthill.

➤ Encourage children to create ants on construction paper and paste them to the diagram. Have children copy the diagram.

➤ Display the diagram as a word reference for children.

★ *For specific notes on various home languages, see pages xiii–xvii of this Guide.*

3 PRACTICE

Materials:
Student Edition,
page 89

Review the list of short *a* words from *"Looking at Ants"* before doing the writing activity on page 89.

➤ Write the list of short *a* words on the chalkboard. Ask volunteers to read each one aloud.

➤ Read the story aloud once. Talk about the story with ESL learners.

➤ Ask questions such as "Who saw the ants?" and "Did the ants run fast or slow?" Guide children to write one-word answers.

➤ Explain the writing activity and complete it as a group. Review.

4 APPLY

Materials:
Student Edition,
page 90

Assist ESL learners with writing a description of the picture on page 90.

➤ Review words in the box. Use them and others your ESL learners might need (*Jan, Dan, can, has*) to talk about the picture.

➤ Ask questions that will help each child write a description, such as "What does Dad have?" and "Who has a bag?"

➤ Write a class experience chart story together first. This can serve as a model for less-proficient ESL learners.

➤ Help more fluent ESL learners write 2–4 sentences, Then read them.

5 ASSESS

Materials:
Student
descriptions, paper,
pencil

Ask ESL learners to match short *a* words to a corresponding picture. Say the short *a* word. Have children identify the initial, middle, and final sounds.

MORE PHONICS PRACTICE

Set aside class time to read trade books with ESL learners. Preview these books and do a first reading to children.

HADDIE'S CAPS by Christine Economos. Ready Readers, Stage 1 (Modern Curriculum Press, 1996)

WHEN THE ALLIGATOR CAME TO CLASS by Cass Hollander. Discovery Phonics (Modern Curriculum Press, 1992)

AstroWord

Invite children to complete some of the intergalactic activities on the CD-ROM *AstroWord Short Vowels: a, i* (Module 3). Ask small groups of ESL learners and English-speaking children to work together as you focus their efforts on practicing the short sound of *a*. Monitor children's time on the computer for equal participation and progress.

Lesson 43
Reviewing Short Vowel *a*

INFORMAL ASSESSMENT OBJECTIVE

Can children

✔ read short *a* words in the context of a story?

---

1 INTRODUCE

Materials:
English Language Learners/ESL section, *MCP Phonics Teacher Resource Guide,* page 91; pictures of a baseball bat and a flying bat, realia

Introduce *All About Bats* by discussing and acting out the different meanings of the word *bat* with ESL learners.

➤ Write the word *bat* on the chalkboard. Ask a volunteer to read the word aloud and tell the other children what a bat is.

➤ Supplement the child's definition with others from English Language Learners/ESL section on page 91. Show realia and act out definitions.

2 TEACH

Materials:
All About Bats Take-Home Book, Student Edition, pages 91–92

Talk about the *All About Bats* Take-Home Book with ESL learners and review words containing the sound of short *a*.

➤ Assist children in making their Take-Home Books.

➤ Tell children to look at the photographs and talk about bats. Ask "What have you learned about bats?"

➤ Make a word web to organize information about bats.

➤ Read the story together.

➤ Have children look through the story for familiar words that contain the sound of short *a*. Keep a list on the chalkboard of all the words they find. Read the list aloud to children.

➤ Teach/review other important story words such as *what, know, about, fly, catch, eat, fur,* and *brown.*

➤ Have children practice using these words in oral sentences.

★ *For specific notes on various home languages, see pages xiii–xvii of this Guide.*

3 PRACTICE

Materials:
All About Bats Take-Home Book; red, black, blue crayons; Letter Cards *Bb, Cc, Ff, Pp*

Have ESL learners circle words beginning with a specific consonant sound and containing a short *a*.

➤ Hold up a Letter Card; ask volunteers to name the letters.

➤ Read the story one page at a time. For each page, give children a specific task, such as "Listen for words that have the sound of short *a* and circle them in black." or "Underline in red words that begin with the sound of *p*."

➤ Read the story a second time. Have volunteers read aloud.

➤ Ask "How do bats fly?" and "What color is their fur?"

4 APPLY

Materials:
Paper, crayons, markers, glue, tape, clips or staples, nonfiction big book about bats (optional)

After reading *All About Bats*, have children work in groups to create an additional page for the story.

➤ You might wish to use a nonfiction big book about bats to share with the class a list of additional facts about bats, such as they sleep in trees and they hang upside down when they sleep.

➤ Ask ESL learners to draw a picture of one of these facts and to write a sentence about it. Help with vocabulary and spelling.

➤ Make a cover for a class book with a title. Attach the pages. Have children read their sentences aloud and show their drawings.

5 ASSESS

Materials:
All About Bats Take-Home Book

Verify ESL learners' understanding and recall of the story vocabulary by asking children to illustrate a sentence from the story.

MORE PHONICS PRACTICE

Set aside class time to read trade books with ESL learners. Preview these books and do a first reading to children.

SANDY by Cynthia Rothman. Ready Readers, Stage 1 (Modern Curriculum Press, 1996)

A PACK AND A SACK by Cindy and Zach Clements. Phonics Practice Readers (Modern Curriculum Press, 1979)

AstroWord

Some learners will benefit from additional interaction and audiovisual feedback, such as that provided by the CD-ROM *AstroWord Short Vowels: a, i* (Module 3). Encourage native speakers of English and ESL learners to work together to complete activities that interest them using the sound of short *a*. Monitor each group's progress.

Lesson 44
Short *i*

INFORMAL ASSESSMENT OBJECTIVE

Can children

✔ identify pictures whose names contain the sound of short *i*?

★ *Children who speak a language other than English may pronounce* i *like the* e *in* me. *Practice* sit, seat; fit, feet; bin, bean; *and so on.*

---

1 INTRODUCE

Materials:
Letter Card *Ii*; Phonics Picture Cards (numbers 54, 57–60)

Introduce the sound of short *i*, reviewing familiar words that contain the sound and adding new words to children's vocabulary.

➤ Hold up Letter Card *Ii*. Have a volunteer name it. Model the sound of short *i*. Have children practice making the sound.

➤ Display one Picture Card at a time and have ESL learners name the picture. Emphasize the sound of short *i* in each word.

➤ Ask children to say some of the picture names.

➤ Write *did, jig, sit, licks,* and *wig* on the chalkboard; have children read aloud. Display Picture Cards 57–60 and tell them to pick rhyming word(s) from the chalkboard. Review rhyming words.

2 TEACH

Materials:
Student Edition, page 93; large index cards; Rhyme Poster 25 and props from rhyme (optional)

Continue teaching the sound of short *i* by reading and acting out the rhyme on page 93. Use pantomime to convey meanings.

➤ Write *did* and *pink* on the chalkboard. In a cluster, write the rhyming words *big, pig, wig, jig, fig.* Say each aloud.

➤ Act out *put on a wig* and *did a jig* using props to clarify meaning, if necessary. Show a hairpiece and jiglike dance steps.

➤ Hand out one index card per child. Tell them to write one of the words from the chalkboard on their cards.

➤ Have children stand. Read the rhyme. Instruct them to hold their cards in front and sit down when they hear their words. Collect cards, redistribute, and repeat.

➤ Have ESL learners act out the rhyme as they take turns reading a line.

➤ Note ESL learners who have difficulty pronouncing or hearing the short *i*. Target individual instruction.

★ *For specific notes on various home languages, see pages xiii–xvii of this Guide.*

3 PRACTICE

Materials:
Student Edition, page 93

Have ESL learners locate and name pictures whose names contain the sound of short *i*.

➤ Read the direction line aloud.

➤ Randomly call out a number. Ask a volunteer to name the picture. Restate what the child says if the *i* sound is not correct.

➤ Complete items 1–3 aloud together. Ask children to work in pairs to complete items 4–12. Pair children of varying abilities.

➤ Review answers.

4 APPLY

Materials:
Word Flip Books activity, *MCP Phonics Teacher Resource Guide*, page 75m; tagboard; construction paper; markers

Have ESL learners make Word Flip Books for short *i* phonograms or for groups of letters that contain the same phonetic sound. For example, three short *i* phonograms are *-ill*, *-in*, and *-it*.

➤ Cut pieces of tagboard about 10" x 4" (one per child) and 4" squares of construction paper (4–6 per child).

➤ Have children write a short *i* phonogram on the right two thirds of the tagboard. Suggestions include *-it*, *-ig*, *-in*, *-ill*, *-ick*, and *-id*.

➤ Tell children to think of rhyming words using their phonogram. Write the first letter of each on a square of construction paper.

➤ Stack squares on left side of tagboard and affix the top. Use each Word Flip Book to review words together.

➤ Children can add a picture page for words and match picture–word.

5 ASSESS

Materials:
Crayons; Student Edition, page 94

Read directions aloud. Ask a volunteer to name the pictures in item 1. Assist children in determining which picture names rhyme, and have them color the pictures (*bib* and *crib*). Pair children to complete items 2–5. Monitor work for participation. Review answers aloud.

Book Corner

MORE PHONICS PRACTICE

Set aside class time to read trade books with ESL learners. Preview these books and do a first reading to children.

MY TWIN by Nora Fredericks. Ready Readers, Stage 0 (Modern Curriculum Press, 1997)

THE BIG RIG by Linda Hartley. Phonics Practice Readers (Modern Curriculum Press, 1986)

Technology

AstroWord
Some children will benefit from additional practice and feedback, such as that provided by the CD-ROM *AstroWord Short Vowels: a, i* (Module 3). Encourage native speakers of English and ESL learners to work on the Easy level of *Make-a-Word*, where children help alien creatures create words based on a picture clue by inserting the correct vowel. Monitor each group's progress.

Lessons 45–48
Short *i*

1 INTRODUCE

Materials:
Phonics Picture Card number 59 or a toy pig; Student Edition, pages 95–96

Activate prior knowledge about pigs as you discuss the short *i*.

➤ Display Picture Card 59 or a toy pig. Ask a volunteer to name the object, sound it out and, with your help, spell it.

➤ Have ESL learners tell what they know about pigs. Ask questions about pigs using picture clues from page 95: "Do pigs wear bibs? drink milk? have wings? sit on hills?" Aim for full-sentence responses. Restate nonsentences in full sentences, using correct grammar, without correcting children formally.

➤ Have children complete the worksheets on pages 95–96 of the Student Edition. Review answers aloud as a group.

2 TEACH

Materials:
Student Edition, pages 97–98; two index cards per child

Teach children to differentiate words following the C-V-C pattern by identifying the vowel and the initial and final consonant sounds.

➤ Have children write *Aa* on one card and *Ii* on the other.

➤ Say words containing short *a* or *i*, one at a time. Have ESL learners hold up the card that corresponds to the vowel sound they hear.

➤ Write a series of C-V-C patterns on the board, omitting vowels: *p_t, b_g, z_g, d_d, h_t, p_n* and so on. Ask volunteers to write and read two words filling in *a* and *i*. Help ESL learners grasp the meaning of words by drawing the item next to each word.

➤ Read directions for the worksheet on page 97. Work with children to complete item 1 and verify understanding of the task. Have them work in pairs to complete the activity.

➤ Read directions for the activity on page 98 and have children complete it independently. Review both activities.

★ *For specific notes on various home languages, see pages xiii–xvii of this Guide.*

3 PRACTICE

Materials:
Student Edition,
pages 100 and 102

Practice short *i* by using the activities on pages 100 and 102.

➤ Ask children to listen and identify beginning and ending sounds of each picture's name on page 100. Assist with items 1–3 to verify comprehension.

➤ Use the worksheet on page 102 as a spelling and vocabulary test. Have children look at the picture clues. Name one of the objects on the page; children are to write the word you say under the picture. Practice procedures. Repeat each word several times.

➤ Complete the worksheet together. Verify that children have correctly written dictated words reviewing them together after the test.

4 APPLY

Materials:
Student Edition,
page 99

Have children fill in the missing words of a sentence to apply spelling and recognition skills.

➤ Discuss giving pets as gifts. (The concept of indoor or household pets may be an unfamiliar concept in some cultures.)

➤ Briefly summarize the plot of the "story" on page 99. Incorporate vocabulary words needed to complete the activity, such as *gift*, not *present* and *dish*, not *bowl*.

➤ Read the directions and ask ESL learners to explain in their own words what they must do. Model item 1 with children.

➤ Have children work in pairs to complete the activity. Review answers, then read the story aloud.

5 ASSESS

Materials:
Student Edition,
page 101

Review/reinforce the words in the word list (at right) on page 101. Ask a volunteer to read the first part of item 1 aloud. Have children silently circle the word that completes the sentence; review aloud. Together, complete items 2–6. Read the entire story when finished.

Book Corner

MORE PHONICS PRACTICE

Set aside class time to read trade books with ESL learners. Preview these books and do a first reading to children.

MAMA HEN, COME QUICK! by Janet Fisher. Ready Readers, Stage 0 (Modern Curriculum Press, 1997)

I CAN SWIM by David McCoy. Ready Readers, Stage 2 (Modern Curriculum Press, 1996)

Technology

AstroWord

Some ESL learners will benefit from additional practice and linguistic interaction, such as that provided by the CD-ROM *AstroWord Short Vowels: a, i* (Module 3). Encourage groups of children to work together to complete the Easy level of *Word Sort,* in which children help alien creatures sort picture clues according to vowel sound. Offer assistance while monitoring progress.

Lesson 49
Short *i*

> **INFORMAL ASSESSMENT OBJECTIVES**
>
> **Can children**
>
> ✔ write short *i* words to finish sentences about a story?
>
> ✔ write about an imaginary race?

1 INTRODUCE

Materials:
Student Edition, page 103; photos of a state fair or carnival, horse race, dog race (optional); butcher paper; crayons

Talk about fairs and races with ESL learners to anticipate the lesson theme. To help comprehension, with the group create a large picture of a fair or carnival on butcher paper. Discuss what items to include, draw them together, then label them in the picture.

➤ Ask children about what types of fairs and carnival-like celebrations they have attended in the United States or their homeland.

➤ Write *Which pigs will win the race around the ring?* Talk about the pig race. If concerned for the animals' well-being, assure children that animals are unharmed by running races.

➤ Ask a volunteer to go to the chalkboard and circle all the *i*'s in the question. Have other volunteers underline target words needed to complete the activity.

2 TEACH

Materials:
Student Edition, page 103; crayons or pencils; paper; butcher paper

Prepare ESL learners for the writing activity on page 103 by discussing and reading *"Swift Pigs"* aloud. Reread as needed.

➤ Read *"Swift Pigs"* aloud to ESL learners. Read the story a second time. Tell children to underline all the words that contain a short *i*, as you walk through the story for a third time.

➤ Ask children to read the story aloud, one line at a time.

➤ Draw a large pig on butcher paper leaving it up as a visual reminder for ESL students. Ask each child to read one of the underlined (short *i*) words from the story and write it inside the pig's body. Have children copy the list on their papers.

★ *For specific notes on various home languages, see pages xiii–xvii of this Guide.*

3 PRACTICE

Materials:
Student Edition,
page 103

Review the list of short *i* words from *"Swift Pigs"* before assigning the writing activity on page 103.

➤ Write on the chalkboard the list of short *i* words that appear in the story. Ask volunteers to read each one aloud.

➤ Read the story aloud. Discuss the story concept with ESL learners.

➤ Check comprehension with questions such as "Are pigs slow?, What do little pigs run in?", and so on. Have children work in pairs to answer your questions in writing.

➤ Explain the writing activity on page 103. Reread the narrative together, then complete items 1–3 as a group. Review answers.

4 APPLY

Materials:
Student Edition,
page 104

Assist ESL learners in writing a description of a pig race.

➤ Review the words in the word box. Supply others words your ESL learners might need (*little, race, run(s),* and so on).

➤ Ask individuals to talk about the picture.

➤ Ask questions that will help each child write a description, such as "What are the pigs doing?" and "Where are they?"

➤ Write a class experience story about a pig race for less-proficient ESL learners to use when completing page 104.

➤ Assist more proficient ESL learners to write 2–4 sentences. Share their writing orally with the class.

5 ASSESS

Materials:
Student
descriptions, paper,
pencil

Review each child's description on page 104 before giving a spelling test of 6–8 words with short *i*. Ask children to read their sentences. Assist with grammar. Say each word and use it in context in a sentence. Use words from *"Swift Pigs"* (page 103) and the word box on page 104.

MORE PHONICS PRACTICE

Set aside class time to read trade books with ESL learners. Preview these books and do a first reading to children.

MR. FIN'S TRIP by Carolyn Clark. Ready Readers, Stage 1 (Modern Curriculum Press, 1996)

MY HAMSTER, VAN by Florence Beem. Ready Readers, Stage 2 (Modern Curriculum Press, 1996)

AstroWord

Invite children to complete some of the intergalactic activities on the CD-ROM *AstroWord Short Vowels: a, i* (Module 3). Ask small groups of ESL learners and English-speaking children to work together as you focus their efforts on continuing practice with the short sound of *i*. Monitor groups for equal participation and progress.

Lesson 50
Reviewing Short Vowels *a, i*

INFORMAL ASSESSMENT OBJECTIVE

Can children

✔ read short *a* and short *i* words in the context of a story?

★ *The kinds of animals kept as pets varies in different cultures. Be sensitive to the varying definitions of pets that your ESL learners bring to class.*

1 INTRODUCE

Materials:
Action photos of cats and dogs; personal pet photos

Introduce *Biff and Bam* by discussing with ESL learners what pet dogs and cats are and do.

➤ Write *Biff, Bam, cat,* and *dog* on the chalkboard. Ask a volunteer to read the words aloud.

➤ Bring to class photos of cats and dogs. (Magazine ads and calendars are good sources of photos of pets doing amazing things.) Display a picture and talk about it. Ask about children's pets or pets they know. Ask what names they would give to a pet cat or dog.

➤ Tell children they will be reading a story about a cat named Biff and a dog named Bam. The pets do bad things. Brainstorm some predictions of what they might be.

2 TEACH

Materials:
Biff and Bam Take-Home Book; Student Edition, pages 105–106; butcher paper or chart paper

Talk about the *Biff and Bam* Take-Home Book with ESL learners and preview words containing the sounds of short *a* and short *i*.

➤ Assist children in making their Take-Home Books.

➤ Tell children to look at the story pictures and summarize orally what they think will happen in the story.

➤ Have children look through the story for familiar words that contain the sounds of short *a* and short *i*. Begin a list on chart paper or butcher paper of all the words they find.

➤ Identify other important story words: *says, over, think, why, things.* Also talk about alternate meanings for *bats* (*hits*) and *laps* (*licks*).

★ *For specific notes on various home languages, see pages xiii–xvii of this Guide.*

3 PRACTICE

Materials:
Biff and Bam Take-Home Book, crayons

Activate children's phonemic awareness and vocabulary recall by assigning ESL learners specific tasks involving the story text.

➤ Read one page at a time. For each, assign specific tasks: "Listen for words that have the sound of short *a* and circle them in green." "Draw a box around words having short *i* sound."

➤ Read the story a second time. Have volunteers read it aloud.

➤ Ask "What does Biff do first?" "What does Bam do?"

➤ Write words from the story on the chalkboard. Ask children to write new words by changing *a* to *i* or *i* to *a*. Read aloud. Discuss the meanings of new words and use them in oral sentences.

4 APPLY

Materials:
Paper, crayons, markers, stapler

After reading about Biff and Bam, have children work in pairs to create an additional page for the story.

➤ Tell children to draw a picture of lunch time at Jill's house.

➤ Write *Biff drinks milk. Bam has ham. Jill has an apple and milk.*

➤ Ask ESL learners to draw a picture for each sentence, then write the sentence beneath the drawing. Provide support, as needed.

➤ When drawings are complete, have volunteers identify the words with short *i* and short *a*.

➤ Staple drawings into a book. Read pages together. Sit in a circle and pass the book around to give children a close look.

5 ASSESS

Materials:
Biff and Bam Take-Home Book

Verify ESL learners' understanding and recall of the story vocabulary by asking children to read a passage aloud. Check for pronunciation and comprehension. Have ESL learners give an oral summary of the story. Ask questions to verify comprehension.

MORE PHONICS PRACTICE

Set aside class time to read trade books with ESL learners. Preview these books and do a first reading to children.

STOP THAT! by Maryann Dobeck. Ready Readers, Stage 1 (Modern Curriculum Press, 1996)

TIM by Linda Hartley. Phonics Practice Readers (Modern Curriculum Press, 1986)

AstroWord

Some learners will benefit from additional interaction and audiovisual feedback, such as that provided by the CD-ROM *AstroWord Short Vowels: a, i* (Module 3). Encourage native speakers of English and ESL learners to work together to complete activities that interest them using the sounds of short *a* and short *i*. Monitor each group's progress.

Lesson 51
Short *u*

1 INTRODUCE

Materials:
Letter Card *Uu*;
Phonics Picture
Cards (numbers 61,
64, 66, 67)

Introduce the sound of short *u* by reviewing familiar words and picture clues and assessing children's ability to pronounce them.

➤ Display Letter Card *Uu*. Have children name the letter.

➤ Hold up one Picture Card at a time and ask a volunteer to name the picture. Emphasize the sound of short *u* in each word.

➤ Ask children with greater English proficiency to write some of the picture names on the chalkboard; have others read them and underline the *u*.

➤ Display Picture Cards 61 and 64 (*bug, jug*), then 66 and 67 (*run, sun*). Point out each of the rhyme pairs and ask what is similar or different about each pair of words.

2 TEACH

Materials:
Student Edition,
page 107; Rhyme
Poster 26 (optional)

Teach words with the sound of short *u* by reading aloud the rhyme on page 107.

➤ Ask children to talk about the rhyme picture on page 107.

➤ Write *-ub: tub, cub, scrub, rub* on the chalkboard. Pronounce the phonogram *-ub* before saying each word. Ask ESL learners to repeat.

➤ Read the rhyme aloud once, pointing to target words as you say them. Encourage children to act out the rhyme as you recite it. Model the actions if necessary.

➤ Have children take turns reading a line. Repeat reading the rhyme.

★ *For specific notes on various home languages, see pages xiii–xvii of this Guide.*

3 PRACTICE

Materials:
Student Edition, page 107; Phonics Picture Card (number 61)

Practice differentiating between short vowel sounds and naming pictures containing the sound of short *u*.

➤ Write *big, bug, bag* on the board. Display Picture Card 61 and ask which word names the picture. Have a volunteer circle the word.

➤ Repeat the words, emphasizing the different vowel sounds.

➤ Write *jump* on the chalkboard as you pronounce it. Tell children to jump each time they hear a word with the sound of short *u* like in *jump*. The words are *sun, sit, cup, hat, run, jam,* and *tub*.

➤ Read the directions on page 107 aloud and model the task with item 1. Ask children to complete the page in pairs. Review answers.

4 APPLY

Materials:
Word Slides activity, *MCP Phonics Teacher Resource Guide,* page 75m; construction paper, markers, scissors

Make a "sound of short *u*" Word Slide as described on page 75m.

➤ Assist children to create art for their slides (*sun, cup, bug*).

➤ Provide an 11" x 2" strip for each slide. Working in pairs, ask children to write five words that contain the sound of short *u* on their strips. Encourage them to draw quick sketches by their words in order to remember what each word means.

➤ Cut vertical slits and feed the strip through. Review words aloud.

5 ASSESS

Materials:
Student Edition, page 108; crayons

Have ESL learners complete page 108 to check their understanding of rhyming words with short *u* sound. Read the directions aloud. Ask a volunteer to name the pictures in item 1. Assist children in determining which picture names rhyme and have them color the pictures. Have children complete items 2–5 in pairs. Review aloud.

MORE PHONICS PRACTICE

Set aside class time to read trade books with ESL learners. Preview these books and do a first reading to children.

LITTLE HOUSE by Polly Peterson. Ready Readers, Stage 0 (Modern Curriculum Press, 1997)

LITTLE BUNNY'S LUNCH by Joanne Nelson. Discovery Phonics (Modern Curriculum Press, 1992)

AstroWord

Some children will benefit from additional practice and feedback on the CD-ROM *AstroWord Short Vowels: e, u* (Module 5). Encourage native speakers of English and ESL learners to work on the Easy level of *Make-a-Word*, where children help alien creatures create words based on a picture clue by inserting the correct vowel. Monitor each group's progress.

Lesson 52–55
Short *u*; Short *a, i, u*

INFORMAL ASSESSMENT OBJECTIVES

Can children

✔ identify picture names and spell words that contain the sound of short *u*, as well as short *a* and short *i*?

✔ blend C-V-C patterns to identify words with the sounds of short *a, i,* and *u*?

✔ spell and write words that contain the sound of short *u*?

✔ write words that contain the sound of short *u* to complete sentences?

1 INTRODUCE

Materials:
Picture Cards (numbers 45, 47–49, 57–59, 61–63, 67–68); four to six realia items with the sound of short *u* (such as *cup, nut, drum*) (optional); Student Edition, pages 109 and 111

Use familiar objects containing the sound of short *u* to assess children's ability to discriminate between short *a, i,* and *u*.

➤ Display an object; ask a volunteer to name it aloud to the group. Have the group identify the vowel sound the word contains and highlight it.

➤ Choose one of the objects (such as *cup*) and write its name plus two other words on the chalkboard (*cap, cup, cub*). Ask a volunteer to circle the correct word.

➤ Explain the activity instructions. Name the objects pictured, if necessary. Have children complete the worksheets on pages 109 and 111 of the Student Edition.

2 TEACH

Materials:
Student Edition, pages 112 and 114

Teach ESL learners to spell words with the sound of short *a, u,* and *i* by identifying initial and final consonant sounds.

➤ Read the directions for the worksheet on page 112. Name the objects pictured. Instruct children to complete item 1 and check their work to verify understanding of the task. Have them work in pairs to complete the activity.

➤ Read the directions for the worksheet on page 114; have a volunteer explain the task. Name objects pictured, if necessary.

➤ Assist with the first item. Have individuals complete items 2–16. Monitor, offering assistance as needed.

➤ Review answers aloud with the group.

★ *For specific notes on various home languages, see pages xiii–xvii of this Guide.*

3 PRACTICE

Materials:
Student Edition, page 116

Structure the activity on page 116 of the Student Edition to practice auditory comprehension, spelling, and writing.

➤ Explain that you will name the objects on the worksheet one at a time. Invite children to write each word you say under the matching picture. Repeat each word several times. Monitor responses. You may wish to have children of varying language proficiency levels work together to complete this activity.

➤ Complete five or six of the target words, in random order, and verify that children have correctly written the words you've dictated. Continue with the rest of the words.

4 APPLY

Materials:
Student Edition, page 115

Apply children's ability to spell and recognize words that contain the sound of short *u* by filling in missing parts of a sentence.

➤ Invite ESL learners to talk about what they know about farms. Give a brief overview of the "story" told on the worksheet on page 115 so that children can anticipate the action.

➤ Read the directions and ask children to explain the activity to you. Assist ESL learners, if necessary, as they complete item 1.

➤ Have children work in pairs to complete the activity. Review answers aloud as a group.

5 ASSESS

Materials:
Student Edition, page 113

Review/reinforce the words *plays, soon, sees,* and *stuck.* Ask a volunteer to read the first part of item 1 on page 113. Tell children to circle the word that completes the sentence. Verify and reinforce correct answers. Continue for items 2–6. Read the entire story when finished. Ask children to speculate about what happens next.

Book Corner

MORE PHONICS PRACTICE

Set aside class time to read trade books with ESL learners. Preview these books and do a first reading to children.

THE TRUCK IS STUCK by Claire Daniel. Ready Readers, Stage 0 (Modern Curriculum Press, 1997)

SANDY by Cynthia Rothman. Ready Readers, Stage 1 (Modern Curriculum Press, 1996)

Technology

AstroWord

Some learners will benefit from additional practice and audiovisual feedback, such as that provided by the CD-ROM *AstroWord Short Vowels: e, u* (Module 5). Encourage native speakers of English and ESL learners to work together to complete the Easy level of *Word Sort,* in which children help alien creatures sort picture clues according to vowel sound. Offer assistance while monitoring progress.

Lesson 56
Short Vowel *u*

INFORMAL ASSESSMENT OBJECTIVES

Can children

✔ write short *u* words to finish sentences about a story?

✔ write a letter to a story character?

1 INTRODUCE

Materials:
Student Edition, page 117; pictures of a bee and a bear cub (optional); chart paper

Talk about bears, bear cubs, and where they live with ESL learners to anticipate the content of the story and to assess usage of short *u*.

➤ Display or draw a picture of a bee on chart paper. Write *bee* under the picture. Ask children to suggest what bugs called bees do.

➤ Write *buzz* on the board; verify that ESL learners recognize this "sound" word. Model natural pronunciation.

➤ Review *bug*, *cub*, and *fun* by asking a volunteer to write each on the chalkboard as you say them. Have a more proficient child write the words *dull* and *lump*. Pantomime meaning. Then have ESL learners repeat.

➤ Tell ESL learners to circle words with short *u* on page 117 of their books. Verify children's work.

2 TEACH

Materials:
Student Edition, page 117; crayons or pencils; chart paper

Prepare ESL learners for the writing activity on page 117 by discussing and reading "The Cub and the Bug" aloud.

➤ Write short *u* words on chart paper: *dull, cub, must, fun, bug, buzz, stung,* and *lump*. Review aloud, modeling and correcting pronunciation.

➤ Read "The Cub and the Bug" aloud to ESL learners. As you read the story a second time, point to each target word and have a volunteer read it aloud after you.

➤ Read the story once again, asking children to read one line at a time to you or practice as a choral reading.

➤ Ask the Think! question. Encourage children to respond using complete oral thoughts. If necessary, restate incomplete thoughts in a correct complete thought to model the intent.

➤ Create a graphic organizer and record children's responses.

★ *For specific notes on various home languages, see pages xiii–xvii of this Guide.*

3 PRACTICE

Materials:
Student Edition, page 117; chart paper

Review the list of short *u* words from "The Cub and the Bug" with ESL learners before beginning the writing activity on page 117.

➤ Display the list on chart paper. (See Teach.) Model pronunciation. Ask the group to read each one aloud after you.

➤ Read the story aloud. Ask comprehension questions such as "Who wants to have fun?" and "What sound does the bug make?"

➤ As a group, explain and complete the activity, and review answers.

4 APPLY

Materials:
Student Edition, page 118

Introduce ESL learners to the mechanics of letter writing before beginning the open-ended activity on page 118.

➤ Explain the parts of a letter—the greeting ("Dear [name]"), the closing ("Your friend"), and the body (middle part).

➤ Review the six words on the word list at right.

➤ Read the activity directions aloud and talk about how to complete it. For ideas for the body, ask, "What can Cub do to have fun?"

➤ Have children work in pairs to complete a sentence orally. Then have partners write their sentences. Ask volunteers to read their letters to you. Display.

➤ Conduct a Group Language Experience to write the letter. Assist children in telling you what to write. Rewrite incomplete responses. Children can copy the group-generated story in their workbooks.

5 ASSESS

Materials:
Paper, pencil

Review "The Cub and the Bug" (page 117). Explain that you are giving a spelling test of 5 or 6 words that contain the short *u* sound. Choose and say each word aloud, repeat, and use it in a sentence (from the story, if possible). Say each word again. Check spelling.

MORE PHONICS PRACTICE

Set aside class time to read trade books with ESL learners. Preview these books and do a first reading to children.

FUN WITH GUM by Janis Asad Raabe. Phonics Practice Readers (Modern Curriculum Press, 1986)

BUD THE TUG by Linda Hartley. Phonics Practice Readers (Modern Curriculum Press, 1986)

AstroWord

Invite children to complete some of the intergalactic activities on the CD-ROM *AstroWord Short Vowels: e, u* (Module 5). Ask small groups of native speakers of English and ESL learners to work together as you focus their efforts on continuing to practice the short sound of *u*. Monitor group members to ensure equal participation and progress.

Lesson 57
Reviewing Short Vowel *u*

INFORMAL ASSESSMENT OBJECTIVE

Can children

✔ read short *u* words in the context of a story?

---

1 INTRODUCE

Materials:
Two slices of bread, cheese, paper plate, picture of a bird feeder

Some ESL learners may not know what a bird feeder is. Bring in pictures of real bird feeders to explain the concept. *Lunch in a Jug* is about constructing a bird feeder in steps; introduce ESL learners to sequential words *first, second, third,* and *last.*

➤ Write *first, second, third,* and *last* on the chalkboard. Assist volunteers in reading each word aloud.

➤ Demonstrate an activity in steps using a familiar sequence, such as making a sandwich. *First, put a slice of bread on a plate. Second, put the cheese on the bread. Third, put the other slice of bread on top. Last, eat lunch!*

➤ Ask ESL learners to explain and act out other simple but sequenced tasks using target words, such as washing their hands or brushing their teeth.

2 TEACH

Materials:
Lunch in a Jug Take-Home Book, pages 119–120 of the Student Edition; book about birds

Talk about birds and the *Lunch in a Jug* Take-Home Book with ESL learners while reviewing words with short *u.*

➤ Write *tails, beaks, two legs, feathers,* and *wings* on the chalkboard. Identify the parts of the bird using the photographs. Ask volunteers to read each word; assist with *feathers* (the only new word).

➤ Display photographs and talk about birds. What do ESL learners know about birds? Help them use their oral language skills to describe.

➤ Assist children in making their Take-Home Books.

➤ Have children look through the story for words that contain the sound of short *u.* Keep a list on the chalkboard as children read.

➤ Preview other important story words, such as *pal, feeder, clean, hole, string, branch,* and *seeds.* Then, have children take turns rereading the story to classmates in small groups.

★ *For specific notes on various home languages, see pages xiii–xvii of this Guide.*

3 PRACTICE

Materials:
Lunch in a Jug Take-Home Book, crayons

Activate ESL learners' phonemic awareness and vocabulary recall by asking them to underline context words and those containing the short sound of *u*.

➤ Read the story one page at a time and assign children a specific task such as, "Which word means *friend*? Draw a blue box around it," or "Underline the words with the sound of short *u*."

➤ Read the story a second time. Have volunteers read aloud.

➤ Check comprehension with directed questions such as, "If we want to make a milk-jug feeder, what do we do first?"

4 APPLY

Materials:
Plastic milk jugs, string, scissors, birdseed

After reading *Lunch in a Jug*, have children work in small groups to construct the feeder described in the story.

➤ Bring supplies to class. Ask volunteers to bring milk jugs.

➤ Have ESL learners read the story again and then explain each step to you.

➤ Assist with cutting the hole in the jug.

➤ Hang the feeder(s) in a tree visible from a classroom window.

5 ASSESS

Materials:
Lunch in a Jug Take-Home Book, chart paper, crayons

Verify ESL learners' understanding and recall of the story vocabulary. Ask children to read a random passage aloud. Monitor pronunciation and comprehension. Instruct children to draw pictures of the milk-jug feeders they made previously. Assist them in writing a sentence or two about the book or the project.

MORE PHONICS PRACTICE

Set aside class time to read trade books with ESL learners. Preview these books and do a first reading to children.

GOOD NIGHT, LITTLE BUG by Cynthia Rothman. Ready Readers, Stage 1 (Modern Curriculum Press, 1996)

JUST LIKE US by Barbara V. Adams. Ready Readers, Stage 2 (Modern Curriculum Press, 1996)

AstroWord

Some learners will benefit from additional interaction and practice such as that provided by the CD-ROM *AstroWord Short Vowels: e, u* (Module 5). Encourage native speakers of English and ESL learners to work together to complete activities that interest them using the sound of short *u*. Offer assistance and monitor each group's progress.

Lesson 58
Short o

INFORMAL ASSESSMENT OBJECTIVES

Can children

✔ identify picture names and words that contain the sound of short *o*?

✔ identify rhyming words?

★ *Native speakers of Spanish, Tagalog, and some Asian languages may not distinguish between the sounds of short* o, *short* a, *and short* u; *practice* **hot, hat, hut** *and* **lock, lack, luck.**

---

1 INTRODUCE

Materials:
Letter Card *Oo*; Phonics Picture Cards (numbers 70, 73–75, and others, at random); realia (optional)

Assess ESL learners' ability to identify words and picture clues that contain the sound of short *o*.

➤ Hold up Letter Card *Oo*; have children name the letter. Model the sound of short *o* with *hot, mop, sock.* Use pantomime or show realia to confirm meaning.

➤ Write *hop* on the chalkboard. Have children stand. Say a series of words; instruct the group to hop on two feet when they hear you say a word with short *o.* Say words such as *stop, fan, hot, lunch, knot, fox, cup,* and *dot.*

➤ Display one short *o* Picture Card with two others, at random (such as *box, bug, bag*). Ask a volunteer to choose the picture whose name contains the short sound of *o.*

➤ Display Picture Cards 70 and 74 *(box, ox),* then 73 and 75 *(mop, top).* Ask how each pair is similar. (They rhyme.) If necessary, review the concept of rhyming with ESL learners.

2 TEACH

Materials:
Student Edition, page 121; index cards; red and black markers; Rhyme Poster 27 (optional)

Read aloud the rhyme on page 121 to ESL learners as you continue teaching words containing short *o.*

➤ Ask children to talk about the rhyme picture on page 121.

➤ Hand out one index card per child. Assist them in drawing and coloring stop signs and writing *STOP!* on the cards.

➤ Read the rhyme aloud. Tell children to listen for words with the sound of short *o* and to hold up their stop signs when they do.

➤ Have the entire group or volunteers read the entire rhyme aloud.

★ *For specific notes on various home languages, see pages xiii–xvii of this Guide.*

3 PRACTICE

Materials:
Student Edition, page 121; highlighter markers

Practice identifying picture names and rhyming words with the sound of short o.

➤ Read aloud the directions for the activity on page 121. Ask children to look at the pictures and tell you the ones for which they do not know the names. Provide needed vocabulary.

➤ Allow children time to work in pairs to complete the activity.

➤ Review the answers aloud.

➤ Hand out three markers to each child. Tell them to cover all pictures whose names rhyme with the word you say. List: *hot* (*pot, knot*), *dock* (*rock, sock, lock*), *fox* (*box*), *stop* (*pop, top, mop*).

4 APPLY

Materials:
Change-a-Letter activity, *MCP Phonics Teacher Resource Guide*, page 75n; red and blue construction paper, markers, masking tape

Adapt the Change-a-Letter activity to add kinesthetic learning.

➤ Work with groups of six children (English proficient and ESL learners).

➤ Write an initial consonant on each sheet of red paper (*l, r, d*) and a short o phonogram (*-ot,-ock, -og*, and so on) on each blue paper. Tape one paper to each child's shirt front (3 red, 3 blue).

➤ Have children stand in groups facing each other. Call a child to choose a partner from the other group whose sound blends with his or her own to make a word and say it.

➤ Redistribute papers. Repeat, making new words.

5 ASSESS

Materials:
Crayons; Student Edition, page 122

Assess understanding of short o rhyming words using the worksheet on page 122. Read the directions aloud. Have a volunteer name the pictures in item 1. Assist children in determining which picture names rhyme and have children color them. Have children complete items 2–5 in pairs. Review answers aloud.

MORE PHONICS PRACTICE

Set aside class time to read trade books with ESL learners. Preview these books and do a first reading to children.

THE FOX AND THE HOG by Dr. Alvin Granowsky. Phonics Practice Readers (Modern Curriculum Press, 1986)

THE POPCORN POPPER by JoAnne Nelson. Discovery Phonics (Modern Curriculum Press, 1992)

AstroWord

Some ESL learners will benefit from additional feedback and practice using the CD-ROM *AstroWord Short Vowels: i, o* (Module 4). Encourage native speakers of English and ESL learners to work on the Easy level of *Make-a-Word*, where children help alien creatures create words based on a picture clue by inserting the correct vowel. Monitor each group's progress.

Lessons 59–62
Short *o*; Short *a*, *i*, *u*, *o*

INFORMAL ASSESSMENT OBJECTIVES

Can children

✔ identify picture names and words that contain the sound of short *o*?

✔ identify and blend C-V-C patterns to make words?

✔ identify the initial and final consonants in words that contain the sound of short *o*?

★ *Native speakers of Spanish and Russian may confuse the sound of short* u *or* o *with the sound of* oo *in* foot. *Assess ESL children's ability to discriminate and pronounce these sounds; provide individualized practice with word pairs, as necessary.*

---

1 INTRODUCE

Materials:
Student Edition, pages 123–124; four to six realia items with the sound of short *o* or Phonics Picture Cards (numbers 71–75); red crayon

Activate children's knowledge and understanding of the sound of short *o* by using familiar objects that model the target sound.

▶ Display an object or Picture Card; ask a volunteer to say the object and identify the vowel sound he or she hears.

▶ Ask another volunteer to write the name of the object on the chalkboard and underline the short *o*.

▶ Have children read aloud the picture names on page 123, providing assistance as needed. Then have children complete the worksheets on these pages individually or in small groups.

2 TEACH

Materials:
Student Edition, pages 128 and 130

Focus your ESL learners on identifying initial and final consonant sounds as they complete the activities on these pages.

▶ Read aloud directions for the worksheet on page 128. Model for children how to complete items 1 and 2; check their work to verify understanding of the task. Have them work in pairs to say the picture names, then complete through item 15 together. Have children complete the last item by themselves.

▶ Read the directions for the worksheet on page 130; have a volunteer explain the task. Correct misconceptions.

▶ Assist with the first item. Have individuals complete items 2–12.

▶ Review answers aloud with the group; then have volunteers write them on the chalkboard. Have children exchange papers and confirm correct picture names.

★ *For specific notes on various home languages, see pages xiii–xvii of this Guide.*

3 PRACTICE

Materials:
Student Edition, pages 125–126

Review and practice distinguishing short vowel sounds *a, i, u, o* in words ESL learners already know.

➤ Review vowel sounds. Write *stand, hum, hop, sit* on the chalkboard. Tell children to act out each word as you say it. Have volunteer(s) identify and circle the vowels.

➤ Read aloud the directions on page 125. Verify comprehension of the task and then have children complete the page in pairs.

➤ Follow up with the worksheet on page 126. Review answers aloud.

4 APPLY

Materials:
Student Edition, page 127

Have children apply their comprehension of words that contain the sound of short *o* by completing the writing activity on page 127.

➤ Ask children to talk about the pictures they see. "Where is Bob?"

➤ Have a volunteer read the directions. Assist ESL learners in completing item 1, if necessary.

➤ Ask children to complete the worksheet in pairs. Review answers aloud.

➤ Brainstorm possible answers to the Think! question. Write children's ideas on the chalkboard or chart paper.

➤ Then, help children write one sentence to answer.

5 ASSESS

Materials:
Student Edition, page 129

Have children work independently to complete page 129 of the Student Edition. Reinforce the words *likes, puts, shoes,* and *very* with ESL learners and use gestures to communicate meaning. Have a volunteer read item 1. Ask children to circle the word at right that completes the sentence. Monitor test-taking skills. Continue for items 2–6.

Book Corner

MORE PHONICS PRACTICE

Set aside class time to read trade books with ESL learners. Preview these books and do a first reading to children.

HOP ON, HOP OFF by Janis Asad Raabe. Phonics Practice Readers (Modern Curriculum Press, 1986)

WHEN THE ALLIGATOR CAME TO CLASS by Cass Hollander. Discovery Phonics (Modern Curriculum Press, 1992)

Technology

AstroWord
Completing some of the activities on the CD-ROM *AstroWord Short Vowels: i, o* (Module 4) will benefit learners who need additional opportunities for reinforcement. Encourage ESL learners and more English-proficient children to work together on *Word Sort,* an activity in which children help alien creatures sort picture clues according to vowel sound. Offer assistance while monitoring progress.

Lesson 63
Short Vowel *o*

INFORMAL ASSESSMENT OBJECTIVES

Can children

✔ write short o words to finish sentences about a story?

✔ write about a picture?

1 INTRODUCE

Materials:
Student Edition, page 131; photos of foxes

Explain to ESL learners that they will learn about foxes. Describe the animals, using words, gestures, and pictures.

➤ Write *fox* and *foxes* on the chalkboard; have a volunteer read.

➤ Ask children to talk about the photos on page 131 and tell what they know about foxes. Confirm information as you gently model correct pronunciation of unfamiliar words.

➤ Have children look for short o words in the story. Have volunteers write them on the chalkboard.

➤ Encourage ESL learners to use these words, the words they know, and the pictures to restate in their own words what they have learned about foxes.

2 TEACH

Materials:
Student Edition, page 131; crayons or pencils; writing paper

Read and talk about "Foxes" with ESL learners before completing the writing activity on page 131.

➤ Write the following concept words (prepositions) on the chalkboard: *on, around, over, in.* Say each word and model as needed. For example, you can walk *around* the desk, sit *on* the desk, and so on. Make a word chart of prepositions.

➤ Read "Foxes" aloud to the group. Ask comprehension questions to confirm understanding. Practice as a choral reading.

➤ Have volunteers take turns reading a line from "Foxes." Together, tally words with short o on the board.

➤ Ask ESL learners to make new sentences about foxes by using concept vocabulary, the picture clues, and the text on page 131.

➤ Make a class story, with all ESL learners contributing to their level of ability, to orally or in writing tell about foxes.

★ *For specific notes on various home languages, see pages xiii–xvii of this Guide.*

3 PRACTICE

Materials:
Student Edition, page 131

Review short *o* words from "Foxes" before completing the activity on page 131.

➤ Ask volunteers to compose a list of words with the short sound of *o* from the reading as a graphic organizer.

➤ Read the story aloud once. Talk about the story with ESL learners.

➤ Check comprehension: "Where do foxes live? What other animal is like a fox?" and so on.

➤ Explain the writing activity, and encourage ESL learners to finish the sentences, working individually. Review answers.

4 APPLY

Materials:
Change-a-Letter activity, *MCP Phonics Teacher Resource Guide,* page 75n; chalkboard and chalk

Adapt the Change-a-Letter activity to tie to the lesson theme.

➤ Write the word *fox* on the chalkboard. Explain that each player will change one letter to make a new word. If children are unable to move the activity along, offer clues such as "Change the *o* to *i.*"

➤ Ask that children use each new word aloud in a sentence.

➤ Repeat, beginning with a word containing the short *o* sound.

5 ASSESS

Materials:
Student Edition, page 132; chart paper

Activate background knowledge by having ESL learners give oral summary of "Foxes" before they write about the picture on page 132. Read directions and brainstorm ideas aloud before children write. Have children write about the picture; support writing as needed. Conduct a Group Language Experience lesson to create text for page 132. Write the text according to children's dictation. Model correct use, then write on chart paper. Children can copy text into their workbooks. Read each description aloud.

Book Corner

MORE PHONICS PRACTICE

Set aside class time to read trade books with ESL learners. Preview these books and do a first reading to children.

LOST IN THE FOG by Donna Taylor. Ready Readers, Stage 1 (Modern Curriculum Press, 1996)

DOT THE DOC by Linda Hartley. Phonics Practice Readers (Modern Curriculum Press, 1986)

Technology

AstroWord

Invite children to complete some of the intergalactic activities on the CD-ROM *AstroWord Short Vowels: i, o* (Module 4). Ask small groups of native speakers of English and ESL learners to work together as you focus their efforts on continuing to practice the short sound of *o.* Monitor activities during group time to ensure equal participation and progress.

Lesson 64
Reviewing Short Vowels

INFORMAL ASSESSMENT OBJECTIVE

Can children

✔ read short vowel words in the context of a story?

★ *Animal sounds are written/represented differently in every language. For example, frogs say "croac" in Spanish and "kvakat" in Russian. ESL learners may offer a variety of animal sounds for this lesson.*

1 INTRODUCE

Materials:
Student Edition, pages 133–134; comic strip

Evaluate ESL learners' ability to pronounce short vowels in a story as they identify the animal characters and talk about speech balloons.

➤ Write the title *Who Is at the Pond?* on the board. Encourage volunteers to read the title (question) aloud. Have them look at the pictures and answer orally.

➤ Invite children to name each animal; write *bug, duck, frog, robin, turtle. Bird* will likely be given instead of *robin*; write *robin* and explain that it is a kind of bird. Have ESL learners identify the short vowels in the target words.

➤ Point out the use of speech balloons in some books to show who is talking; show a comic strip. Explain their use to children.

2 TEACH

Materials:
Who Is at the Pond? Take-Home Book; pages 133–134 of the Student Edition; pictures of a cat, a dog, a rooster, and other animals

Talk about animal noises with children as you continue reviewing words that contain short vowels. Discuss animal sounds represented in languages other than English. You can create a class book of animal sounds in different languages based on children's answers.

➤ Assist children in making their Take-Home Books.

➤ Display pictures of a dog or cat, and ask what sound the animal makes. Explain that the sound is *bow-wow or woof* or *meow* and write it on the board.

➤ Have children name the animals in the story again.

➤ Talk about the sound words that appear in the speech balloons and what they mean. Make sure children don't confuse real animal sounds with some of the sounds in this book. Have children read each word and identify and circle any short vowels.

➤ Review other important story words, such as *by, little, lily, drink, into,* and *warm.*

★ *For specific notes on various home languages, see pages xiii–xvii of this Guide.*

3 PRACTICE

Materials:
Who Is at the Pond?
Take-Home Book,
crayons

Review short vowel words in context as you read *Who Is at the Pond?* with a choral line-by-line reading.

➤ Have volunteers read a passage aloud.

➤ Give children specific phonemic tasks to perform such as, "Draw a green box around words with the sound of short *o*."

➤ Have children help read the story for a second time.

➤ Check comprehension by having volunteers give an oral summary of what each animal did at the pond that day. Children can use actions or their words (phrases, sentences) as their abilities allow.

4 APPLY

Materials:
Construction paper,
magazines, crayons
and markers,
scissors, glue

Children will create a page for a classroom book about animals.

➤ Review animals, animal sounds, and speech balloons in books.

➤ Tell children to draw (or cut and paste) a picture of an animal they like that is performing an action. Have children draw a speech balloon (follow page 133); then help them write a short vowel word to describe the action. (Suggestions include *munch, crunch, chomp,* and *hiss.*)

➤ Have children each write a sentence to describe their animal.

➤ Make a class book. Have children take turns reading aloud.

5 ASSESS

Materials:
Who Is at the Pond?
Take-Home Book,
chart paper, pencils

Confirm ESL learners' pronunciation, understanding, and recall of the story. Have children summarize aloud *Who Is at the Pond?* Ask them to write two sentences about the story that answer the Talk About It question on page 8 of their Take-Home Book. Assist less proficient ESL learners with writing by engaging them in a Group Language Experience lesson to create the story on chart paper.

MORE PHONICS PRACTICE

Set aside class time to read trade books with ESL learners. Preview these books and do a first reading to children.

THE MERRY-GO-ROUND by Judy Nayer. Ready Readers, Stage 1 (Modern Curriculum Press, 1996)

MR. WINK by Claire Daniel. Ready Readers, Stage 2 (Modern Curriculum Press, 1996)

AstroWord

Some learners will benefit from additional interaction and practice such as that provided by the CD-ROM *AstroWord Short Vowels: i, o* (Module 4). Encourage native speakers of English and ESL learners to work together to complete activities that interest them using the sound of short *o.* Offer assistance and monitor each group's progress.

Lesson 65
Short e

INFORMAL ASSESSMENT OBJECTIVES

Can children

✔ identify picture names and words that contain the sound of short e?

✔ identify rhyming words with the sound of short e?

★ *Native speakers of Tagalog might pronounce written e like the ay in say. Practice let, late; pen, pain; and so on. Since no similar vowel sound exists in Korean, offer additional practice and support.*

1 INTRODUCE

Materials:
Letter Cards *Aa, Ee, Ii, Oo, Uu;* Phonics Picture Cards (numbers 78–84)

Assess ESL learners' ability to make the sound of short e by using rhyming words and practice distinguishing short vowel sounds.

➤ Hold up Letter Card *Ee* and one of the Picture Cards. Have a volunteer name the letter and the picture clue. Model the sound of short e for children to pronounce chorally. Review the remaining Picture Cards in the same way.

➤ Display all the vowel Letter Cards on a desk. Tell ESL learners you will say a word and they are to point to the letter that stands for the short vowel sound they hear. The words are: *bed, bat, mitt, dog, cub, men, sun, set, shell, box,* and *jump.*

➤ Print the words *bet, hen,* and *red* on the chalkboard. Ask a volunteer to read one of the words and supply a rhyming word. Review with children what rhyming words are. You may need to assist less proficient ESL learners by supplying a pair of words and asking if they rhyme (for example, *red/bed* and *hen/bet*). Repeat until children can distinguish rhyming pairs easily.

2 TEACH

Materials:
Student Edition, page 135; Rhyme Poster 28 (optional); Phonics Picture Card 80

Teach and review short e words by reading the rhyme on page 135.

➤ Write *Jen* and *hen* on the chalkboard. Say each aloud.

➤ Point out that the girl in the rhyme and the picture is named *Jen.*

➤ Ask children to talk about the picture at the top of page 135.

➤ Discuss the different meanings of *pen* (such as a writing instrument and a fenced area to hold animals).

➤ Have ESL learners take turns reading a line of the rhyme aloud.

➤ Ask the group what they think might be inside the red hen's pen; display Picture Card 80 (*eggs*) as a clue.

★ *For specific notes on various home languages, see pages xiii–xvii of this Guide.*

3 PRACTICE

Materials:
Student Edition,
page 135

Challenge ESL learners to locate and name picture clues containing the sound of short *e* and rhyming words in the activity on page 135.

➤ Read (or ask a volunteer to read) the directions aloud.

➤ Randomly call out an item number; have a child name the picture clue. Provide vocabulary words as needed.

➤ Pair children to complete the activity. Review answers orally.

➤ Tell children to find pairs of pictures whose names rhyme (such as *ten, hen, pen, men; net* and *jet*).

4 APPLY

Materials:
Auditory/Kinesthetic
Learners section,
*MCP Phonics Teacher
Resource Guide,* page
136; Consonant
Letter Cards; index
cards

Adapt the activity for Auditory/Kinesthetic Learners for use with ESL learners.

➤ Prepare several index cards by printing one short *e* phonogram on each (*-ed, -en, -est,* and so on). Make duplicate cards for frequently used phonograms.

➤ Display consonant cards face up in grid form. Place phonogram cards face down in a pile.

➤ Have children pick a card from the pile and choose a beginning sound card to form a word. Have them say each word aloud.

➤ Shuffle cards. Repeat.

5 ASSESS

Materials:
Student Edition,
page 136; crayons

Read the directions aloud for page 136. Ask a volunteer to name the pictures in item 1. Assist children in determining which picture names rhyme and have them color each one (*jet* and *net*). Have children complete items 2–5 in pairs according to levels of English proficiency. Monitor each pair for equal participation. Review orally.

MORE PHONICS PRACTICE

Set aside class time to read trade books with ESL learners. Preview these books and do a first reading to children.

RED HEN by Janis Asad Raabe. Phonics Practice Readers (Modern Curriculum Press, 1986)

NELL GETS A PET by Linda Hartley. Phonics Practice Readers (Modern Curriculum Press, 1986)

AstroWord

Some children will benefit from additional practice and feedback, using the CD-ROM *AstroWord Short Vowels: e, u* (Module 5). Encourage native speakers of English and ESL learners to work together on *Make-a-Word*, where children help alien creatures create words based on picture clues by inserting the correct vowel. Monitor each group's progress.

Lessons 66–69
Short *e;* Reviewing Short Vowels *a, i, u, o, e*

INFORMAL ASSESSMENT OBJECTIVES

Can children

✔ recognize the sound of short *e* in picture names?

✔ identify short *e* words?

✔ identify and blend C-V-C patterns to make short *a, i, u, o,* and *e* words?

✔ identify picture names and spell words that contain the sound of short *e*?

✔ write words that contain the sound of short *e*?

1 INTRODUCE

Materials:
Student Edition, page 137; four to six realia items that model the sound of short *e*

Identify ESL learners' ability to say and write the names of everyday objects (*pen, belt, net, desk, bell*) containing the sound of short *e*.

▶ Display an object; have a volunteer identify and write its name on the chalkboard.

▶ When all objects have been named, choose one and write its name plus two other similar words on the board. Have children identify the object name by circling the correct word choice. Model as needed.

▶ Tell children to work in pairs to complete the activity on page 137. Have them follow the same steps they followed to identify the realia to complete the worksheet items.

2 TEACH

Materials:
Student Edition, page 138; crayons and markers

Discuss hens and eggs with children; follow up with the activity on page 138.

▶ Print *hen* and *eggs* on the chalkboard. Talk about buying eggs at the market and where they come from.

▶ Write *draw* on the chalkboard, and have a volunteer read it aloud and model what it means. Tell children the activity they will be doing includes drawing. Have six volunteers read the sentences on page 138, one sentence each. Explain unfamiliar words and model pronunciation, as needed.

▶ Read the directions aloud. Have children work individually. Check work for reading comprehension and accuracy.

★ *For specific notes on various home languages, see pages xiii–xvii of this Guide.*

3 PRACTICE

Materials:
Student Edition,
pages 142 and 144

Practice C-V-C word patterns, spelling, writing, and listening comprehension by adapting the activities on pages 142 and 144.

➤ Encourage volunteers to read the directions and summarize for you what they are to do in the activity on page 142.

➤ Have children work in pairs. Say a picture name and instruct children to finish the word under the matching picture.

➤ Continue with the activity on page 144. Complete half of the items. Check to see that ESL learners have correctly written the words you've dictated.

➤ Circulate, answer questions, and monitor equal participation and progress.

4 APPLY

Materials:
Student Edition,
pages 139–140

Apply children's cumulative knowledge of short vowels by completing the activities on pages 139–140 as follows.

➤ Review short vowel sounds; have volunteers name a vowel, model the short sound, and say a word containing the sound.

➤ Complete the activity on page 139; review answers together.

➤ Assign pairs to complete both steps of the worksheet on page 140 together. Offer assistance only if needed; monitor progress.

5 ASSESS

Materials:
Student Edition,
pages 141 and 143

Assess ESL learners' ability to complete a sentence with the correct short e word. Review children's knowledge of *picks, draws, hangs* (page 141) and *have, use, likes* (page 143). Ask a volunteer to read aloud the first part of item 1 on page 141. Children circle the word that completes the sentence and print it on the line. Continue for items 2–6. Repeat for page 143.

Book Corner

MORE PHONICS PRACTICE

Set aside class time to read trade books with ESL learners. Preview these books and do a first reading to children.

A WET HEN by Dr. Alvin Granowsky. Phonics Practice Readers (Modern Curriculum Press, 1986)

THE TRIP by Leya Roberts. Ready Readers, Stage 2 (Modern Curriculum Press, 1996)

Technology

AstroWord

Some learners will benefit from additional practice and audiovisual feedback, such as that provided by the CD-ROM *AstroWord Short Vowels: e, u* (Module 5). Encourage native speakers of English and ESL learners to work together to complete the Easy level of *Word Sort*, in which children help alien creatures sort picture clues according to vowel sound. Offer assistance while monitoring progress.

Lesson 70
Short Vowels

INFORMAL ASSESSMENT OBJECTIVES

Can children

✔ spell and write words with short vowels?

✔ write a postcard using spelling words?

★ *Some ESL learners may require additional support and practice with specific short vowels. Review previous lessons and encourage oral practice.*

---

1 INTRODUCE

Materials:
Chart paper; colored markers

Review the five short vowel sounds and familiar words before doing the activity on page 145. Practice orally and by reading and writing.

➤ Print *map, sink, tub, dog, and web* without the vowels (*m_p,* and so on) on the chart paper. As you say each word, ask volunteers to supply the missing vowels.

➤ Have children brainstorm other words that contain each short vowel sound and review, as above.

➤ Review the concept of riddles with children. Create short vowel riddles: "Say two words that contain the sound of short *u* that name something you can put water in (*tub, mug, cup*)." Other ideas include short *e* things to wear (*dress, vest*), short *a* things on your head (*hat, cap*), and short *o* things in the kitchen (*mop, pot*). Provide picture clues for less proficient ESL learners.

2 TEACH

Materials:
MCP Phonics Teacher Resource Guide:
Short Vowel Bingo activity, page 75l;
Unit 2 Word List (one copy per child), page 75k;
playing grid; game markers

Play Short Vowel Tic-Tac-Toe by adapting the Short Vowel Bingo activity.

➤ Prepare a large, nine-square tic-tac-toe grid and make a copy for each child.

➤ Provide children with words from the Unit 2 Word List found on page 75k. Tell them to write one word in each of the nine tic-tac-toe grid squares.

➤ Hand out game markers to cover squares. Call out words from the Word List at random as children cover matching words. Have them call "Tic-Tac-Toe" when they match three in a row.

➤ Repeat with other words from the Unit 2 Word List.

★ *For specific notes on various home languages, see pages xiii–xvii of this Guide.*

3 PRACTICE

Materials:
Student Edition,
page 145

Practice identifying picture names and writing words with short vowels by completing the activity on page 145.

➤ Copy the word list onto the chalkboard and review with children with their books closed.

➤ Ask volunteers to read the directions on page 145.

➤ Work together with children to complete item 1. Have them finish the activity independently. Offer support, as requested.

➤ Review answers aloud as a group. Then challenge ESL learners to use each answer in context in an oral or written sentence.

4 APPLY

Materials:
Student Edition,
page 146; postcards

Activate children's background knowledge and experiences with travel before beginning to write the postcards.

➤ Ask volunteers to talk about a trip they may have taken to brainstorm ideas for the writing activity.

➤ Display postcards. Explain that a postcard is a short letter.

➤ Read the directions for the activity. Have children work in pairs to write three sentences describing a real or an imaginary trip.

5 ASSESS

Materials:
Unit 2 Word List,
*MCP Phonics
Teacher Resource
Guide,* pages 75j
and 146

Give a spelling test featuring words from the lessons in Unit 2 containing short vowel sounds. Use the spelling word list and context sentences found on pages 75j and 146, or create your own list using short vowel C-V-C pattern words. Say the word, repeat it, use it in context in a sentence, and repeat it once more. Check work, verify comprehension, and identify problem areas that need review.

MORE PHONICS PRACTICE

Set aside class time to read trade books with ESL learners. Preview these books and do a first reading to children.

TOO HIGH! by Judy Nayer. Ready Readers, Stage 1 (Modern Curriculum Press, 1996)

MAX by Janis Asad Raabe. Phonics Practice Readers (Modern Curriculum Press, 1986)

AstroWord

Have groups of ESL learners and more English-proficient children work on a variety of activities on the CD-ROMs *AstroWord Short Vowels: a, i; Short Vowels: i, o;* and *Short Vowels: e, u* (Modules 3–5). Have each child report back on which activities she or he has completed and some of the short vowel words used. Monitor progress and offer assistance as needed.

Lesson 71
Reviewing Short Vowels

INFORMAL ASSESSMENT OBJECTIVE

Can children

✔ read short vowel words in the context of a story?

1 INTRODUCE

Materials:
Student Edition,
pages 147–148

Introduce *Amazing Fish* by discussing the topic with ESL learners before you assign the story.

➤ Print the letters *h i f s* on the chalkboard. Challenge ESL learners to unscramble the letters and make the word *fish*.

➤ Ask children to tell what they know about fish, where they live, what they eat, and so on. Help them create a list of words associated with fish that might appear in the story. Story vocabulary includes *think, most, amazing, frog, land, fast, smaller, called, catches, spits, hide, here,* and *well.* Use synonyms, gestures, visuals, and pantomime to clarify the meaning of unfamiliar words, writing them on the chalkboard as you help children sound them out.

➤ Discuss different meanings of the word *fish* (verb and noun).

2 TEACH

Materials:
Amazing Fish Take-Home Book, pages 147–148 of the Student Edition

Talk about the *Amazing Fish* Take-Home Book with ESL learners and review words containing the sounds of short vowels.

➤ Assist children in making their Take-Home Books.

➤ In sequence, ask children to look at the photographs and talk about what they see in each picture. Practice reading each page.

➤ Have children look through the story for words that contain the sounds of short vowels. Keep a list on the chalkboard of all the words they find. Review new words from the story and the Introduce activity, above.

➤ Review these important story words: *amazing, which, think, smaller, about.*

★ *For specific notes on various home languages, see pages xiii–xvii of this Guide.*

3 PRACTICE

Materials:
Blackline Master 15, *MCP Phonics Teacher Resource Guide*, page 75o; number cube or spinner, game markers

To review all short vowel sounds, have ESL learners and their peers play Follow the Path.

➤ Copy the Follow the Path game board found on page 75o.

➤ Have children take turns rolling the number cube and moving their markers along the path. Each child is to make a word from the clues on the "stone" he or she lands on by filling in a vowel.

➤ Ask children to use the words they create in oral sentences.

➤ Clarify rules of play, as needed. Repeat the game several times.

4 APPLY

Materials:
Amazing Fish Take-Home Book, crayons

Engage children's phonemic awareness and vocabulary recall by having ESL learners perform specific tasks as they read *Amazing Fish*.

➤ Ask volunteers to read the story aloud, one page at a time. Support reading and pronunciation effort through praise and correction.

➤ After each page is read, give children a specific task to perform, such as "Circle three words that begin with the sound of *f* and contain a short vowel sound."

➤ Assess comprehension through content-related questions.

5 ASSESS

Materials:
Amazing Fish Take-Home Book

Verify ESL learners' comprehension and retention of story vocabulary. Ask children to read a passage aloud at random. Talk about the text and the photo related to the passage. Check for pronunciation and comprehension. Have children read the last page of the story and answer the Talk About It question.

Book Corner

MORE PHONICS PRACTICE

Set aside class time to read trade books with ESL learners. Preview these books and do a first reading to children.

FISH IN A DISH by Cindy and Zach Clements. Phonics Practice Readers (Modern Curriculum Press, 1979)

GUS by Janis Asad Raabe. Phonics Practice Readers (Modern Curriculum Press, 1986)

Technology

AstroWord
Display vowel cards face down. Divide children into groups, each of which contains one or more ESL learner. Ask one member from each group to choose a card. Have the group work together to complete several intergalactic activities on the corresponding CD-ROMs *AstroWord Short Vowels: a, i; Short Vowels: i, o; Short Vowels: e, u* (Modules 3–5). Monitor each group's progress.

Lesson 72
Reviewing Short Vowels

INFORMAL ASSESSMENT OBJECTIVES

Can children

✔ identify picture names and words that contain short vowel sounds?

✔ distinguish among short vowel sounds?

✔ read words that contain short vowel sounds?

1 INTRODUCE

Materials:
Unit 2 Checkup worksheet, Student Edition, page 149; sticky notes

Do a warm up before completing the worksheet on page 149.

➤ Hand out a self-stick note on which you have written a vowel.

➤ Tell children to stick their notes on classroom objects whose names contain their short vowel sounds. Verify word choices.

➤ Review the names of picture clues. Explain unfamiliar objects.

➤ Pair children who need support with those who understand the concept. Have them work together to complete page 149. Review answers aloud and correct misconceptions orally.

2 PRACTICE

Materials:
Unit 2 Checkup worksheet, Student Edition, page 150; Phonics Picture Cards (numbers 47, 49, 59, 71)

Practice distinguishing among short vowel sounds by having ESL learners choose the correct form of a word.

➤ Display Picture Card 49 (cat); print *cat* and *cot* on the board. Ask a volunteer to select the correct word. Continue with Cards 59 (pig, peg), 71 (dig, dug, dog), and 47 (bug, bag, big).

➤ Look at the pictures together. Be sure that ESL learners know the vocabulary they will need to understand the sentences.

➤ Read directions for the activity on page 150. Work with children to complete item 1. Children should do the activity individually.

➤ Review answers with the entire group.

Book Corner

MORE PHONICS PRACTICE

Set aside class time to read trade books with ESL learners. Preview these books and do a first reading to children.

WHEN WE ARE BIG by Marilyn Minkoff. Ready Readers, Stage 2 (Modern Curriculum Press, 1996)

THE APPLE FARM by Claire Daniel. Ready Readers, Stage 2 (Modern Curriculum Press, 1996)

NIGHT AND DAY by Marilyn Minkoff. Ready Readers, Stage 2 (Modern Curriculum Press, 1996)

Assessment Strategy Overview

Throughout Unit 3 you have opportunities to assess ESL learners' ability to read and write words with long vowel sounds. Some of your ESL learners may require additional assessment strategies to meet their special language needs. Vowel sounds may be especially problematic for ESL learners. Note pronunciation difficulties but assess based on children's ability to distinguish vowel sounds when pronounced by a native speaker.

FORMAL ASSESSMENT

Before you start Unit 3, complete the Unit 3 Pretest, found on pages 151e–151f of *MCP Phonics Teacher Resource Guide*. Children's scores will help you assess their knowledge base before beginning the unit and alert you to areas for further support. Complete the Student Progress Checklist on page 151i. Based on their responses to the Unit 3 Pretest, note with which long vowel sounds children are struggling. Monitor performance.

◆ Some children may understand a concept but have difficulty reading the written directions. Read the directions aloud to the group and model how the Pretest is to be completed.

◆ Before beginning the Pretest, preview the visuals on pages 151e–151f so children are familiar with the picture names. Then they can focus on matching the vowel sounds in the answer choices to the picture clues.

INFORMAL ASSESSMENT

Review pages, Unit Checkups, and Take-Home Books are effective tools to evaluate children's progress. Following are other suggestions for informal ways to assess children's understanding of the concepts.

◆ Many of the visuals may be unfamiliar to your ESL learners. Engage in creative story-telling, tall tales, and "imagine if" opportunities for ESL learners to use language to talk about the items they are asked to recognize visually.

◆ Bring to class realistic props. Say and write each word as you identify it. Have children identify the letter that stands for each long vowel sound.

PORTFOLIO ASSESSMENT

Portfolio

Portfolio Assessment opportunities are identified by the logo shown here. In addition to collecting the pages mentioned on page 151c, gather other examples of children's work for comparison and evaluation at critical periods in the unit, as indicated below.

◆ **Initial practice** Encourage ESL learners to write lists, riddles, and sentences and add to portfolios. Evaluate entries on a regular basis to identify areas of strength and weakness. Early efforts can include skills such as handwriting, prewriting, and emergent writing skills, and beginning word activities.

◆ **Midunit classwork** Have children use rhymes, riddles, jingles, and songs to convey meaningful information as they practice sounding out and writing words containing long vowels.

◆ **Final products or projects** Review progress in completing the Curriculum Connections Portfolio activities. Compare later entries with earlier work. Use Student Progress Checklist on page 151i to assess areas of difficulty.

STUDENT PROGRESS CHECKLIST

Photocopy and attach the checklist on page 151i of *MCP Phonics Teacher Resource Guide* to each child's portfolio. Evaluate growth and areas of weakness from your assessment tools. Then use the strategies and activities suggested in this Guide to build a strong phonics foundation for your ESL learners.

Administering and Evaluating the
Pretest and Posttest

➤ Read the information on page 151d of *MCP Phonics Teacher Resource Guide*. Answers for the Pretest and the Posttest are provided on page 151d.

➤ Record test results on the Student Progress Checklist on page 151i after children complete the Pretest.

➤ Record results again on the same form after children take the Posttest.

➤ Compare the results of the two tests. Use the Performance Assessment Profile at the bottom of page 151d to help you draw conclusions about children's performance. Opportunities to reteach each specific skill in the unit are identified by page number.

TEST OBJECTIVES

The objectives of both the Unit 3 Pretest and Posttest in *MCP Phonics Teacher Resource Guide* are to read and to write words with long vowel sounds. ESL learners may find that some sounds in their native languages (especially Vietnamese, Khmer, Hmong, and Spanish) are different than certain long vowel sounds in English. Have children practice saying the picture clues aloud; reinforce with frequent reading and spelling opportunities throughout the unit.

UNIT 3 PRETEST, pages 151e–151f

Page 151e of *MCP Phonics Teacher Resource Guide* focuses on identifying the long vowel sound in the names of picture clues and darkening the bubble of words that have the same vowel sound. Support ESL learners by modeling or demonstrating any of the following suggestions prior to beginning the Pretest.

◆ **Practice test-taking skills.** Some ESL learners may not recognize the picture clues on page 151e and therefore may not be able to pronounce the word names on their own. Ask them to listen to a picture name as you say it, then listen as you say aloud the word that contains the same vowel sound. Slowly and clearly pronounce the four words at right, always pointing to the correct picture clue.

◆ **Adjust pacing.** Some ESL learners may feel intimidated by children who appear to complete the tests more quickly or more easily than they do. Conduct the Pretest one-on-one with children who need special pacing and provide frequent encouragement and support for their efforts. Administer the test orally if children are unable to read the print.

◆ **Provide models.** Read the direction lines aloud. Demonstrate how to mark the correct response. On the chalkboard, using an overhead projector, or on a sheet of paper at a child's desk, provide one or more opportunities to practice testing-taking procedures. Model for children how to fill in the bubbles on page 151e. Complete several items together as you monitor ESL learners' work.

- **Test orally.** Some ESL learners may not be ready to take the test on their own and complete all the tasks asked of them. For these children, try working one-on-one as you name aloud the picture clues and the word choices that may contain the same vowel sounds.

Page 151f focuses on matching the picture name to the word that represents it. You may wish to incorporate these strategies.

- **Preview answer choices.** Use word lists, charts, and word wheels to provide pretest practice of the long and short vowel variances. This will familiarize children with the words, allowing them to select the best picture-print match.

- **Work in groups.** The Pretest on page 151f requires children to independently discriminate long from short vowel sounds, then match an answer choice to the visual above. If the tasks are too overwhelming, work in small groups or one-on-one and complete the test in two or three sittings.

- **Simplify tasks.** If this activity is too complex for some children, break it down into separate tasks. If children cannot identify the picture clues, name them aloud. Then read aloud with children the answer choices. Provide prompts and pronunciation support as determined by children's ability levels.

- **Work one-on-one.** Children who are unable to read print independently in English can complete the activity orally with you, during class or at a separate time. At a later time, work on developing print fluency.

UNIT 3 POSTTEST, pages 151g–151h

The Unit 3 Posttest of *MCP Phonics Teacher Resource Guide* requires children to discriminate between long and short vowel sounds and read words containing each. Check scores on the Pretest on page 151f. Identify areas of difficulty and adapt test-taking strategies as needed. Use these suggestions as ESL learners complete pages 151g–151h.

- **Confirm that children understand directions.** Read aloud the directions for each page and ensure that children know how to proceed. Model what they are expected to do, working one-on-one with ESL learners who need that level of support.

- **Emphasize important directions.** Help children read the directions silently as you read them aloud. Confirm that children understand that they are to select either *short vowel* or *long vowel*, depending on the name of each picture. They are not to match the picture clue to one of the answer choices.

- **Eliminate overwhelming tasks.** Some children may be unable to read well enough in English to complete page 151h alone. Read the incomplete sentence (and answer choices, if necessary) aloud. Or, conduct the test orally, allowing ESL learners to give verbal responses.

- **Create context.** Some children may be distracted by the "text heaviness" of page 151h. Point out that the sentences tell a story. Summarize the plot so children can anticipate the action. Then read aloud each sentence. Read the answer choices aloud to children and guide them to select the best choice.

Spelling Connections

Pages 151j–151k of *MCP Phonics Teacher Resource Guide* provide a collection of activities and suggestions to actively incorporate spelling into your phonics program. It is recommended that ESL learners reach the intermediate fluency level of English proficiency before focusing on spelling.

* **Anticipate spelling problems.** Anticipated areas of difficulty for children who speak Spanish, Korean, Hmong, Khmer, Russian, Cantonese, or Vietnamese are noted by a star in the Informal Assessment Objectives box at the beginning of each lesson. You may wish to refer to these notes as you progress through specific lessons, especially as you make the link between oral and written language. These notes include letters, sounds, and positions of letters in words that may not exist, may be spelled differently, or may sound different in the native languages of your ESL learners.

* **Create personalized picture dictionaries or spelling cards.** Allow ESL learners to identify which words are new to them. Have them draw or cut-and-paste a picture of each word on individual pages (or cards) and print the word name beneath each picture. Have children use an alphabet chart to put the words in order.

* **Provide frequent mini-lessons.** Repeated misspellings often indicate children do not understand how to spell words correctly. Provide ESL learners with customized mini-lessons in which they can be taught phonics skills. First provide examples of words. Then explain a rule that is a source of misspellings. Then, provide written, oral, and physical (gestures, pantomime) reinforcement and examples. Supplement with practice in the form of short drills, writing charts, and opportunities to write independently.

* **Link speaking to spelling.** To ensure building a link between oral sounds and the written forms of words, speak in simple, full sentences and at a natural rate of speech. Provide frequent opportunities for ESL learners to connect visuals, sounds, and printed (spelled) words by posting picture clues with the spelled words beneath them throughout your classroom. Use the picture clues to introduce, model, and prompt meaning. Then, if your ESL learners are at the intermediate level of proficiency, you may wish to cover up the printed words to assess spelling mastery of words in the Unit Word List.

* **Practice taking dictation.** Dictation of words or sentences and spelling tests may be unfamiliar classroom procedures for ESL learners. Practice test-taking skills related to spelling before you administer the Pretest for each long vowel. Once ESL learners are confident with the process and can focus on the task, continue with steps 1–3 of the Introduction on page 151j.

✳ **Make spelling fun.** Use fun writing mediums such as shaving cream, paints, clay, twine and sandpaper, and sand to practice spelling new or unfamiliar words. Children will have fun with the materials and enjoy writing the words you ask them to spell. Correct spelling before children "erase" their responses.

✳ **Incorporate games and flashcards into spelling practice.** Have ESL learners copy the words from the word list onto individual flashcards. Distribute words by specific long vowel list to small groups of children. Have children take turns playing "teacher" and quizzing the other group members orally on the words in their set. After all children have had a chance to spell each word in a set, exchange with another group.

✳ **Attach meaning to words.** Allow children to acquire meaning before they focus on spelling the word. As a group, introduce the long vowels *a, i, u, o,* and *e* separately, as they are grouped in the lessons. You may wish to focus on one vowel per day to minimize confusion for some ESL learners.

✳ **Incorporate games and flashcards into spelling practice.** Have ESL learners copy the words from the word list onto individual flashcards. Distribute words in specific letter patterns to small groups of children. Have children take turns playing "teacher" and quizzing the other group members orally on the words in their set. After all children have had a chance to spell each word in a set, exchange sets with another group.

✳ **Incorporate journal writing in your class.** Encourage ESL learners to free-write in English and to use spelling words as a prompt for free expression. Have children review their journal writing with you one-on-one and decorate their pages with artwork, photos, pictures, or realia.

Blackline Master 22 (page 151k) requires that children have sufficient command of English and contextual background to sound out and spell the 30 words on the Unit Word List. For ESL learners, introduce the words and their meanings, three or four at a time, through visuals or realia. Provide ample practice overtime and contextual background when introducing the words.

Unit 3

Phonics Games, Activities, and Technology

Pages 151l–151n of *MCP Phonics Teacher Resource Guide* provide a collection of ideas and opportunities to actively engage children as they develop or reinforce phonics skills. Many of the activities provided on these pages can be implemented with little or no modification for children whose native languages are not English. However, be alert to picture clues that are unfamiliar in contexts or in their names. Multistep directions may also be difficult for some ESL learners to understand or follow. You may need to take a longer time and make sure children understand one step before moving onto the next step.

To ensure comprehension of activity directions, speak in simple, complete sentences and at a natural, not exaggerated, pace. Incorporating visuals and props, audiotapes, and CDs provides additional contexts and clues for new learners of English. For activities that require a written response, determine whether children have sufficient command of written print to complete the activities. Be aware that some children may write in cursive letters.

● **That's My Word** (page 151l) and **Word Clues** (page 151n) require that children be familiar with a wide variety of English words and their rhyming patterns. Simplify this activity by having children select words from the Unit 3 Word List, found on pages 151j–151k, or those of previous units and match by long or short vowel sounds.

▲ **"Put the Sounds Together" Song** (page 151l) provides opportunities for ESL learners to practice saying long vowel words. Model the activity by writing the letters *f, e, e, t* on the board. Sing the words as you point to the letters and the sounds they make. Repeat for other long vowel words on the Unit 3 Word List.

◆ **Word Flip Books** (page 151l) can help ESL learners practice the pronunciation of new words. Use the phonograms you assemble for the Flip Books as a resource for children's **Long Vowel Books** (page 151l). For ESL learners who are ready for a reading challenge, suggest the **Silly-Sentence Game** (page 151m), which is patterned after the flip-book concept.

■ **Interesting Words** (page 151l) can be simplified for ESL learners by limiting the scope of their "long vowel sound" word search to the Take-Home Book activity pages in the Student Edition or to the Book Corner selections suggested in each lesson. Have groups of ESL learners reading the same selection work together to create their charts.

- **Word Relays** (page 151m) requires that children have oral fluency in English in order to participate successfully. Assist ESL learners by working with them to create a list, or by providing for them a working list of words. Assign children to work in teams; ask them to offer one response per team, on your signal. This allows all children to participate and benefit from the interaction, instead of focusing on the speed of the response.

- ▲ **Word Beads** (page 151m) may be difficult for ESL learners who cannot write long vowel words from memory. Permit them to select one word from each column of the Unit 3 Word List to copy onto their pasta. Reading one another's necklaces will reinforce target spelling words.

- ◆ **Go and Stop** (page 151m) and **Feed the Dog a Bone** (page 151n) can be more supportive to ESL learners by having the class respond whether the card has a long or short vowel word on it. Children respond on the group's cue instead of independent production.

- ■ **Sound-Alikes** and **Zap Words** (page 151n) work best by introducing the word pairs on several occasions before conducting the activity.

Technology

Use children's interest in technology to their advantage in learning English. If possible, allow ESL learners to work in small groups on the appropriate *AstroWord* CD-ROM Module before or after class or during center time. Preview skill levels and supervise the groups directly to eliminate frustration and to guide phonics development. You may wish to add your observations to the Student Progress Checklist, found on page 151i, *MCP Phonics Teacher Resource Guide*, as well as use the software suggested on page 151n to provide additional phonics practice for ESL learners.

Lessons 73–78
Long *a*

INFORMAL ASSESSMENT OBJECTIVES

Can children

✔ identify pictures whose names contain the sound of long *a*?

✔ distinguish between short *a* and long *a* picture names?

✔ identify words and pictures whose names contain the sounds of short or long *a*?

★ *In many languages each letter or symbol stands for only one sound; thus, help children by pronouncing/spelling long* a *vs. short* a. *Native speakers of Spanish will likely write* e *instead of long* a *in words.*

---

1 INTRODUCE

Materials:
Student Edition, page 153; realia (or pictures): hay, a cake, a tail; Rhyme Poster 29

Introduce the sound of long *a* using familiar objects and the rhyme on page 153 of the Student Edition.

➤ Display one object at a time; have volunteers name each aloud. Repeat, emphasizing the long *a* sound.

➤ Write *hay, cake, tail* on the board. Ask ESL learners which vowel they see in each word and what sound it stands for.

➤ Read aloud the rhyme on page 153. Ask children to listen first for words with the sound of long *a*. Read it again; point to target words on the Rhyme Poster. Have children read/repeat.

➤ Have children find the words that rhyme with *hay, cake,* and *tail* in the Rhyme Poster. List the rhyming words with their pairs on the chalkboard. Have children practice saying rhyming pairs aloud.

2 TEACH

Materials:
Student Edition, pages 153–155, 157; realia: a cap and a cape (optional)

Emphasize sound-to-letter distinctions of long *a* versus short *a*, and work with children on aural discrimination between long *a* and short *a*.

➤ Display realia. Print *cap* and *cape* on the board. Have ESL learners name the objects.

➤ Ask which different vowel sounds they hear in each word; have them supply a rhyming word for each.

➤ Explain to children that a word has a long vowel sound when it has two vowels. The first vowel usually stands for the long sound, and the second vowel is silent.

➤ Use the worksheet activities on pages 153–155 and 157 to check comprehension.

★ *For specific notes on various home languages, see pages xiii–xvii of this Guide.*

3 PRACTICE

Materials:
Student Edition, pages 158, 159, 161, 163

Review the rule for spelling words with long vowels; remind children as they write words to listen for beginning/ending consonant sounds.

➤ Have ESL learners identify the vowel they hear, the second (silent) vowel, and the initial/final consonants in: *tape, pain, wait, safe, bay.*

➤ Practice the lesson strategies with worksheets on pages 158, 159, 161, 163.

4 APPLY

Materials:
Word Beads activity, *MCP Phonics Teacher Resource Guide,* page 151m; string or yarn, large tube pasta, felt-tip markers, buttons (optional)

Have ESL learners make Word Beads, as described on page 151m. Model the process for children.

➤ Hand out five or six pieces of pasta to each child.

➤ Print five or six long *a* phonograms on the board (*-ait, -ane, -ale,* and so on). Have children write one word with each phonogram on a piece of pasta.

➤ String together; separate macaroni with colorful buttons (optional). Review words.

5 ASSESS

Materials:
Student Edition, pages 160, 162, 164

Complete these activities with ESL learners to verify understanding and assess children's mastery of lesson content. Read directions; explain the task. Have children complete page 160 in pairs and pages 162 and 164 individually. Review answers aloud and ask volunteers to write each answer on the board. Offer a one-on-one review of the worksheets with ESL learners who need additional support.

MORE PHONICS PRACTICE

Set aside class time to read trade books with ESL learners. Preview these books and do a first reading to children.

DALE AND THE CAVE by Linda Hartley. Phonics Practice Readers (Modern Curriculum Press, 1986)

WHEN BOB WOKE UP LATE by Robin Bloksberg. Ready Readers, Stage 2 (Modern Curriculum Press, 1996)

AstroWord
Invite children to complete some of the intergalactic activities on the CD-ROM *AstroWord Long Vowels: a, i* (Module 7). Ask small groups of English-speaking children and ESL learners to work together as you focus their efforts on continuing practice with the sound of long *a.* Monitor groups for equal participation and progress.

Lesson 79
Long Vowel *a*

INFORMAL ASSESSMENT OBJECTIVES

Can children

✔ write long *a* words to finish sentences about a story?

✔ write a newspaper story about a game?

★ *In most cultures, football is the term used instead of soccer.*

1 INTRODUCE

Materials:
Sports page or sports-related magazine, audiotape or videotape of sports news (optional)

Introduce the theme of the lesson's reading selection by discussing sports that ESL learners are familiar with; soccer and baseball will be the best known.

➤ Have volunteers talk about sports they know well. Bring in the sports section from the newspaper, a magazine that deals with the subject, or a video or audiocassette of a sports program to prompt interest and activate background knowledge.

➤ Talk about newspaper articles that deal with sports. What information is generally given? (Names of teams, who won, schedule of games, and so on).

➤ Read a simple sports article aloud to ESL learners (four or five sentences). Ask basic information questions: Who won? What was the sport? Where was the game played? and so on.

2 TEACH

Materials:
Chalkboard and chalk

Teach children guidelines for spelling words with long *a* while reviewing words from the reading text.

➤ Print the words *bat, ball, home plate* on the board. Have a volunteer read each aloud. Ask what sport the words pertain to. Offer *base* and *safe* as further clues.

➤ Review the rule for long vowels on the Teach section of page 128 of this Guide. Write *base, safe, sail, wait, day* on the board. Instruct children to identify the long vowel sounds they hear and the silent second vowels. Explain to ESL learners that the letter *y* also stands for a vowel sound in words like *day*.

★ *For specific notes on various home languages, see pages xiii–xvii of this Guide.*

3 PRACTICE

Materials:
Student Edition, page 165

Assess children's recognition of long *a* words as you read "Hooray for Ray!" with ESL learners.

➤ As you and ESL learners read the story, have them list, name, or point to words with long *a*.

➤ Ask them to identify by pointing to the silent vowel as well as the beginning/ending consonant sounds in each word. Then have them complete comprehension items 1–3.

➤ Discuss the Think! question aloud in small groups.

4 APPLY

Materials:
Long Vowel Books activity, *MCP Phonics Teacher Resource Guide*, page 151l; white paper, crayons, markers

Begin making Long Vowel Books for each ESL learner as described on page 151l.

➤ Hand out art supplies.

➤ Ask children to create a caption that they will illustrate; assist as needed. Write some sample captions on the board like *Kate and Jake bake a cake; Jay and Gail read the mail;* and so on to give visual clues to non-readers.

➤ Collect long *a* pages. File away until all long vowels have been presented.

5 ASSESS

Materials:
Student Edition, page 166

Check ESL learners' progress by having them complete the writing assignment on page 166. To assist ESL learners, brainstorm ideas aloud by asking basic information questions: Who plays what sport? Where and when is it played? and so on. Write their responses on chart paper or the chalkboard. Encourage children to use these responses as reference for their writing. If children are challenged by content, have them write about a sport they know (explain rules, narrate a time they played, and so on).

Book Corner

MORE PHONICS PRACTICE

Set aside class time to read trade books with ESL learners. Preview these books and do a first reading to children.

THE NAME IS THE SAME by Kana Riley. Ready Readers, Stage 2 (Modern Curriculum Press, 1996)

CAT GAMES by Dr. Alvin Granowsky. Phonics Practice Readers (Modern Curriculum Press, 1986)

Technology

AstroWord

Ask groups of children (ESL learners and native speakers of English) to explore the activities included on the CD-ROM *AstroWord Long Vowels: a, i* (Module 7). Encourage them to work together to complete activities that interest them. Offer support, monitor group progress, and ask directed questions about long vowel sounds and vowel recognition.

Lesson 80
Reviewing Long Vowel *a*

INFORMAL ASSESSMENT OBJECTIVE

Can children

✔ read long *a* words in the context of a story?

---

1 INTRODUCE

Materials:

Safe Skating Take-Home Book, Student Edition, pages 167–168; pictures of in-line skates, pads and helmets, skaters, ice skates

Introduce *Safe Skating* Take-Home Book by discussing different types of skating and skating equipment with ESL learners.

➤ Talk about different games and hobbies children enjoy and some of the rules for safe play like wearing helmets for riding bicycles, wearing lifesavers when swimming, and so on.

➤ Display pictures of skates and skating equipment (mail-order catalogues are a good source); have ESL learners identify the objects and talk about skating: Do they skate? When and where? and so on.

➤ Ask children what they think some skating safety tips might be.

2 TEACH

Materials:

Safe Skating Take-Home Book, pages 167–168 of the Student Edition; teacher-prepared worksheet

Talk about the *Safe Skating* Take-Home Book with ESL learners and review words containing the sound of long *a*.

➤ Assist children in making their Take-Home Books.

➤ Tell children to look at the photographs and talk about them.

➤ Prepare a worksheet using incomplete words from the story that contain long and short *a*. Use: *c_n, p_l, p_ds, f_st; r_ce, s_fe, m_ke, pl_y, sk_te*. Ask children to fill in the missing letters; have them look through *Safe Skating* to locate the words. Review aloud.

➤ Review other important story words: *thick, should, alone, people* to help understanding.

➤ Read the book with the class, sentence by sentence in a choral reading.

★ *For specific notes on various home languages, see pages xiii–xvii of this Guide.*

3 PRACTICE

Materials:
Safe Skating Take-Home Book; Letter Cards *Ll, Mm, Pp, Rr, Ss*

Engage children's phonemic awareness and vocabulary recall by having them supply rhyming words and substitute ending sounds.

➤ Have ESL learners read the story with more English-proficient peers. Monitor that they take turns reading a page at a time.

➤ With ESL learners, print *race, skate, make, safe, play* on the board. Display a Letter Card and have them create rhyming words by substituting the new initial consonant: *lace, late, lake*, and so on. Cover word endings and have them create new words ending in *-il* (*rail, mail, sail*), *-te*, and so on.

➤ Read the story a second time. Have volunteers read it aloud.

➤ Discuss *Talk About It* on page 8 of the Take-Home Book.

4 APPLY

Materials:
Paper, crayons, markers, glue, tape, clips or staples

After reading *Safe Skating*, have children work in groups to create a "safe skating" gallery of pictures.

➤ Ask ESL learners to draw and color (or cut and paste) a picture of themselves, family members, and friends skating safely. Have children write about their drawings. Assist with vocabulary and the spelling of new words.

➤ Create a bulletin board or class gallery for the pictures.

5 ASSESS

Materials:
Safe Skating Take-Home Book

Verify ESL learners' comprehension and recall of the story and target vocabulary. Have ESL learners retell the story orally. Ask children to read a random passage aloud. Check for pronunciation and comprehension.

BOOK Corner

MORE PHONICS PRACTICE

Set aside class time to read trade books with ESL learners. Preview these books and do a first reading to children.

JANE AND GAIL'S SHOW by Linda Hartley. Phonics Practice Readers, Series B, Set 2 (Modern Curriculum Press, 1986)

THE BABY WHO GOT ALL THE BLAME by JoAnne Nelson. Discovery Phonics (Modern Curriculum Press, 1992)

KATE AND JAKE by Janis Asad Raabe. Phonics Practice Readers (Modern Curriculum Press, 1986)

Technology

AstroWord

Some ESL learners will benefit from additional practice and linguistic interaction, such as that provided by the CD-ROM *AstroWord Long Vowels: a, i* (Module 7). Encourage groups of children (native speakers of English and ESL learners) to work together on Listen & Write, in which children listen to clues and write the appropriate response. Offer assistance while monitoring progress.

Lessons 81–85
Long *i*

INFORMAL ASSESSMENT OBJECTIVES

Can children

✔ identify pictures whose names contain the sound of long *i*?

✔ distinguish between short *i* and long *i* picture names?

✔ identify initial and final consonants in words that contain the sounds of short or long *i*?

✔ identify words and pictures whose names contain the sounds of short or long *i*?

★ *Native speakers of Spanish may spell this vowel sound as* ai. *Practice with pairs of words like* rain, ride; tail, tire; fair, fire; *and so on.*

---

1 INTRODUCE

Materials:
Student Edition, page 169; realia (or pictures) of a kite, a tie, a dime, a knife, numerals 5 and 9; Rhyme Poster 30 (optional)

Present long *i* by first reviewing the rhyme and target words, then reinforcing with an oral review of visuals.

➤ Say/model the sound of long *i* as in *kite, dime, bike,* and so on.

➤ Read the rhyme aloud, tracking the sentences on the Rhyme Poster. Instruct ESL learners to listen and identify words with the sound of long *i*. Read it again; have children chart or read along.

➤ Display each object; ask a volunteer to name it aloud. Print each word on the board.

➤ Ask each child to say a word they know with long *i*. Cue for rhyming words: *tie, pie; dime, time,* and so on.

➤ Explain that in some words the long *i* is spelled with the two vowels together as in *pie*, and in other words there's a consonant between the vowels, as in *dime*.

2 TEACH

Materials:
Student Edition, pages 169, 170, 173

Teach the sound of long *i*, emphasizing aural discrimination and the sound-to-letter contrast of long *i* versus short *i*.

➤ Create pairs of words with long *i* and short *i*; have children say whether the vowel sounds are "same" or "different": *kite, time; pin, right;* and so on.

➤ With children who need practice with long *i* versus short *a*, repeat the activity.

➤ Verify understanding of long *i* by having children complete the activities on pages 169, 170, 173 as you monitor the group's work.

134

★ *For specific notes on various home languages, see pages xiii–xvii of this Guide.*

3 PRACTICE

Materials:
Student Edition, pages 171, 172, 174, 176, 178

Ask ESL learners to review the rule for spelling words with long vowels and to listen for and identify beginning/ending consonant sounds.

➤ Work with ESL learners to identify the vowel they hear (the first vowel), the silent vowel (the second vowel), and the initial/final consonants in *kite, dive, nine, mile*. Have them use several words in context, in oral sentences.

➤ Practice the lesson strategies with pages 171, 174, 176, 178.

➤ Adapt the crossword puzzle on page 172 by having ESL learners simply name the pictures for items 1–8, write each, then write one to three sentences using target vocabulary.

4 APPLY

Materials:
Word Clues activity, *MCP Phonics Teacher Resource Guide,* page 151n; index cards, marker

Adapt the Word Clues activity to offer additional practice with long *i*.

➤ Print several words with long *i* (such as *Mike, file, pine*) on separate index cards.

➤ Prepare a set of beginning sound cards by printing a consonant on the far right edge of each card.

➤ Ask word clue questions like the ones on the Word Clues activity. If ESL learners need support, use the consonant card to cover the first letter of each long *i* word. Repeat.

5 ASSESS

Materials:
Student Edition, pages 175, 177

Read the directions for each activity aloud before you assign them. Have each child work individually to complete the worksheets. Begin with page 175, which offers visual cues to support children's efforts. Review answers aloud and ask volunteers to write each answer on the board. Ask each child to respond orally to the Think! questions.

Book Corner

MORE PHONICS PRACTICE

Set aside class time to read trade books with ESL learners. Preview these books and do a first reading to children.

DIVE IN! by Lilly Ernesto. Ready Readers, Stage 2 (Modern Curriculum Press, 1996)

IF I COULD by Judy Nayer. Discovery Phonics (Modern Curriculum Press, 1986)

Technology

AstroWord
Some children will benefit from additional practice and feedback by using the CD-ROMs *AstroWord Long Vowels: a, i* (Module 7) and *Long Vowels: i, o* (Module 8). Encourage native speakers of English and ESL learners to work on the Easy level of *Make-a-Word,* where children help alien creatures create words based on a picture clue. Monitor each group's progress.

Lesson 86
Long Vowels

INFORMAL ASSESSMENT OBJECTIVES

Can children

✔ write long *i* words to finish sentences about a story?

✔ write a description of a kite?

★ *In many languages like Spanish and Khmer, each letter or symbol stands for one sound; thus, children may need support with pronouncing and spelling long versus short vowel sounds.*

1 INTRODUCE

Materials:
Kites or pictures of kites (optional)

Introduce the theme of the reading selection by talking about kites and when kites are flown in different cultures. Use pictures of kites to explain what they are to children who are not familar with them.

➤ Discuss different types of kites and kite flying with ESL learners. Have they ever flown kites?

➤ Draw a kite on the board and label *kite, tail, line*. Have children read labels aloud and name the long vowel sounds they hear.

2 TEACH

Materials:
Student Edition, page 179; chalkboard and chalk

Discuss the rules for spelling words with long *a* and long *i* while reviewing words from the reading on page 179 of the Student Edition.

➤ Print the words *kite, like, line* on the board. Have a volunteer read each aloud. Ask which long vowel sound children hear in each and which silent vowel is present.

➤ Teach that *-igh* also stands for the sound of long *i*. Print *high* and *tight* as examples; ask ESL learners to supply rhyming words for *tight* (*night, light, fight*).

➤ Review additional words: *everywhere, special* for children who need more vocabulary support.

➤ If ESL learners note the long *i* sound of *y* in *fly*, explain that the letter *y* also has the vowel sound in words like *fly*; *y* as a vowel is actively taught in Lessons 125–126. (See pages 259–262 of the Student Edition and of the *MCP Phonics Teacher Resource Guide*.)

★ *For specific notes on various home languages, see pages xiii–xvii of this Guide.*

3 PRACTICE

Materials:
Student Edition,
page 179

The reading offers ESL learners the opportunity to read words with long vowels *a* and *i* in context.

➤ As ESL learners read the story, have them find and identify words with long *i* and long *a*.

➤ Ask them to point to the silent vowel as well as the beginning/ending consonant sounds in each word. Then have them complete comprehension items 1–3.

➤ Talk about the Think! question in small groups.

4 APPLY

Materials:
Long Vowel Books
activity, *MCP Phonics
Teacher Resource
Guide,* page 151l;
white paper,
crayons, markers

Make a long *i* page of the Long Vowel Books activity for ESL learners to create a book.

➤ Distribute art supplies.

➤ Tell children to create a sentence that they will illustrate; assist as needed. Suggestions: *Mike likes to ride his bike; I fly my kite high.*

➤ Collect long *i* pages. Then together with children, make a group book to put in the class reading center.

5 ASSESS

Materials:
Student Edition,
page 180

Assess ESL learners' ability to use long *a* and long *i* words in context by having them write a description of a kite. Brainstorm ideas together before they write. Write responses on chart paper. Allow children to use your writing as a reference for their own. If children are challenged by content, ask leading questions: What color is the kite? What shape? and so on. Have ESL learners read their descriptions aloud.

MORE PHONICS PRACTICE

Set aside class time to read trade books with ESL learners. Preview these books and to a first reading to children.

THE BABY WHO GOT ALL THE BLAME by JoAnne Nelson. Discovery Phonics (Modern Curriculum Press, 1992)

DIVE IN! by Lilly Ernesto. Ready Readers, Stage 2 (Modern Curriculum Press, 1996)

AstroWord
Some ESL learners will benefit from additional interaction and audiovisual feedback, such as that provided by the CD-ROM *AstroWord Long Vowels: a, i* (Module 7). Encourage native speakers of English and ESL learners to work together to complete activities that interest them using the sounds of long vowels *i* and *a*. Monitor each group's progress.

Lesson 87
Reviewing Long Vowels *a, i*

INFORMAL ASSESSMENT OBJECTIVE

Can children

✔ read long *a* and long *i* words in the context of a story?

★ *In many languages like Spanish and Khmer, each letter or symbol stands for one sound; thus, children may need support with pronouncing and spelling long versus short vowel sounds.*

---

1 INTRODUCE

Materials:
Photos of fishing equipment (or realia): pole, line, flies, and so on.

Talk about the theme of fishing with ESL learners to activate background knowledge and experience before reading *Ty's Line*.

➤ Display realia or photos and invite children to comment on and talk about fishing: Have they ever gone fishing? When?

➤ Encourage children who have fished to explain how they do it. Assist with vocabulary if necessary.

➤ Explain to children from other cultures that fishing can be someone's job but that it is also a popular hobby or pastime in the United States.

➤ Ask critical-thinking questions: Why do people fish? Is fishing fun or boring? Why?

2 TEACH

Materials:
Ty's Line Take-Home Book; Student Edition, pages 181–182

Talk about spelling rules for words with long vowels (see Teach section of page 128 of this Guide) while preparing children to read *Ty's Line*.

➤ Assist children in making their Take-Home Books.

➤ Brainstorm a list of words with long *a* and *i* related to fishing: *line, bait, wait, lake*. Ask ESL learners to explain why each word has a long vowel.

➤ Teach/review other important story words: *getting, pulls, catch, throws, water, flowers*.

➤ Ask children to look at the story pictures and tell what they think will happen in the story.

★ *For specific notes on various home languages, see pages xiii–xvii of this Guide.*

3 PRACTICE

Materials:
Ty's Line Take-Home Book, chart paper and pencil

Practice reading and writing words with long *a* and long *i* in context, using the *Ty's Line* Take-Home Book.

➤ Read the story one page at a time. Have each child find and point out words containing target sounds after reading a passage.

➤ Discuss the story; then read the story a second time.

➤ Check comprehension with content-related questions.

➤ Print words from the story (*line, waits, late, and so on*) on the board. Create a sentence with each word for oral practice. Then have children choose three or four words and write a sentence with each one.

4 APPLY

Materials:
Orange and yellow construction paper, scissors, crayons, markers

Have children make a "rhyming school of fish" based on story words from *Ty's Line*.

➤ Draw and cut out several fish, using orange paper. Print a long *i* or long *a* phonogram on each fish (*-ine, -ake, and so on*)

➤ Assist children with cutting out yellow fish (three or four per child). Have them find words in the story that contain each phonogram and print them on the fish (*line, takes*). Then ask them to print one or two more words that rhyme on other fish (*fine, fakes*).

➤ Display "rhyming fish" together on bulletin boards or separate poster boards.

5 ASSESS

Materials:
Ty's Line Take-Home Book

Verify ESL learners' understanding and recall of the story vocabulary. Ask children to read passages aloud. Check for pronunciation and comprehension. Have ESL learners retell the story orally. Give a brief spelling test (five or six words), using long *a, i* words from the story and/or Unit 3 Word List (*MCP Phonics Teacher Resource Guide*, page 151k).

Book Corner

MORE PHONICS PRACTICE

Set aside class time to read trade books with ESL learners. Preview these books and do a first reading to children.

ALL MINE by Linda Hartley. Phonics Practice Readers (Modern Curriculum Press, 1986)

THE NAME IS THE SAME by Kana Riley. Ready Readers, Stage 2 (Modern Curriculum Press, 1996)

Technology

AstroWord

Some ESL learners will benefit from additional practice and linguistic interaction such as that provided by the CD-ROM *AstroWord Long Vowels: a, i* (Module 7). Encourage groups of native speakers of English and ESL learners to work together on *Listen & Write*, in which children listen to clues and write the appropriate response. Offer assistance while monitoring progress.

Lessons 88–93
Long *u*

INFORMAL ASSESSMENT OBJECTIVES

Can children

✔ identify and distinguish among words and pictures whose names contain the sounds of short or long *u*?

✔ identify rhyming words that contain the sounds of short and long *u*?

✔ identify and distinguish between the sounds of long *u*, *a*, and *i* and the sound of short *u* in words and pictures?

✔ identify words and pictures whose names contain the sounds of short or long vowels?

★ *Children who speak Cantonese or Vietnamese may pronounce a "round," French-sounding* u; *offer additional oral practice. Spanish speakers may have trouble with the /yu/ sound of long* u *as in* cube *and* use *(pronouncing* coob, ooze).

1 INTRODUCE

Materials:
Student Edition, page 183; realia (or pictures): glue, a tube, a cube, a ruler; Rhyme Poster 31 (optional)

Emphasize target words in the rhyme and use appropriate realia to introduce to ESL learners the sound of long *u*.

➤ Print on the board and say aloud *Lu used the glue*; point out the sound of long *u*. Read the rhyme; ask ESL learners to hold up a ruler each time they hear a word with long *u*. Read it again; have children read and repeat.

➤ Display one object at a time; have volunteers name each aloud. Repeat, emphasizing the sound of long *u*.

➤ Write each word on the board. Ask ESL learners to circle the target vowel in each word.

2 TEACH

Materials:
Student Edition, pages 183–185

Teach long *u*/short *u* discrimination as well as the two long *u* sounds.

➤ Print *nut, cup, suit, cube*. Point out the different vowel sounds that *u* stands for.

➤ Talk about the "silent vowel" rule; ask children to indicate which words contain a silent vowel.

➤ Discuss the different long *u* sounds in *suit* and *cube*. Ask for/offer additional examples. (Words with initial *c, f, h, m, u* have the /yu/ sound.)

➤ Practice these strategies on pages 183–185 of the Student Edition.

140

★ *For specific notes on various home languages, see pages xiii–xvii of this Guide.*

3 PRACTICE

Materials:
Blue paper; objects whose names model long and short *u*; Letter Cards *Aa, Ii, Uu*; Student Edition, pages 186–191

Practice long *u* versus short *u* and long vowel (*a, i, u*) discrimination.

▶ Display about eight objects. Have children place those whose names contain long *u* on the blue paper.

▶ Say a series of words with long vowels. Tell children to point to the correct Letter Card. Words are *mail, mule, mile, cube, cave, kite, blue, safe,* and *suit.*

▶ Most activity pages can be completed by ESL learners with support and direction. Adapt page 186 (the coded words) by modeling how to use the codes, providing a word list as reference. Then have children select the best word to finish each sentence.

4 APPLY

Materials:
Sound-Alikes activity, *MCP Phonics Teacher Resource Guide,* page 151n; index cards, marker

Encourage ESL learners to play the Sound-Alikes game.

▶ Prepare pairs of cards with rhyming long and short *u* words (*use, fuse; nut, cut; fruit, suit;* and so on).

▶ Place cards face down in a grid. Have children match pairs of rhymes by turning two cards at a time (Concentration-style).

▶ When finished, mix the cards and repeat.

5 ASSESS

Materials:
Student Edition, pages 192–194

Read the directions; have ESL learners restate in their own words for the group. Have each child work individually. Allow ESL learners to skip the word-search puzzle on page 194 if it poses a problem; instead, have them complete items 1–6 only. Review answers aloud and have volunteers write each response on the board for verification.

MORE PHONICS PRACTICE

Set aside class time to read trade books with ESL learners. Preview these books and do a first reading to children.

TRUE OR FALSE? by Susan McCloskey. Ready Readers, Stage 2 (Modern Curriculum Press, 1996)

WHO SAID BOO? by Cass Hollander. Discovery Phonics (Modern Curriculum Press, 1992)

AstroWord

Some ESL learners will benefit from additional practice and linguistic interaction, such as that provided by the CD-ROM *AstroWord Long Vowels: e, u* (Module 9). Encourage native speakers of English and ESL learners to work together to complete the Easy level of *Word Sort,* in which children help alien creatures sort picture clues according to vowel sound. Offer assistance while monitoring progress.

Lesson 94
Reviewing Long Vowels *a, i, u*

INFORMAL ASSESSMENT OBJECTIVES

Can children

✔ write long *u* words to finish sentences about a story?

✔ write a story about playing?

★ *In many foreign languages, each letter or symbol stands for one sound; thus, children may need support with pronouncing and spelling long versus short vowel sounds.*

1 INTRODUCE

Materials:
Chalkboard, chalk; pictures of bears and cubs (optional); video clip of bears from National Geographic videos (optional)

Talk about bears and bear cubs with ESL learners in anticipation of the reading on page 195.

➤ Have volunteers tell what they know about bears. Bring pictures to class to stimulate children's imagination and invite input.

➤ Talk about what bears eat: insects, honey, fish, fruit. Print *fruit* and *blueberries* on the chalkboard. Point out the sound of long *u*.

➤ Have ESL learners explain how to play hide-and-seek to make sure they understand the game.

2 TEACH

Materials:
Student Edition, page 195

Review the rule for spelling words with long vowels and have children write words from the story on Student Edition page 195.

➤ Review the rule for long vowels that appear on the Teach section of page 128 of this Guide. Write *blue, suit, smile, tail* on the board. Tell children to identify the long vowel sounds they hear and name the silent second vowel in each word.

➤ Read the story "The Blue Suit" aloud chorally with ESL learners.

➤ Ask ESL learners to read the story and make a list of words that contain long vowel sounds. Review each child's list one-on-one; reinforce spelling rules of English and focus on individual needs.

★ *For specific notes on various home languages, see pages xiii–xvii of this Guide.*

3 PRACTICE

Materials:
Student Edition, page 195; blue crayon or marker

Practice vowel sound recognition and have children identify long and short vowels they know as they read "The Blue Suit."

➤ During a second oral reading, have children point out words with long *a, i, u.*

➤ Ask them to underline words with the sound of long *u* in blue; have them also identify the silent vowels and initial and final consonant sounds in various words.

➤ Complete comprehension items 1–3. Discuss the Think! question in small groups.

4 APPLY

Materials:
Long Vowel Books activity, *MCP Phonics Teacher Resource Guide,* page 151l; white paper, crayons, markers

Continue making Long Vowel Books as described on page 151l. Prepare a page for the long sound of *u.*

➤ Hand out art supplies.

➤ Ask children to create oral sentences. Then help them write the sentences and illustrate them; assist as needed. Suggestions include *Lu likes fruit juice* and *Luke and June wear blue suits.*

➤ Collect the long *u* pages. File until you assemble books.

5 ASSESS

Materials:
Student Edition, page 196

Ask ESL learners to complete the writing assignment on page 196. First, brainstorm ideas asking content questions. Write childrens' ideas on chart paper. Encourage them to refer to the chart. If children are challenged by the suggested topic, have them write about a "huge blue monster." Offer assistance with vocabulary; encourage learners to use language they know. Have volunteers read their sentences aloud.

Book Corner

MORE PHONICS PRACTICE

Set aside class time to read trade books with ESL learners. Preview these books and do a first reading to children.

JULES THE MULE by Cindy and Zach Clements. Phonics Practice Readers (Modern Curriculum Press, 1986)

SUE AND JUNE by Janis Asad Raabe. Phonics Practice Readers (Modern Curriculum Press, 1986)

Technology

AstroWord
Ask groups of children (ESL learners and native speakers of English) to explore the activities on the CD-ROMs *AstroWord Long Vowels: e, u* and *Long Vowels: a, i* (Modules 7, 9). Encourage them to complete activities that interest them. Assign specific tasks to children who need additional practice. Monitor each group for equal participation and progress.

Lesson 95
Reviewing Long Vowels *a, i, u*

INFORMAL ASSESSMENT OBJECTIVE

Can children

✔ read long *a, i,* and *u* words in the context of a story?

★ *Many languages other than English do not have long and short vowel sounds. Pay particular attention to areas of difficulty for individual ESL learners; provide opportunities for correction and practice using the words from the word list on page 151j–151k of the MCP Phonics Teacher Resource Guide.*

1 INTRODUCE

Materials:
Student Edition, pages 197–198; flashlight or projector; chart paper; tape; markers

Discuss the story theme with children by making some of the hand shadows shown in the photos.

➤ Talk about light and shadows as you demonstrate with a lamp and your hands.

➤ Have children look at the photos in the *Hand Games* Take-Home Book and name the animals they see. Assist with verbal identification and model pronunciation, as needed.

➤ Tape a large sheet of chart paper to the board. Shine the light on the paper and make one of the shadow figures. Ask ESL learners to trace the shape onto the paper. Assist them with labeling each figure made by the shadows. Have children name figures aloud.

2 TEACH

Materials:
Hand Games Take-Home Book, Student Edition, pages 197–198; Letter Cards

Talk about and review spelling rules for words with long vowel sounds while preparing children to read *Hand Games*.

➤ Assist children in making their Take-Home Books.

➤ Provide a set of Letter Cards. Ask ESL learners to look through the Take-Home Book and, using the Letter Cards, spell out words they find with the sounds of long *a, i,* and *u*. Have them say each word they spell.

➤ As a challenge, ask ESL learners to write the words they hear and raise their hand when they can pronounce the words. Have children challenge each other to a spelling bee. Correct, or have volunteers correct, spelling or pronunciation errors.

➤ Review other less familiar story words: *shadow, pictures, rabbit, swan* and comparatives *bigger, smaller.*

★ *For specific notes on various home languages, see pages xiii–xvii of this Guide.*

3 PRACTICE

Materials:
Hand Games Take-Home Book, teacher-prepared worksheet

Have ESL learners work toward mastery and comprehension of the theme by reading *Hand Games* silently and completing a related task.

➤ You may want to read the book aloud first to model correct pronunciation.

➤ Tell children to read the story silently to themselves.

➤ Remind them that good readers use the photos as clues to what they are reading about.

➤ Prepare a three-or-four item worksheet using incomplete sentences that children complete by filling in a word with long *a*, *i*, or *u*, such as *Shine a ___ on your hands.*

➤ Monitor each child's progress and offer verbal support, as needed.

4 APPLY

Materials:
Go and Stop activity, *MCP Phonics Teacher Resource Guide,* page 151m; chalk; word cards

Conduct the Go and Stop activity with small groups of children to review long and short *a, i, u.*

➤ Prepare a set of word cards modeling long and short *a, i, u.*

➤ Review each target vowel sound with children before play begins.

➤ After the game, have each child select a word card and print on the board a sentence using the word.

5 ASSESS

Materials:
Hand Games Take-Home Book, light source

Have ESL learners read the story aloud in small groups. Check for pronunciation and ask content-related questions. Then have ESL learners retell the story orally. Use a light source and model making shadow figures larger and smaller as you discuss the Talk About It question.

Book Corner

MORE PHONICS PRACTICE

Set aside class time to read trade books with ESL learners. Preview these books and do a first reading to children.

IF I COULD by Judy Nayer. Discovery Phonics (Modern Curriculum Press, 1992)

CAT'S TRIP by Sharon Fear. Ready Readers, Stage 2 (Modern Curriculum Press, 1996)

Technology

AstroWord
Some learners will benefit from additional interaction and audiovisual feedback such as that provided by the CD-ROMs *AstroWord Long Vowels: a, i* (Module 7) and *Long Vowels: e, u* (Module 9). Encourage native speakers of English and ESL learners to work together to complete activities that interest them using the long vowel sounds in review. Monitor each group's progress.

Lessons 96–102
Long o

INFORMAL ASSESSMENT OBJECTIVES

Can children

✔ identify rhyming words and pictures whose names contain the sound of long o?

✔ identify the letters in words that stand for the sound of long o?

✔ identify words that contain the sound of long o to complete sentences?

✔ identify pictures whose names contain the sounds of long a, i, u, and o and distinguish among these long vowel sounds?

★ *Emphasize the difference between pronouncing/spelling long* o *versus short* o; *have children say and write* cot, coat; hop, hope; not, note. *Children who speak Asian languages may confuse and assimilate long* o *with the sound of* aw *in* awful; *practice* low, law; so, saw.

1 INTRODUCE

Materials:
Realia (or pictures): a bone, a bow, a robe, a rope, a soap; objects whose names contain long a, i, u, or short o (such as *glue, box*); self-stick notes

Introduce long o by using familiar objects and having children label them.

➤ Print *Joe has an old coat.* Read aloud. Have children repeat. Ask them to circle words containing the target sound.

➤ Display seven or eight objects on a table. Explain that children will say the name of each. If it has the same vowel sound as *Joe* and *coat*, they will print o on a self-stick note and label the object.

➤ When finished, review object names aloud. Correct mispronunciations and reinforce the sound of long o.

2 TEACH

Materials:
Student Edition, page 199; Rhyme Poster 32 (optional); realia: soap, a bowl, a cone; Phonics Picture Cards (numbers 91, 93, 103, 108–112)

Teach spelling and recognition of long o words while using visual clues and rhyming words.

➤ Read the rhyme on page 199 as a warm up to teaching the sound of long o. Have children listen for and repeat target words.

➤ Hold up an object; have ESL learners say the name. Print *soap, bowl,* and *cone* on the board. Review the rule for spelling words with long vowels, and ask volunteers to underline the two letters that stand for the sound of long o.

➤ Mix the Picture Cards and place face down in a pile. As ESL learners turn over a card, have them say the name of the picture and sort out the long o words.

★ *For specific notes on various home languages, see pages xiii–xvii of this Guide.*

3 PRACTICE

Materials:
Student Edition, pages 199–203, 205–207, 209, 211

Practice target strategies and goals using worksheets and activities from the lesson pages.

➤ Practice pronunciation by having children name picture clues aloud; model pronunciation as needed. Complete pages 199–201, 207.

➤ Review spelling long o words and the sequences *ow, oa, oe*; practice with activities on pages 202, 203, 206, 209, 211.

➤ Say a long *o*/short *o* word and have children supply a rhyming word. Use *coat, top, hole, cone,* and *hot*. Complete page 205.

4 APPLY

Materials:
Word Flip Books activity, *MCP Phonics Teacher Resource Guide*, page 151l; construction paper, markers

Offer additional practice with spelling rules and rhyming words with long o by making Word Flip Books.

➤ Assist children with making a long o phonogram Word Flip Book. Use *-oat, -ole, -one, -ow,* and so on. For less proficient ESL learners, suggest they draw pictures of words made to ensure comprehension.

➤ Review each word aloud. Have ESL learners use each in a sentence in context. Ask content questions that model correct pronunciation, if needed.

➤ Collect the Word Flip Books, redistribute, and repeat the activity.

5 ASSESS

Materials:
Student Edition, pages 204, 208, 210

Check vocabulary comprehension and ESL learners' use of long o words in written context. Ask children to work in pairs as they complete the activity on page 204. Complete pages 208 and 212 together with children, working with small groups or pairs. Assign page 210 as an individual activity; review answers aloud in small groups.

Book Corner

MORE PHONICS PRACTICE

Set aside class time to read trade books with ESL learners. Preview these books and do a first reading to children.

BO THE SHOW OFF by Linda Hartley. Phonics Practice Readers (Modern Curriculum Press, 1986)

THE TOAD AND THE GOAT by Dr. Alvin Granowsky. Phonics Practice Readers (Modern Curriculum Press, 1986)

Technology

AstroWord

Some children will benefit from additional practice and feedback, using the CD-ROM *AstroWord Long Vowels: i, o* (Module 8). Encourage native speakers of English and ESL learners to work on the Easy level of *Make-a-Word*, where children help alien creatures create words based on a picture clue. Monitor each group's progress.

Lesson 103
Long Vowels

INFORMAL ASSESSMENT OBJECTIVES

Can children

✔ write long o words to finish sentences about a story?

✔ write a sign announcing a show?

---

1 INTRODUCE

Materials:
Magician's hat, ads for shows or playbills, video of a magic show or TV program that uses magicians (optional)

Encourage ESL learners to share stories about magic acts, shows they've seen, and amusing things pets do.

➤ In some cultures, animals are not kept as pets but raised strictly to provide food or labor. You may need to introduce the concept of pets and explain the interaction between owner and pet.

➤ Have volunteers talk about the lesson topics. Provide visuals to stimulate children's imagination and encourage input. Model and correct pronunciation and word choice indirectly, by using the terms correctly in rephrased sentences.

➤ Give children a brief overview of the story they will be reading. Use the illustrations to help clarify your introduction.

2 TEACH

Materials:
Student Edition, page 213

Review words from the story with the sound of long o and have children read "Joe's Show."

➤ Ask ESL learners to follow the story as you read and to underline words they know that contain the sound of long o. Have them pronounce the words aloud, and model correct pronunciation if children mispronounce.

➤ Print the words on the chalkboard. Have volunteers circle the letters that stand for the sound of long o.

➤ Tell children to match orally rhyming words from the story (*Joe, show, go, no; Rose, nose*).

➤ Read the story aloud in small groups. Discuss the Think! question.

★ *For specific notes on various home languages, see pages xiii–xvii of this Guide.*

3 PRACTICE

Materials:
Student Edition, pages 213–214; crayons, markers, pencils; realia of a sign announcing a show

Practice lesson objectives by having children complete the worksheets with oral modeling and support from you.

➤ Ask each ESL learner to contribute one thing she or he remembers about "Joe's Show." Assist with sequence of events by asking "Who wanted to have a show?" and "Who came to Joe's home?"

➤ Have pairs complete items 1–3 on page 213, then read the completed sentences to one another. Model correct pronunciation as needed.

➤ Brainstorm ideas for the writing task on page 214. Bring a sign to class and talk about information to include. Guide the discussion as needed. Create a Language Experience chart story using children's ideas. Have the chart available when children write their own stories to provide extra support for spelling and sentence structure.

4 APPLY

Materials:
Long Vowel Books activity, *MCP Phonics Teacher Resource Guide,* page 151l; white paper, crayons, markers

Continue making Long Vowel Books as described on page 151l. Prepare a page for the sound of long o. Distribute art supplies.

➤ Guide ESL learners as they write a sentence using words with long o. Ask them to draw a picture about the sentence.

➤ Collect the long o pages to assemble the Long Vowel Books.

5 ASSESS

Materials:
Spelling section, *MCP Phonics Teacher Resource Guide,* page 214

Refer to the spelling test and list on page 214. Say each word, repeat it, read the sentence in context, and say the word again. After checking work, have children write short context sentences using the words or, for those less proficient, construct the sentences orally, then model how to write. Have children copy the sentences and reread. Ask volunteers to read several sentences; correct usage and model acceptable pronunciation.

MORE PHONICS PRACTICE

Set aside class time to read trade books with ESL learners. Preview these books and do a first reading to children.

WHEN IT SNOWS by JoAnne Nelson. Discovery Phonics (Modern Curriculum Press, 1992)

MR. WINK by Claire Daniel. Ready Readers, Stage 2 (Modern Curriculum Press, 1996)

AstroWord
Ask groups of children (ESL learners and native speakers of English) to explore the activities included on the CD-ROMs *AstroWord Long Vowels: a, i* (Module 7); *Long Vowels: i, o* (Module 8); and *Long Vowels: e, u* (Module 9). Encourage them to work together to complete activities that interest them. Offer support, monitor group progress, and ask directed questions about long vowel sounds and vowel recognition.

Lesson 104
Reviewing Long Vowels *a, i, u, o*

INFORMAL ASSESSMENT OBJECTIVE

Can children

✔ read long *a, i, u,* and *o* words in the context of a story?

---

1 INTRODUCE

Materials:
Soccer ball, jump rope, jacks, yo-yo (optional)

Remind ESL learners that the theme for Unit 3 is Let's Play. In preparation for reading the Take-Home Book, talk about games that children in the United States enjoy.

➤ Bring small toys, board or video games, and sports equipment to class. Have volunteers tell about each.

➤ Ask children what types of games they play in their culture. Invite them to bring small toys and games to class or illustrate them and talk about them.

➤ Provide opportunities for children to play games from different cultures as they use key vocabulary for each activity.

2 TEACH

Materials:
Games Around the Globe Take-Home Book, Student Edition, pages 215–216; Letter Cards *Gg, Ll, Pp, Rr;* globe or world map

Discuss the *Games Around the Globe* Take-Home Book with ESL learners and review words containing the long vowel sounds.

➤ Assist children in making their Take-Home Books.

➤ With a globe or map, help children locate Turkey, Mexico, Holland, and countries that your ESL learners come from. Mention that people from Holland are Dutch.

➤ Ask ESL learners to find and pronounce for you each country name (and the word *Dutch*) in the text and talk about the photo from that country.

➤ Read the story to children, modeling correct pronunciation.

➤ Pronounce and define for ESL learners less familiar story words, such as *children, many, called, also,* and *clapping.*

➤ Have children pick a Letter Card and read the story for a word that begins with the letter and contains a long vowel (such as *game, globe, play, places, like,* and *rope*).

★ *For specific notes on various home languages, see pages xiii–xvii of this Guide.*

3 PRACTICE

Materials:
Games Around the Globe Take-Home Book

Determine which skills individual ESL learners need more practice with and implement the Take-Home Book accordingly.

➤ First model correct pronunciation for ESL learners who need additional support with pronunciation. Then have them read the story aloud and review target or problem sounds.

➤ Build vocabulary by asking volunteers to define story words.

➤ Check comprehension by asking content-related questions that contain the target words or sounds. Discuss the Talk About It question in small groups.

4 APPLY

Materials:
Zap Words activity and Blackline Master 23, *MCP Phonics Teacher Resource Guide,* pages 151n–151o

Practice the sounds of long and short *a, i, u,* and *o* with the Zap Words activity on pages 151n–151o.

➤ Duplicate Blackline Master 23 and cut apart the cards.

➤ Adapt the activity for ESL learners to practice skills specific to each individual's areas of weakness, such as read/say the words aloud, add the e and print the new words, or write sentences using activity words.

5 ASSESS

Materials:
Games Around the Globe Take-Home Book, teacher-prepared worksheet

Prepare a worksheet of three to five fill-in sentences from the story for children to complete using target words in context. Hand out worksheets. Allow children to use the book to find the words. Have children read their completed sentences aloud to one another. Ask children to give a brief oral summary of the story. (You may wish to assess this portion separately.) Again, assess skill development by observing and noting areas of strength and weakness.

Book Corner

MORE PHONICS PRACTICE

Set aside class time to read trade books with ESL learners. Preview these books and do a first reading to children.

YES, I CAN! by Irma Singer. Ready Readers, Stage 1 (Modern Curriculum Press, 1996)

KATE'S TRAIL by Dr. Alvin Granowsky. Phonics Practice Readers (Modern Curriculum Press, 1986)

Technology

AstroWord

Some ESL learners will benefit from the additional practice and linguistic interaction provided by the CD-ROMs *AstroWord Long Vowels: a, i; Long Vowels: i, o;* and *Long Vowels: e, u* (Module 7–9). Encourage native speakers of English and ESL learners to work together to complete the Easy level of *Word Sort,* in which children help alien creatures sort picture clues. Offer assistance while monitoring progress.

Lessons 105–109
Long e

INFORMAL ASSESSMENT OBJECTIVES

Can children

✔ identify pictures whose names contain the sound of long e?

✔ identify words and picture names that contain the sounds of short and long e?

★ *Children who speak Asian languages or Spanish may confuse long e and short i; practice saying* feet, fit; Pete, pit; *and* seen, sin.

1 INTRODUCE

Materials:
Student Edition, page 217; Rhyme Poster 33 (optional)

Introduce the sound and most common spellings of long e by reading the rhyme on page 217 of the Student Edition.

➤ Model the sound of long e. Have children repeat.

➤ Print ee and ea on the chalkboard. Tell children that many words containing the sound of long e are spelled with these sets of letters. Give examples; have ESL learners repeat each one after you.

➤ Read the rhyme aloud; have ESL learners listen for target words.

➤ Instruct children to look for words spelled with ee or ea in the rhyme, read them aloud, and print them on the board. Words are *tree, neat, green, leaves,* and *see.*

➤ Have ESL learners complete the worksheet on page 217 on their own as much as they can. Provide support as requested. Work with ESL learners to discover and correct their own mistakes.

2 TEACH

Materials:
Student Edition, page 221

Teach and review long e versus short e, i and expand ESL learners' lexicon of words with long e by creating a food menu.

➤ With ESL learners who need practice differentiating among long e, short e, and short i, do an activity to practice discrimination. Say a list of words; have children clap when they hear the sound of long e. Words are *green, seat, hen, grin, tree, fit, feet, three, ten, bead.*

➤ Complete the activity on page 221 to reinforce the concept.

➤ Print on the board *We eat* and *We feed deer.* Explain that you will name a food and children must decide which category it fits in. Have ESL learners print the words on the board. Words are *meat, leaves, beans, seeds, peaches,* and *peas.*

★ *For specific notes on various home languages, see pages xiii–xvii of this Guide.*

3 PRACTICE

Materials:
Student Edition, pages 218–220, 222–223, 225

Adapt these pages to review and practice target strategies with ESL learners.

➤ Use the activities on pages 219, 223, and 225 to practice naming pictures containing the target sound(s). Expand vocabulary by asking volunteers to use target words in sentences.

➤ Ask ESL learners to explain what rhyming words are. Say a word and have children supply a rhyming word. If supplying a word is difficult, say two words and ask children to say whether they rhyme.

➤ Have children complete pages 218 and 222 in pairs. Review answers. Adapt the maze activity on page 220 by having children read each word, circle the words with long e, and connect the circled words.

4 APPLY

Materials:
Word Clues activity, *MCP Phonics Teacher Resource Guide,* page 151n; index cards, teacher-prepared word clues

Work with small groups of ESL learners and English-proficient peers on the Word Clues activity.

➤ Prepare six index cards by printing one long e word on each. Prepare a list of two clues for each word used.

➤ Hand out one index card to pairs of children.

➤ Say a clue. Tell children that whoever has the answer to the clue must stand together and read the word aloud.

➤ Collect cards, redistribute, and repeat the activity.

5 ASSESS

Materials:
Student Edition, pages 224, 226

Ask a child to read and paraphrase the directions. Have children complete page 224 in pairs and page 226 individually. Review answers aloud, and ask volunteers to write each answer on the board. Assist ESL learners in writing short answers to the Think! questions. Provide individual support, as needed.

Book Corner

MORE PHONICS PRACTICE

Set aside class time to read trade books with ESL learners. Preview these books and do a first reading to children.

EYES ARE EVERYWHERE by Polly Peterson. Ready Readers, Stage 2 (Modern Curriculum Press, 1996)

WHAT DO YOU SEE? by Judy Nayer. Discovery Phonics (Modern Curriculum Press, 1992)

Technology

AstroWord
Invite children to complete some of the intergalactic activities on the CD-ROM *AstroWord Long Vowels: e, u* (Module 9). Ask small groups of ESL learners and English-speaking peers to work together as you focus their efforts on continuing practice with the sound of long e. Monitor groups for equal participation and progress.

Lesson 110
Long e; Reviewing Long Vowels a, i, u, o, e

INFORMAL ASSESSMENT OBJECTIVES

Can children

✔ identify pictures whose names contain the sounds of short and long e?

✔ distinguish among the sounds of long a, i, u, o, and e?

1 INTRODUCE

Materials:
Chart paper; markers

Begin with a review of long e and short e where ESL learners supply rhyming words.

➤ Print *web* and *tree* on the board. Ask a volunteer to read each aloud and circle the vowels.

➤ Point out the difference between the sounds of e, stressing the labels *long* and *short*.

➤ Say a word. Have ESL learners tell whether the sound is long or short and then supply a rhyming word. Have available on chart paper a list of rhyming words for added support. Words include *heat, sled, feel, keep, wet, nest, ten, reed, lean,* and *sell.*

2 TEACH

Materials:
Unit 3 Word List, *MCP Phonics Teacher Resource Guide,* page 151k; Vowel Letter Cards; tape

Use words from the Unit 3 Word List to review and reinforce the five long vowel sounds.

➤ Review the rule for long vowel sounds and second (silent) vowels on the Teach section of page 128 of this Guide. Print *may, mile, cute, boat, seat* on the board. Have ESL learners read each word aloud and indicate by circling the long and silent vowels.

➤ Tape vowel cards to the board a few feet apart.

➤ Say a word from the word list. Tell ESL learners to stand under the letter that stands for the long vowel sound they hear.

➤ For ESL learners who need additional practice with spelling and writing, have them print the word you say on the board under the correct vowel card.

★ *For specific notes on various home languages, see pages xiii–xvii of this Guide.*

3 PRACTICE ···*·*·*··*·*···*·*··*··*··*·*·*··*·*·*·

Materials:
Student Edition, pages 227–228; crayons; chart paper and pencils

Adapt the worksheets on pages 227–228 to offer additional practice for the lesson objectives.

➤ Before ESL learners complete page 227, have them name each picture aloud and say whether the vowel sound is long e or short e.

➤ After coloring the correct pictures on page 228, ask ESL learners to write the name of a picture you point to. Encourage ESL learners to use each answer word in a context sentence.

4 APPLY ···*·*·*··*·*··*·*·*·*··*··*·*··*··*·*·*·

Materials:
Long Vowel Books activity, *MCP Phonics Teacher Resource Guide,* page 151l; white and colored construction paper, crayons, markers, paper clips or stapler, Vowel Letter Cards

Complete the Long Vowel Books with ESL learners. Prepare a page for the sound of long e and have children read their books aloud in small groups.

➤ Distribute art supplies.

➤ Tell children to write a sentence using words with long e. Have them draw a picture about the sentence.

➤ Assist ESL learners in writing [*Name's*] *Long Vowel Book* on a sheet of colored construction paper (the cover). Assemble books.

➤ In small groups, have each child pick a vowel card and read the corresponding page aloud. Repeat for practice.

5 ASSESS ···*·*·*··*·*··*·*·*·*··*·*·*·*··*·*·*·

Materials:
Letter Cards *Aa, Ee, Ii, Oo, Uu*; Phonics Picture Cards 85–120; complete set of Letter Cards

Assess each ESL learner's progress and use the materials as follows. *Oral practice:* Select Picture Cards that correspond to the vowel sound each ESL learner needs to practice. *Spelling:* Have ESL learners select a Phonics Picture Card and arrange Letter Cards to spell the word. *Discrimination:* Display Vowel Letter Cards. Ask ESL learners to pick Phonics Picture Cards, name the objects aloud, and stack them next to the letter that stands for the long vowel sound.

Book Corner
MORE PHONICS PRACTICE

Set aside class time to read trade books with ESL learners. Preview these books and do a first reading to children.

THE APPLE FARM by Claire Daniel. Ready Readers, Stage 2 (Modern Curriculum Press, 1996)

WHAT DO YOU SEE? by Judy Nayer. Discovery Phonics (Modern Curriculum Press, 1992)

Technology

AstroWord
Some ESL learners will benefit from additional practice and linguistic interaction, such as that provided by the CD-ROMs *AstroWord Long Vowels: a, i; Long Vowels: i, o;* and *Long Vowels: e, u* (Modules 7–9). Encourage native speakers of English and ESL learners to work together on *Listen & Write,* in which children listen to clues and write the correct response. Offer assistance while monitoring progress.

Lessons 111–113
Reviewing Short and Long Vowels

INFORMAL ASSESSMENT OBJECTIVES

Can children

- ✔ distinguish among short and long vowels?
- ✔ identify and complete the names of pictures that contain the sounds of long vowels?
- ✔ spell and write words with long vowels?
- ✔ write a letter using spelling words?

1 INTRODUCE

Materials:
Index card with *e* printed on it, blank card; Phonemic Awareness activity, *MCP Phonics Teacher Resource Guide,* page 229

Confirm that ESL learners can recognize and say long and short vowel sounds while practicing worksheet tasks.

➤ Print *pin, tub, can, not* on the board. Have ESL learners read each aloud. Then hold up the e card at the end of the word and ask children to read the new words.

➤ Implement the Phonemic Awareness activity. If ESL learners need more practice, adapt the activity: print words on the board and cover the first letter with a blank index card.

2 TEACH

Materials:
Chalk and chalkboard

Review long vowel combinations with ESL learners and explore letter substitution to create new words.

➤ Talk about the long vowel spelling rules: one long vowel sound and one silent vowel.

➤ Ask ESL learners to supply a word with each long vowel sound. Allow them to scan the Student Edition to find pictures; spontaneously supplying a word is difficult. Have them tell which vowel makes the long sound and which is silent.

➤ Point out the following combinations: *ay, ai, ee, ea, ow, ui.* Ask ESL learners to supply words with each combination. Point out that a final e is the most common silent letter.

➤ Print incomplete words on the board, such as *t_ne, t_me, p_n, c_t,* and so on. Have volunteers fill in possible vowels, say the words they make, and define/use in a context sentence.

★ *For specific notes on various home languages, see pages xiii–xvii of this Guide.*

3 PRACTICE

Materials:
Student Edition, pages 229–234; crayons

Use the worksheets in these lessons to track ESL learners' progress in target objectives.

➤ Review the picture clues on page 229 together to avoid confusion.

➤ Have ESL learners print all words on page 230 before doing the matching task.

➤ Offer additional assistance and support with the "Short Vowel" portion of the activity on page 232, as some ESL learners are likely to supply rhyming words instead of doing vowel substitution.

➤ Give the writing task on page 234 a "real life" context by having children write letters to each other. Write a sample letter on chart paper for children. Draw names from a hat. Assist less proficient writers in writing their letters. Pair children to read letters to each other.

4 APPLY

Materials:
Feed the Dog a Bone activity, *MCP Phonics Teacher Resource Guide,* page 151n; toy dog, dog dish, construction paper, marker

Use the Feed the Dog a Bone activity to practice long and short vowel recognition.

➤ Hand out several paper bones to each ESL learner. Ask them to print a long or short vowel word on each.

➤ Proceed with the activity as described.

5 ASSESS

Materials:
MCP Phonics Teacher Resource Guide, page 234

Assess ESL learners' mastery of Unit 3 spelling words by giving a cumulative spelling test using the 30 words in sentences. Give an oral test for additional speaking/pronunciation practice or if writing is still too complex, point to a word on the ESL learner's paper and have the child read it aloud and use it in a context sentence.

MORE PHONICS PRACTICE

Set aside class time to read trade books with ESL learners. Preview these books and do a first reading to children.

ICE FISHING by Julie Alperen. Ready Readers, Stage 3 (Modern Curriculum Press, 1996)

ZEKE by Janis Asad Raabe. Phonics Practice Readers (Modern Curriculum Press, 1986)

AstroWord

Ask ESL learners and English-proficient children to explore the activities included on the *AstroWord* CD-ROMs (Modules 3–5 and 7–9) that cover long and short vowels. Encourage them to work together to complete activities that interest them. Assign specific vowel sounds that children need to practice further. Offer support, monitor group progress, and ask directed questions that use long vowel sounds.

Lesson 114
Reviewing Long Vowels *a, i, u, o, e*

INFORMAL ASSESSMENT OBJECTIVE

Can children
✔ read long *a, i, u, o,* and *e* words in the context of a story?

1 INTRODUCE

Materials:
Realia associated with sleep and bedtime (pajamas, a teddy bear, an alarm clock, and so on)

Since *No Sleep* is about trouble falling asleep, have ESL learners practice oral language skills to discuss what happens when they have trouble falling asleep.

➤ Ask ESL learners to talk about when they are tired, what makes them tired, and what they do at bedtime.

➤ Hold up objects one at a time and have volunteers name it and tell what it is used for, relating it to sleep and bedtime.

➤ Narrate your own story of a night you had trouble falling asleep; ask comprehension questions, like "Why do you think I had trouble falling asleep?"

2 TEACH

Materials:
No Sleep Take-Home Book; Student Edition, pages 235–236

Talk about the *No Sleep* Take-Home Book with ESL learners while reviewing words with long vowel sounds.

➤ Assist children in making their Take-Home Books. Give a brief overview of how to proceed as they follow your oral instructions.

➤ Have ESL learners look through the story for words they know or think contain long vowel sounds. Ask them to print the words on the board.

➤ Teach/review other important story words: *trying, along, knees, tangled, loud.*

➤ Read the story to children as they follow in their books.

★ *For specific notes on various home languages, see pages xiii–xvii of this Guide.*

3 PRACTICE

Materials:
No Sleep Take-Home Book, crayons

Activate ESL learners' phonemic awareness and vocabulary recall by asking them to circle context words containing long vowels.

➤ Have children read the story silently, using the illustrations as clues.

➤ Check comprehension; assess how much information ESL learners gleaned from reading the story independently.

➤ Have them read the story aloud to you.

➤ Give specific phonemic and vocabulary-related tasks: circle the words that mean a part of the body, underline the long e words, and so forth.

➤ Pair children to reread the story. Monitor individuals' reading abilities.

4 APPLY

Materials:
Phonics Picture Cards (numbers 85–120), buttons or plastic chips ("counters")

Review words with long vowel sounds using the How Many Sounds? activity found on page 75l of the *MCP Phonics Teacher Resource Guide*.

➤ Ask ESL learners to determine how many sounds are in each word; have them "dissect" the word, telling which beginning, middle, and ending sounds they hear. Ask which letters stand for each sound.

➤ Have children who need practice with writing/spelling print each picture name.

5 ASSESS

Materials:
No Sleep Take-Home Book, realia props

Verify ESL learners' understanding of the story by having them create, narrate, and act out a similar story. Children can prepare skits in pairs or groups of four. Offer support and brainstorm ideas together. For example, two children can be a noisy truck that awakens another child, two can be a barking dog, and so on. Have groups perform for you alone at first to avoid stage fright.

Book Corner

MORE PHONICS PRACTICE

Set aside class time to read trade books with ESL learners. Preview these books and do a first reading to children.

JUMP RIGHT IN by Maryann Dobeck. Ready Readers, Stage 1 (Modern Curriculum Press, 1996)

MR. JONES AND MR. BONES by Janis Asad Raabe. Phonics Practice Readers (Modern Curriculum Press, 1986)

Technology

AstroWord

Select one of the *AstroWord Long Vowels* CD-ROMs (Modules 7-9) according to which long vowel sound your ESL learners need to practice most. Have children work one-on-one with a more English-proficient child to complete activities that interest them. Offer assistance and monitor each pair's progress.

Lesson 115
Reviewing Long Vowels

INFORMAL ASSESSMENT OBJECTIVES

Can children

✔ identify picture names that contain long vowel sounds?

✔ distinguish between words that contain long and short vowel sounds to complete sentences?

1 INTRODUCE

Materials:
Self-stick notes;
Student Edition,
page 237; Checkup
activity, *MCP Phonics
Teacher Resource
Guide*, page 237

Confirm ESL learners' ability to identify classroom items whose names contain long vowels before completing the worksheet on page 237.

➤ Give each ESL learner a self-stick note on which you have written a vowel.

➤ Tell children to stick their notes on objects whose names model that long vowel. Review names aloud. Model pronunciation.

➤ Reinforce with Preparing for the Checkup activity on page 237. Model directions and have children complete. Review.

➤ Review picture names aloud together before beginning the activity. Allow children who are challenged to work with a more proficient peer on items 1–6, then complete 7–12 individually.

2 PRACTICE

Materials:
Student Edition,
page 238

Reviewing the "two vowel" spelling rule for long vowels will greatly facilitate ESL learners' ability to complete the review worksheet.

➤ After children complete the task, have them go back and underline all the words that contain long vowel sounds.

➤ As you review answers, ask ESL learners to explain the difference between the correct answer and the incorrect choice.

Book Corner

MORE PHONICS PRACTICE

Set aside class time to read trade books with ESL learners. Preview these books and do a first reading to children.

MR. WINK by Claire Daniel. Ready Readers, Stage 2 (Modern Curriculum Press, 1996)

DALE AND THE CAVE Phonics Practice Readers, (Modern Curriculum Press, 1992)

Assessment Strategy Overview

Throughout Unit 4 you have opportunities to assess ESL learners' ability to read and write words with consonant blends and with *y* as a vowel. Some of your ESL learners may require additional assessment strategies to meet their special language needs.

FORMAL ASSESSMENT

Before you start Unit 4, administer the Unit 4 Pretest, found on pages 239e–239f of *MCP Phonics Teacher Resource Guide.* Children's scores will help you assess their knowledge base before beginning the unit and alert you to areas for further support. Complete the Student Progress Checklist on page 239i. Based on their responses to the Unit 4 Pretest, note with which consonant blends children are struggling.

♦ Some children may understand a concept but have difficulty reading directions. Assess children's ability to interpret directions. If necessary, read them aloud to the group and model how the Pretest is to be completed.

♦ Before administering the Pretest, preview the picture clues on page 239e so that children are familiar with the picture names. Then, they can focus on matching the answer choices to the picture clues.

INFORMAL ASSESSMENT

Review pages, Unit Checkups, and Take-Home Books are effective ways to evaluate children's progress. Following are other suggestions for informal ways to assess children's understanding of the concepts.

♦ Gather realia or pictures of objects that reflect children's areas of difficulty. Allow them to select a visual and name it. Have children match each item to its counterpart letter on an alphabet chart.

♦ Bring to class props that use the target sounds. Say and write each word as you identify it. Have children identify the letters that stand for the sounds of each consonant blend.

Portfolio

PORTFOLIO ASSESSMENT

Portfolio Assessment opportunities are identified by the logo shown here. In addition to collecting the pages mentioned on page 239c, gather other examples of children's work for comparison and evaluation at critical periods in the unit, as indicated below.

♦ **Initial practice** Children are now using sentences and rhymes to communicate meaning as well as to practice phonics. Encourage ESL learners to write lists, riddles, and sentences, and add to portfolios. Analyze entries to identify areas of strength and weakness. Early efforts can include skills such as handwriting, prewriting and emergent writing skills, and beginning word activities.

♦ **Midunit classwork** Have ESL learners create personalized picture dictionaries in which they use consonant blends and the sounds of *y* as a vowel to write about topics of interest. Assess their "books" to determine areas that need reinforcement.

♦ **Final products or projects** Review ESL learners' progress in completing the Curriculum Connections Portfolio activities in the *MCP Phonics Teacher Resource Guide.* Compare later entries to earlier work. Use the Student Progress Checklist on page 239i to assess.

STUDENT PROGRESS CHECKLIST

Photocopy and attach the checklist on page 239i of *MCP Phonics Teacher Resource Guide* to each child's portfolio. Evaluate growth from your assessment. Use activities suggested in this Guide to build a strong phonics foundation.

Administering and Evaluating the
Pretest and Posttest

➤ Read the information on page 239d of *MCP Phonics Teacher Resource Guide*. Answers for the Pretest and the Posttest are provided on page 239d.

➤ Record test results on the Student Progress Checklist on page 239i after children complete the Pretest.

➤ Record results again after children take the Posttest.

➤ Compare the results of the two tests. Use the Performance Assessment Profile at the bottom of page 239d to help you draw conclusions about children's performance. Opportunities to reteach each specific skill in the unit are identified by page number.

TEST OBJECTIVES

The objectives of both the Unit 4 Pretest and Posttest of *MCP Phonics Teacher Resource Guide,* are to read and write words with consonant blends and *y* as a vowel. ESL learners may confuse *r* blends and *l* blends (especially Vietnamese, Korean, Khmer, Hmong, and Cantonese), pronouncing them the same way. Have children practice saying the picture clues aloud; reinforce with frequent reading and spelling opportunities throughout the unit.

UNIT 4 PRETEST, pages 239e–239f

Page 239e of *MCP Phonics Teacher Resource Guide* focuses on identifying and naming picture clues that contain consonant blends or the sounds of *y* as a vowel. Support ESL learners by implementing any of the following suggestions prior to administering the Pretest.

♦ **Practice test-taking skills.** Some ESL learners may not recognize the picture clues on page 239e and therefore may not be able to pronounce the word names on their own. Ask them to listen to a picture name as you say it aloud. Have children repeat after you. Follow this process for items 1–12.

♦ **Adjust pacing.** Some ESL learners may feel intimidated by children who appear to complete the tests more quickly or more easily than they do. Conduct the Pretest one-on-one with children who need special pacing and provide frequent encouragement and support for their efforts. Administer the test orally if children are intimidated by print.

♦ **Test orally.** Some ESL learners may not be ready to test on their own and complete all the tasks asked of them. For these children, try working one-on-one as you name aloud the picture clues and the word choices that may contain the same vowel sounds.

Page 239f focuses on comprehension of specific word clues that contain the target sounds. You may wish to incorporate these strategies as you administer the test.

- **Read the prompts aloud to ESL learners.** Items 13–20 require children to read the hints. If necessary, read them aloud to ESL learners and pantomime the meanings for children to respond to. Then have them discriminate among the answer choices for the correct words.

- **Preview answer choices.** Use word lists, charts, and word wheels to provide pretest practice of consonant blends and *y* as a vowel. This will familiarize your ESL learners with the words, allowing them to focus on selecting the best picture-print matches.

- **Work in groups.** The Pretest on page 239f requires children to read the text and then select the best answer that is an example of the hint. If these tasks are too overwhelming, work in small groups or one-on-one and read aloud, or have children read the answer choices. Provide prompts and pronunciation support as determined by children's ability levels. Complete the test in two or three sittings.

- **Work one-on-one.** Children who are unable to read print independently in English can complete the activities orally with you during class or at a separate time. At a later time, work on developing print fluency.

UNIT 4 POSTTEST, pages 239g–239h

Check ESL learners' scores on the Unit 4 Pretest on page 239f. Confirm areas of difficulty and adapt test-taking strategies as needed. You may wish to use these suggestions for ESL learners as they complete pages 239g–239h.

- **Confirm that children understand directions.** Read aloud the directions for each page and ensure that children know how to proceed. Model what they are expected to do, working one-on-one with ESL learners who need undivided attention.

- **Eliminate overwhelming tasks.** Even by the end of the unit, some ESL learners may be unable to read well enough in English to complete page 239h alone. For children who experience difficulties, read each incomplete sentence aloud (and answer choices, if necessary) and emphasize the blend (or sound of *y*). Or conduct the test orally, allowing ESL learners to give verbal responses.

- **Create context.** Some children may be distracted by the "text-heaviness" of page 239h. Point out that the sentences all form a story. Summarize the plot of the story so that children can anticipate the action. Then read aloud each sentence separately. Read the answer choices aloud to children and guide them to select the best choice.

Spelling Connections

Pages 239j–239k of *MCP Phonics Teacher Resource Guide* provide a collection of ideas and opportunities to actively incorporate spelling into your phonics program. It is recommended that ESL learners reach the intermediate fluency level of English proficiency before focusing on spelling.

✳ **Anticipate problem words.** Anticipated areas of difficulty for children who speak Spanish, Korean, Hmong, Khmer, Russian, or Vietnamese are noted by a star in the Informal Assessment Objectives box at the beginning of each lesson in this Guide. You may wish to refer to these notes as you progress through specific lessons, especially as you make the link between oral and written forms.

✳ **Incorporate rhymes and songs.** Rhymes, songs, and poems are helpful for introducing new spelling words because of their repetitive nature. Introduce the rhymes in lessons 116, 118, 120, 122, and 125 and have children repeat them often. In their Student Books, have children identify the similarities and differences among words and highlight the target sounds of the lesson. Have children spell the words on a daily basis.

✳ **Enhance meaning with visuals.** To ensure a link between oral speech and the written form of words, speak in simple, complete sentences and at a natural, not exaggerated, pace. Have children connect the visuals, the sounds, and the spelling words by posting throughout your classroom picture clues with the spelled words beneath them. Use the picture clues to introduce, model, and prompt meanings. Then cover up the printed words to assess spelling mastery and conduct an oral or written spelling test of new spelling words in the unit.

✳ **Develop personalized spelling lists.** Encourage children to add to their lists of new words those with which they have difficulty or are unfamiliar. Accustom children to writing new words on their lists. Review regularly with ESL learners and have children sound them out and spell them for you, first by sight-reading, then from memory. Encourage children to make a quick sketch next to difficult words to ensure they know the meanings of words.

✳ **Link sounds and print.** Incorporating listening tools such as audiotapes and CDs provides additional modalities through which ESL learners can acquire English. Have children work with partners to say the spelling words into a tape recorder. Have children record the words; then replay the tape as they practice writing the words they hear. Have ESL learners check their work against their Unit Spelling Lists.

✳ **Read it, write it, remember it.** Encourage ESL learners to commit spelling to memory. Ask ESL learners to copy the words from the Unit Word List onto individual index cards. Have them study four or five words daily at frequent intervals—before recess and lunch, during center time, and at home.

* **Conduct oral spelling drills.** Use oral repetition as a large group or in smaller groups at a listening station. Provide quick drill opportunities to reinforce similarities, differences, or other word associations.

* **Make writing fun.** Use fun writing mediums such as shaving cream, paints, clay, twine and sandpaper, and sand to practice spelling new or unfamiliar words. Children will have fun with the materials and enjoy writing the words you ask them to spell. Correct spelling before children "erase" their responses.

* **Incorporate games and flashcards into spelling practice.** Have ESL learners copy the words from the word list onto individual flashcards. Distribute words in specific letter patterns to small groups of children. Have children take turns playing "teacher" and quizzing the other group members orally on the words in their set. After all children have had a chance to spell each word in a set, exchange with another group.

* **Practice taking dictation.** Model the activity with words the children already know and can spell. Preteach new words a few at a time, using visuals, props, gestures, and contexts to enhance meanings. Write the words for children and allow them to trace each one as they sound it out aloud. Then, continue with Steps 1–3 of the Introduction on page 239j.

* **Incorporate journal writing in your class.** Encourage ESL learners to free-write in English and to use spelling words as prompts for free expression. Have children review their journal writings with you one-on-one and decorate their pages with artwork, photos, pictures, or realia.

Blackline Master 30 (page 239k) contains 31 words grouped by letter pattern. For ESL learners, introduce the words in each group separately and have children focus on the pattern itself as a spelling key. Have children sound out the words, then underline or highlight the consonant blend or use of *y* as a vowel.

Unit 4

Phonics Games, Activities, and Technology

Pages 239l–239n of *MCP Phonics Teacher Resource Guide* provide a collection of ideas and opportunities to actively engage children as they develop or reinforce phonics strategies. Many of the activities provided on these pages can be implemented with little or no modification for children whose native languages are not English. However, be alert to picture clues that are unfamiliar in context or in their names. Multistep directions may also be difficult for some ESL learners to understand or follow.

To ensure comprehension of activity directions, speak in simple, complete sentences and at a natural slow pace. Incorporating visuals and props, audiotapes, and CDs provides additional contexts and clues for new learners of English. For activities that require a written response, determine whether children have sufficient command of written print to complete the activities. Be aware that some children may write in cursive letters.

● **Word Wheels** (page 239l) can be simplified for ESL learners by adding picture clues of words containing the long *i* and *e* sounds to the wheels for children to pronounce. When they have mastered this version, pair ESL learners to play the game, using the Unit 4 Word List as a reference.

▲ **"Put the Sounds Together" Song** (page 239l) can focus ESL learners on blending sounds to form words. Have ESL learners work with you to adapt the sample rhyme to include words on the Unit 4 Word List.

◆ **Switch** (page 239l) relies on quick recognition and comprehension of blends for success. Have ESL learners work together in a group and eliminate the child who is "it."

■ **Add a Letter** (page 239l) can be simplified for ESL learners by practicing words that contain the blends before trying the activity. Display the words to be practiced on cards or charts as children say and spell the words and then identify the blends. To increase the level of difficulty, hide the visual prompts.

● **Treasure Word Hunt** (page 239m) can be completed successfully by having ESL learners work in pairs. Have one child find the words and the partner verify them before they cut out and paste their "treasures."

▲ **Using Describing Words** and **Blending Objects** (page 239m) require that ESL learners have strong vocabularies. Prompt memory of words ESL learners may have been introduced to but have forgotten with flashcards of describing words, picture clues cut out from magazines, or photographs that model the word clues.

◆ **Y Books** (page 239m) will be more successful for ESL learners if children work in groups with the Unit 4 Word List and Book Corner literature selections as sources for words that end in y. If children cannot apply the rules for y representing the sound of long *i* or long *e*, complete lessons 125 and 126 before assigning this activity.

■ **Stop Sign** (page 239m) works best by introducing the action words on several occasions before conducting the activity. Write the words on tagboard and, next to them, provide a visual clue of each action. Post so ESL learners can see as they play the activity.

● **Blend Shuffle** (page 239m), **Blend Chains** (page 239n) can be made less complex for ESL learners by preparing a second pile of cards (or set of paper strips), in a second color, that form actual words using the initial consonant blends. For the paper strips, you may reserve one color for this purpose only. Have a child turn over two cards, then continue turning over the second pile until he or she makes a match and forms an actual word. Have other group members confirm responses.

▲ **Toss a Word** and **Sneaky Snakes** (page 239n) require that ESL learners have the ability to recognize and spell words containing specific blends. Allow children to use picture clues, word lists, or their personalized picture dictionaries as references for these activities.

Technology

Use children's interest in technology to their advantage in learning English. If possible, allow ESL learners to work in small groups at the computer before or after class or during center time using the specific *AstroWord* CD-ROM Modules suggested in each lesson. Preview skill levels and supervise the groups directly to eliminate frustration and to guide phonics development. You may wish to add your observations to the Student Progress Checklist found on page 239i of *MCP Phonics Teacher Resource Guide* as well as use the software suggested on page 239n to provide additional phonics practice for ESL learners.

Lessons 116–117
r Blends

INFORMAL ASSESSMENT OBJECTIVES

Can children

✔ identify picture names and words that contain *r* blends?

✔ spell words that contain *r* blends?

★ *Speakers of Vietnamese, Hmong, Korean, Khmer, and Cantonese may confuse* r *blends and* l *blends. Have children pronounce* grow, glow; braid, blade; *and* fright, flight. *Initial* r *blends are relatively common in Spanish, Tagalog, and Russian. Monitor pronunciation for the "tap r" sound. Be sure children do not separate the two consonants with an intervening schwa sound (where* froze *might sound like* for Rose).

---

1 INTRODUCE

Materials:
Student Edition, pages 241–244; food pyramid chart

Assess ESL learners' ability to pronounce *r* blends clearly by having children name the picture clues on pages 241–244.

➤ Concentrate ESL learners' efforts on initial *r* blends by having them practice and repeat blend + vowel sound words, such as *grow, tree, brew, cry, pray, free,* and *dry.*

➤ Discuss the unit theme, Everybody Eats, using a food pyramid chart. Incorporate words containing *r* blends in your description (*grapes, grain, bread, fruits* that *grow* on *trees, cream,* and so on) and have ESL learners repeat and print each word.

2 TEACH

Materials:
Student Edition, pages 241–244

Review spelling and assess ESL learners' recognition of *r* blend words by having children go on a "hunt" for *r* blends.

➤ Print the seven *r* blends on the board and draw a large circle around each. Review the sound of each, using familiar words. Point out that *r* is always the second letter in each blend.

➤ Have ESL learners look through pages 241–244 and identify a picture clue for each initial *r* blend. Ask them to name the picture and point to the blend on the chalkboard. More proficient children can write the word.

➤ For children who need additional practice with auditory discrimination, say a series of words and have them clap when they hear an *r* blend. Words include *go, grow, block, friend, crab, clap, broom, door, drawer,* and *pretzel.*

★ *For specific notes on various home languages, see pages xiii–xvii of this Guide.*

3 PRACTICE

Materials:
Student Edition, pages 241–243; markers (buttons, pennies, and so on); crayons

Adapt the worksheets to serve "double duty" as you assess ESL learners' progress and comprehension of lesson content.

➤ Before children complete page 241, play a bingo game by calling out words and having children cover the corresponding pictures with markers.

➤ After completing page 242 in pairs, ask individuals to identify the initial blends in all the pictures that are not colored.

➤ Quickly review the rule for long vowel sounds (second silent vowel) with ESL learners as well as the long and short sound of each vowel as preparation for the activity on page 243.

4 APPLY

Materials:
Blend Shuffle activity, *MCP Phonics Teacher Resource Guide,* page 239m; Student Edition, pages 241–243; index cards, marker

Tailor the Blend Shuffle activity to your ESL learners' specific needs.

➤ Print one blend on each card: *br, cr, dr, fr, gr, pr, tr.* Have ESL learners name the letters that form each blend and say a word beginning with the blend. Allow children to look through the Student Edition pages 241–243 for picture clues.

➤ Print several phonograms on the board. Have children pick a card and make words by holding the blend in front of each. Phonograms: *-ick, -ow, -ain, -ess, -ee, -ize, -ab*

➤ Challenge children to use each word in a context sentence.

5 ASSESS

Materials:
Student Edition, page 244

Have ESL learners complete page 244 to assess their ability to use *r* blends. As children look at page 244, say an incomplete sentence and have children fill in the missing word to practice vocabulary in context. (*I baked a pie for a contest and won a __; Francie spilled juice on her favorite __.* Proficient children can write missing words as a spelling test.

MORE PHONICS PRACTICE

Set aside class time to read trade books with ESL learners. Preview these books and do a first reading to children.

AT THE TRACK by Gary Pernick. Ready Readers, Stage 2 (Modern Curriculum Press, 1996)

WHAT CAN A CRAB GRAB? by Dr. Alvin Granowsky. Phonics Practice Readers (Modern Curriculum Press, 1986)

AstroWord

Invite children to complete some of the intergalactic activities on the CD-ROM *AstroWord Consonant Blends and Digraphs* (Module 6). Ask small groups of English-speaking children and ESL learners to work together as you focus their efforts on continued practice with *r* blends. Monitor groups for equal participation and progress.

Lessons 118–119
l Blends

INFORMAL ASSESSMENT OBJECTIVES

Can children

✔ identify picture names and words that contain *l* blends?

✔ identify initial *l* blends to name pictures and complete sentences?

★ *Korean, Khmer, Hmong, Cantonese, or Vietnamese ESL learners may confuse* l *blends and* r *blends. Have children practice pronouncing* play, pray; clown, crown; flea, free; *and so on. Spanish-speaking children might pronounce a* short e *before* sl *words since Spanish lacks this initial blend.*

1 INTRODUCE

Materials:
Phonemic Awareness and Sound to Letter activities, *MCP Phonics Teacher Resource Guide*, page 245; Student Edition, pages 245–247

Assess ESL learners' proficiency levels with *l* blends while discussing different homophones in the target language.

➤ Implement the Phonemic Awareness and Sound to Letter activities. Use only short words beginning with *l*, as using word parts (such as *lum* for *plum*) may confuse children. (They may think that *lum* is a new word.) Words to use include *lip, lap, low, lock,* and *late.*

➤ Create contexts for new words by talking about different meanings for target words. (Noun and verb: *fly, plant, block, flash, glue, plug;* different noun meanings: *glass, club*)

2 TEACH

Materials:
Letter Cards *b, c, f, g, p, s;* Student Edition, page 245; Rhyme Poster 36 (optional)

Continue practicing pronunciation of *l* blends while teaching spelling and word recognition to ESL learners.

➤ Print several incomplete words, such as *_lip* and *_lant* on the chalkboard. Have ESL learners select a Letter Card and hold it up to form a word with the initial *l* blend.

➤ Point out that *l* is always the second letter in each blend. Assess comprehension and work with each child on *l* blends that pose problems in pronunciation or recognition.

➤ Use the rhyme on page 245 for further practice with identifying *l* blends and/or pronunciation practice. Have ESL learners identify target words, read them aloud in isolation, then read them again in the context of the rhyme.

★ *For specific notes on various home languages, see pages xiii–xvii of this Guide.*

3 PRACTICE

Materials:
Student Edition, pages 245–247; bingo markers

Use the following practice and review strategies to prepare ESL learners to complete the Student Edition activities on pages 245–247.

➤ For children who need support in spelling and recognition, print a series of consonant blends on paper: *bl, fl, dl, tl; gl, cl, jl, pl*. Say a word and have ESL learners point to or say the correct blend.

➤ For children who confuse *r* and *l* blends, repeat using *gl, bl, gr, tr, br*, and so on. Provide as much practice time as needed.

➤ To practice identifying picture clues, play a game of bingo by calling out words and having children cover the corresponding pictures (from pages 245–247) with markers.

4 APPLY

Materials:
Word Wheels, *MCP Phonics Teacher Resource Guide*, page 239l; paper plates, tagboard, brads, markers

Have each ESL learner make an *l* blend Word Wheels as described on page 239l.

➤ Construct word wheels. Print an *l* blend (*bl, cl, fl, gl, pl*) on each plate.

➤ Draw 4–5 rules on the tagboard circle and have children fill in word endings appropriate to the *l* blend on the wheel.

➤ Review each word on a wheel; verify recognition, pronunciation, and understanding. Redistribute wheels and repeat the activity.

5 ASSESS

Materials:
Student Edition, page 248

Use the worksheet on page 248 and a spelling test to assess ESL learners' mastery of *l* blends. The activity on page 248 will indicate if children need practice in matching a printed word to a visual clue or if there is confusion with target vocabulary used in context. ESL learners may require small group or individual practice ahead of time to successfully complete the spelling test with the rest of the class.

Book Corner

MORE PHONICS PRACTICE

Set aside class time to read trade books with ESL learners. Preview these books and do a first reading to children.

PLANTING A GARDEN by Jennifer Jacobson. Ready Readers, Stage 2 (Modern Curriculum Press, 1996)

A GLOB OF GLUE by Dr. Alvin Granowsky. Phonics Practice Readers (Modern Curriculum Press, 1986)

Technology

AstroWord

Some children will benefit from additional practice and feedback, using the CD-ROM *AstroWord Consonant Blends and Digraphs* (Module 6). Encourage native speakers of English and ESL learners to work on the Easy level of *Make-a-Word,* where children help alien creatures create words based on picture clues. Monitor each group's progress.

Lessons 120–121
s Blends

INFORMAL ASSESSMENT OBJECTIVES

Can children

✔ identify picture names and spell words that contain s blends?

✔ write words that contain s blends to complete sentences?

★ *Children whose home languages are Vietnamese, Cantonese, Khmer, Hmong, or Korean might have trouble with initial s blends, since they do not exist in these languages. Spanish-speaking children may pronounce a short e before all s blends, while Russian speakers might pronounce a voiced z sound in some blends (zboon for spoon).*

---

1 INTRODUCE

Materials:
Sound to Letter activity, *MCP Phonics Teacher Resource Guide,* page 249; realia whose names model initial s blends; Letter Card Ss

Build on ESL learners' mastery of initial consonants to activate knowledge of s blends.

▶ Use the Sound to Letter activity on page 249, but expand the activity to include the words *tar, tone, nail, lip, lap, kit,* and *pot* to provide additional practice. Have an ESL learner hold up the *Ss* card for the group to create new words and read them aloud.

▶ Use familiar objects from home for further practice, such as *sweater, skirt, spice, spoon,* and *stamp.*

▶ Make ESL learners familiar and more comfortable with two-letter s blends before embarking on the more difficult three-letter blends, such as *squ-, scr-,* and *str-.*

2 TEACH

Materials:
Student Edition, page 249; Rhyme Poster 37 (optional); teacher-prepared worksheet

ESL learners may require more reinforcement, practice, and review with s blends than with r or l blends. First work with individual blends, then expand to two or three s blends.

▶ Ask children first to circle in their books all the s blends in the rhyme on page 249. Have them read the rhyme in pairs to each other, then discuss it with them.

▶ Prepare a worksheet with related s blend words. Have ESL learners draw a picture for each word, then match the "partner" words and use them in context sentences. Possible pairs: *skirt, sweater; swing, slide; sled, snow; spill, scrub; skunk, smell.*

172

★ *For specific notes on various home languages, see pages xiii–xvii of this Guide.*

3 PRACTICE

Materials:
Student Edition, pages 249–251; *s* blend cards

Have ESL learners complete the worksheets on these pages to identify specific problems they might have with *s* blends. Record on the Student Progress Checklist for this unit.

➤ Hold up an *s* blend card (such as *sl*) and ask children to identify pictures whose names begin with the target sound (*sled, sleep, slide, slippers*). They can then complete page 249 individually.

➤ Use page 250 to assess recall and recognition. Have children read all the words aloud to a partner. Monitor reading and provide assistance as necessary.

➤ If ESL learners cannot complete page 251 correctly, review all or specific *s* blends and give them a similar task to complete.

4 APPLY

Materials:
Blend Chains activity, *MCP Phonics Teacher Resource Guide,* page 239n; strips of colored paper, markers, paste or tape

Have ESL learners work on the Blend Chains activity without using books or visual clues to assess their ability to produce words with *s* blends on their own.

➤ Distribute seven strips of paper and a marker to each ESL learner.

➤ Print *s* blends on the board. Have children print one word beginning with each *s* blend on the strips, using words they can produce. Offer support as needed.

➤ Assemble chains and review words aloud.

5 ASSESS

Materials:
Phonics Picture Cards (numbers 140, 143–145, 147, 148, 151, 152); Student Edition, page 252

Assess mastery of *s* blends by displaying the Picture Cards, one at a time, to individual ESL learners. Verify correct pronunciation of the initial *s* blends, and have children use the words in context to check comprehension. Have ESL learners complete the activity on page 252 with an English-proficient peer; review as a small group.

MORE PHONICS PRACTICE

Set aside class time to read trade books with ESL learners. Preview these books and do a first reading to children.

MY LOST TOP by Diane Engles. Ready Readers, Stage 2 (Modern Curriculum Press, 1996)

SCAT, CAT! by Janis Asad Raabe. Phonics Practice Readers (Modern Curriculum Press, 1986)

AstroWord

Some learners will benefit from additional practice and linguistic interaction such as that provided by the CD-ROM *AstroWord Consonant Blends and Digraphs* (Module 6). Encourage native speakers of English and ESL learners to work together to complete the Easy level of *Word Sort,* in which children help alien creatures sort picture clues according to initial consonant blends. Monitor progress.

Lesson 122
Final Blends

INFORMAL ASSESSMENT OBJECTIVE

Can children

✔ identify pictures whose names end with final *mp, sk, nk, st,* and *ng* blends?

★ *Children who speak Cantonese, Khmer, or Korean will be familiar with* ng, *but the other final blends may pose problems. Learners whose home language is Tagalog or Spanish might "clip" the blend, pronouncing only the first consonant of each.*

---

1 INTRODUCE

Materials:
Student Edition, page 253; realia or Picture Cards of target words (optional)

Assess ESL learners' ability to discriminate among the different blend sounds by doing a "same or different" activity.

➤ Introduce and clearly model each final blend sound using words ESL learners know. Bring realia to class or use Picture Cards of target words on page 253.

➤ Have children practice pronouncing and identifying each final blend. Work with *nk* vs. *ng*, *sk* vs. *st*, and final *m* or *n* vs. *mp*. Model pronunciation and have children repeat.

➤ Practice word pairs such as *sing, sink; bang, bank; ring, rink; hung, trunk; desk, nest; fast, ask; disk, list; hum, hump; stem, stamp;* and *run, jump.*

2 TEACH

Materials:
Student Edition, page 253; Rhyme Poster 38 (optional); Letter Cards *Gg, Kk, Ll, Mm, Nn, Pp, Ss, Tt*

Focus initial instruction on having children recognize and master the vowel + final blend combinations in the Student Edition.

➤ Begin with *-amp* and *-ump* (*stamp, lamp, hump, jump*). As ESL learners become proficient, you may wish to introduce other combinations, for example *-imp* (*limp*) and *-omp* (*stomp*). Final *st* offers the most choices (*fast, test, list, lost, must*).

➤ The rhyme offers limited practice with final blends. Provide additional practice material by creating original sentences: *The lamp and the stamps are on the desk*, for example.

➤ Verify recognition by saying a word or pointing to a picture clue and having ESL learners arrange Letter Cards that stand for the final blend.

★ *For specific notes on various home languages, see pages xiii–xvii of this Guide.*

3 PRACTICE

Materials:
Student Edition, pages 253–254; markers (buttons, pennies, and so on); index cards

Adapt the worksheets to serve "double duty" as you assess ESL learners' progress and comprehension of final blends.

► Play bingo by calling out a word and having each child cover the corresponding picture with a marker. Or, make final blend cards, hold one up, and have ESL learners cover all the corresponding picture clues that match the word clues you say.

► Make word puzzles by printing target words on index cards and cutting the letters apart. Scramble the pieces, say the word, and ask ESL learners to rearrange the letters to spell, then say, the word.

► Have ESL learners complete page 253 with a peer partner.

4 APPLY

Materials:
Blending Objects activity, *MCP Phonics Teacher Resource Guide*, page 239m; realia whose names model final blends; chart paper; pencils; Picture Cards

Adapt the Blending Objects activity on page 239m to provide vocabulary recall and spelling practice with final blends.

► Bring to class several objects, such as a stamp, a ring, and so on, that represent at least four of the final blends in this lesson.

► Have ESL learners do the activity independently without using the Student Edition and Picture Cards. Provide support.

► Allow children who need additional practice to redo the activity, this time using the Student Edition and/or Picture Cards.

5 ASSESS

Materials:
Student Edition, page 254; Unit 4 Word List

Use page 254 to assess ESL learners' comprehension of final blends. After completing the activity and reviewing answers, give ESL learners a brief "test" using words from the worksheet. Say an incomplete sentence and have children fill in the missing word to practice vocabulary, using the vocabulary from the worksheet in context. (*I like to eat cookies with cold __. Before I go shopping I make a __.*)

Book Corner

MORE PHONICS PRACTICE

Set aside class time to read trade books with ESL learners. Preview these books and do a first reading to children.

THAT PIG CAN'T DO A THING by Carolyn Clark. Ready Readers, Stage 2 (Modern Curriculum Press, 1996)

AT THE POND by Janis Asad Raabe. Phonics Practice Readers (Modern Curriculum Press, 1986)

Technology

AstroWord

Ask groups of children (ESL learners and native speakers of English) to explore the activities included on the CD-ROM *AstroWord Consonant Blends and Digraphs* (Module 6). Encourage them to work together to complete activities that interest them. Assign specific tasks to children who need additional practice with final blends. Monitor each group for equal participation and progress.

Lesson 123
Blends

INFORMAL ASSESSMENT OBJECTIVES

Can children

✔ identify initial blends to name pictures?

✔ identify final blends to name pictures?

★ *Native speakers of Spanish may be more familiar with initial consonant blends, which are common in that language.*

1 INTRODUCE

Materials:
Index cards, markers

Begin reviewing initial and final blends simultaneously as an informal assessment of ESL learners' recall and mastery of unit content.

➤ Prepare 10–12 blend cards, using both initial and final blends. Print the letters only (such as *sl* and *ng*) in the center of the card. (In both positions *st* and *sk* are correct.) Place cards face down.

➤ Tell ESL learners to select a card and identify the blend (beginning, ending, or both). Have them name two words that contain the blend. Allow children to use their Student Editions to find words containing the blends.

➤ Recycle the cards in another session. Display them face up, say a word, and have ESL learners point to the blend they hear in the word; or pair a more proficient child with a less proficient learner and have them play the game together.

➤ Use the activities to assess which skills ESL learners must practice and review further: spelling, recognition, pronunciation.

2 TEACH

Materials:
Sound to Letter activity, *MCP Phonics Teacher Resource Guide,* page 255; Student Edition, page 255

Adapt the Sound to Letter activity on page 255 to be more visually oriented for ESL learners who need visual support.

➤ Use word puzzles. Print a word on a card or a strip of paper (*sled*), cut it apart (*sl - e - d*), and display the pieces on a desk.

➤ Begin with the pieces close together. Have ESL learners look at the word and read it aloud as you slide the pieces apart.

➤ Ask children to slide the pieces back together and read the word again. Repeat with several words; then repeat the activity for words with final blends.

176

★ *For specific notes on various home languages, see pages xiii–xvii of this Guide.*

3 PRACTICE

Materials:
Student Edition,
pages 255–256

Use the worksheets on pages 255–256 as follow-up practice and comprehension checks for strategies suggested in Teach.

➤ Review the task by using the *sled* word puzzle. Have children complete page 255 individually.

➤ After reviewing answers, ask ESL learners to circle the other picture that begins with the same sound (for example, in item 1, *slide*).

➤ Have ESL learners review picture clues on page 256 before completing the worksheet. Remind them to listen to the ending sounds.

4 APPLY

Materials:
Treasure Word Hunt activity, *MCP Phonics Teacher Resource Guide,* page 239m; newspapers and magazines, scissors, tape or paste, cardboard "coins" or index cards, box or bag

Use the Treasure Word Hunt activity for additional practice with lesson content and vocabulary.

➤ Have children prepare three to five coins each. If cardboard coins are not available, have them paste their words on index cards.

➤ Drop "word coins" into "treasure chest." Ask each ESL learner to take out a coin and read the word. To practice recognition of blends, have them identify beginning/final blends; to practice recall and pronunciation, have them supply rhyming words.

➤ Remind children they can use the pictures from the Student Edition to find another word with the target blend.

5 ASSESS

Materials:
Index cards, six-eight objects whose names have blends

Have children identify and associate names of visuals with consonant blends they hear. Display objects (a ring, a star, a flag). Prepare one card for each object and print the appropriate blend on the card (*ng, st, fl*). Shuffle cards and have ESL learners place each next to the correct object. Have them create a blend list by printing each name. Have children read their lists to a partner. Review misconceptions.

Book Corner

MORE PHONICS PRACTICE

Set aside class time to read trade books with ESL learners. Preview these books and do a first reading to children.

WHERE DOES THE RABBIT HOP? by Cass Hollander. Ready Readers, Stage 2 (Modern Curriculum Press, 1996)

HUNK OF JUNK by Janis Asad Raabe. Phonics Practice Readers (Modern Curriculum Press, 1986)

Technology

AstroWord
Some learners will benefit from additional practice and linguistic interaction, such as that provided by the CD-ROM *AstroWord Consonant Blends and Digraphs* (Module 6). Encourage native speakers of English and ESL learners to work together on *Listen & Write,* in which children listen to clues and write the appropriate responses. Offer assistance while monitoring progress.

Lesson 124
Blends

INFORMAL ASSESSMENT OBJECTIVES

Can children

✔ write words containing initial and final blends to finish sentences about a story?

✔ write a get-well note?

★ *In some cultures, animals customarily are not kept as pets. Explain to ESL learners that many people in the United States care for animals as if they were members of the family.*

1 INTRODUCE

Materials:
Realia and visuals pertaining to pets (such as dishes and pet beds)

Encourage ESL learners to share personal experiences about caring for sick family members or pets.

➤ Have volunteers talk about the lesson topics. Bring visuals to class to stimulate children's imagination and encourage oral participation.

➤ Give the group an oral preview of the story. Use facial expressions, gestures, synonyms, and visuals to introduce new story vocabulary. (For example, introduce broth as a kind of soup.)

2 TEACH

Materials:
Student Edition, page 257

Review words from the story with initial and final blends and have children read "A Friend in Need."

➤ Ask ESL learners to scan the story and underline words they know that contain consonant blends. Verify and then have children say the words.

➤ Print the words on the chalkboard. Have volunteers circle the letters that stand for the blend sounds. Correct misconceptions orally.

➤ Prompt children to find words with blends other than those studied in the previous lessons, such as *soft, cold, Champ,* and *fresh.*

➤ Read the story aloud in small groups. Discuss the Think! question.

★ *For specific notes on various home languages, see pages xiii–xvii of this Guide.*

3 PRACTICE

Materials:
Student Edition,
pages 213–214

Practice target objectives by having ESL learners complete the worksheets in pairs.

➤ Ask each ESL learner to contribute one thing she or he remembers about "A Friend in Need." Assist by asking related questions.

➤ Have pairs complete the sentences on page 257; then have them read their sentences to one another. Assist with pronunciation.

➤ With ESL learners who need support, review the story and brainstorm ideas for the writing task on page 258. Create a Language Experience Chart Story with less proficient ESL learners. Allow children to use the chart story as a reference when writing.

➤ Ask children to identify blends in each word in the list.

➤ Have pairs of children exchange notes and read them aloud.

4 APPLY

Materials:
Toss a Word activity
and Blackline Master
31, *MCP Phonics
Teacher Resource
Guide,* pages
239n–239o

Have groups play Toss-a-Word to practice spelling words with blends.

➤ Reproduce Blackline Master 31 on page 239o and cut the cards apart. Make the cube or cover a number cube with masking tape and print the consonant blends on each side.

➤ Model playing Toss-a-Word before asking ESL learners to play.

➤ Have ESL learners practice pronouncing and using the words they form in context sentences.

5 ASSESS

Materials:
*MCP Phonics
Teacher Resource
Guide,* pages 239k,
258

Give spelling test using Unit 4 Word List to assess ESL learners' ability to write words with blends. Refer to guidelines and list on the page 258. After checking work, return papers and have children write context sentences using the words. Work with them to create sentences. Encourage oral production, but assist with correct sentence construction. Ask them to read several sentences. Verify correct usage and pronunciation.

MORE PHONICS PRACTICE

Set aside class time to read trade books with ESL learners. Preview these books and do a first reading to children.

GLENDA THE LION by Gary Pernick. Ready Readers, Stage 2 (Modern Curriculum Press, 1996)

WEST WIND by Marjorie Eberts and Margaret Gisler. Phonics Practice Readers (Modern Curriculum Press, 1986)

AstroWord

Ask ESL learners and native speakers of English to explore the activities included on the CD-ROM *AstroWord Consonant Blends and Digraphs* (Module 6). Encourage them to work together to complete activities that interest them. Offer support, monitor group progress, and ask focus questions to elicit answers containing the target blends.

Lessons 125–126
y as a Vowel

> **INFORMAL ASSESSMENT OBJECTIVES**
>
> **Can children**
>
> ✔ discriminate between the consonant and vowel sounds of *y*?
>
> ✔ identify picture names and spell words that contain the vowel sounds of *y*?
>
> ✔ write words that contain *y* as a vowel to complete sentences?
>
> ★ *Native speakers of Spanish will have little trouble with the sounds of* y, *since* y *functions as a consonant and vowel in Spanish as well. However, they may confuse the sound of* j *in English with the sound of* y *in Spanish. Provide practice opportunities if you note native-language interference.*

1 INTRODUCE

Materials:
Phonics Picture Cards (numbers 7, 42, 137); Student Edition, pages 260 and 262

Use Picture Cards in order to activate background vocabulary and to illustrate the three sounds that the letter *y* stands for.

➤ Display the Picture Cards one at a time. Have children name them aloud and print the words on the board. Offer assistance.

➤ As you say each word, indicate the sound that the *y* stands for. Ask ESL learners to say other words they know that contain a *y* with the same sound.

➤ Tell children to name the picture clues on pages 260 and 262. Ask them to tell which sound the *y* in each word stands for (the sound they hear).

2 TEACH

Materials:
Student Edition, page 259

Assess ESL learners' comprehension of the sounds of *y* as you focus their efforts on the two target vowel sounds of *y*.

➤ Summarize the rules for ESL learners: When *y* is at the beginning of a word, it stands for a consonant sound, as in *yes, yell*. When it is part of a one-syllable word, it stands for the long *i* sound, as in *sky, try*. When it is at the end of a two-syllable (or more) word, it stands for the long *e* sound, as in *baby, happy*.

➤ Have ESL learners scan the rhyme on page 259 and sort *y* words into three lists (consonant, long *i* sound, long *e* sound). They should then work in pairs and compare their lists.

★ *For specific notes on various home languages, see pages xiii–xvii of this Guide.*

3 PRACTICE

Materials:
Phonics Picture Cards (numbers 7, 42, 137); Student Edition, pages 259, 260, 262; game markers

Practice using the sounds of *y* with Picture Cards as visual clues and stressing the sound-to-letter functions of *y*.

➤ Review the sounds of *y*. Hold up each Picture Card, and have ESL learners cover all words on page 259 that contain the same sound of *y*. Then ask individuals to complete the worksheet per directions.

➤ Have ESL learners identify the picture clues on pages 260 and 262 before they complete the tasks. Remind children to listen for and identify the beginning sounds as well as the sounds of *y* to determine the correct spelling of each picture's name.

4 APPLY

Materials:
Y Books activity, *MCP Phonics Teacher Resource Guide*, page 239m; construction paper; markers; crayons

Prepare *Y* Books in small groups as a vocabulary review apparatus, focusing on words with the vowel sounds of *y*.

➤ Ask children to work in pairs or small groups to brainstorm lists of words.

➤ Prepare the books as described in page 239m.

➤ Review the books and have ESL learners say or write context sentences using the target words.

5 ASSESS

Materials:
Student Edition, page 261; index cards

Adapt page 261 for ESL learners to practice in pairs. Prepare activity word flash cards to review with ESL learners before they complete the worksheet on page 261. Have children check their own work (before you do) by reading their completed sentences to one another and verifying the correct words from the list of choices. Check their work; then give the spelling test in a later session.

Book Corner

MORE PHONICS PRACTICE

Set aside class time to read trade books with ESL learners. Preview these books and do a first reading to children.

SALLY'S SPACESHIP by Susan McCloskey. Ready Readers, Stage 2 (Modern Curriculum Press, 1996)

PING-PONG KING by Marjorie Eberts and Margaret Gisler. Phonics Practice Readers (Modern Curriculum Press, 1986)

Technology

AstroWord

Invite children to complete some of the intergalactic activities on the CD-ROM *AstroWord Consonant Blends and Digraphs* (Module 6). Ask small groups of English-speaking children and ESL learners to work together as you focus their efforts on continued practice with the vowel sounds of *y*. Monitor groups for equal participation and progress.

Lesson 127
Consonant Blends

1 INTRODUCE

Materials:
Student Edition, page 263; index cards

Review consonant blend sounds and familiar words before completing the activity on page 263 in small groups.

➤ Print *lamp, step, milk,* and so on on index cards, one word per card. Ask volunteers to read the words aloud. Explain the meanings of words, as needed. Reinforce pronunciation by having ESL learners repeat the words.

➤ Cut the word cards apart and scramble the letters. Prompt responses with incomplete sentences for each word, such as *I make a sandwich with _____.*

➤ Have ESL learners work together in pairs, assisting them as needed with unscrambling the words on page 263. Then complete items 1–6. Verify responses aloud.

2 TEACH

Materials:
MCP Phonics Teacher Resource Guide: Short Vowel Bingo activity, page 75l; Unit 4 Word List, page 239k (one copy per child), playing grid, game markers or buttons

Play Blend Tic-tac-toe by adapting the Short Vowel Bingo activity found on page 75l.

➤ Prepare a large, nine-square tic-tac-toe grid and copy (one copy per child).

➤ Provide children with words from the Unit 4 Word List. Instruct them to write one word in each of the nine grid squares. Make sure ESL learners know the meanings of the words they choose.

➤ Hand out game markers to cover squares. Call out words from the Word List at random as children cover matching words. Have them call out "Tic-tac-toe" and read off the covered words aloud when they match three in a row.

★ *For specific notes on various home languages, see pages xiii–xvii of this Guide.*

3 PRACTICE

Materials:
Student Edition, page 263; teacher-prepared worksheet

Use page 263 of the Student Edition to provide small-group reading practice for ESL learners.

➤ Copy the word list on the chalkboard and do a closed-book review with ESL learners. Challenge children to supply additional words containing the same target sound (*fresh: fry, friend,* and so on).

➤ Have two or three children read the sentences aloud to each other.

➤ Prepare a worksheet (four to six sentences) that employs the same format and strategy. Choose known words. Ask children to complete it individually. Check ability to complete the task.

4 APPLY

Materials:
Using Describing Words activity, *MCP Phonics Teacher Resource Guide,* page 239m; chalkboard, chart paper, pencils, crayons

Have children practice critical-thinking and writing skills by adapting the Using Describing Words activity.

➤ Work with small groups of ESL learners of varying language proficiency. (Include fluent English-speaking children, if possible.)

➤ Brainstorm a list of describing words; cue children by providing a target sound and an example (such as *y: happy, tidy; sl: sly, slow*).

➤ Talk about what each word means. Orally brainstorm a sentence for each word. Ask children to write several sentences using describing words from the list; then draw a picture to illustrate each sentence.

5 ASSESS

Materials:
Student Edition, page 264; newspaper flyers, supermarket circulars, and coupons

Have ESL learners create shopping lists to use acquired vocabulary to practice lesson objectives. Provide flyers, ads, or grocery coupons to stimulate ideas. Talk about shopping and have children share items they would buy from the visuals you provided. Have each ESL learner create a shopping list by writing the list or cutting and pasting pictures. Help children write words to go with their picture lists.

Book Corner

MORE PHONICS PRACTICE

Set aside class time to read trade books with ESL learners. Preview these books and do a first reading to children.

A FUN PLACE TO EAT by Beth Jenkins Grout. Ready Readers, Stage 2 (Modern Curriculum Press, 1996)

STAN THE SQUID by Janis Asad Raabe. Phonics Practice Readers (Modern Curriculum Press, 1986)

Technology

AstroWord

Some children will benefit from additional practice and feedback, using the CD-ROM *AstroWord Consonant Blends and Digraphs* (Module 6). Encourage native speakers of English and ESL learners to work on *Make-a-Word,* where children help alien creatures create words based on a picture clue. Monitor each group's progress.

Lesson 128
Reviewing Blends

INFORMAL ASSESSMENT OBJECTIVE

Can children

✔ read words with consonant blends and *y* as a vowel in the context of a story?

1 INTRODUCE

Materials:
Cookbook with color photos; pizza

Point out to ESL learners that the theme for Unit 4 is Everybody Eats. Talk about foods that children enjoy to introduce the Take-Home Book.

➤ Display a picture of one of your favorite foods. Tell ESL learners which ingredients are needed to prepare it.

➤ Ask children what types of foods they eat in their culture. Invite ESL learners to talk about them and tell how they are prepared.

➤ Since many ESL learners will probably have tasted pizza, ask which toppings are their favorites. Make a list of the most popular ones on the chalkboard. Have children read them aloud after you. Chart favorite responses. Enjoy pizza samples in class.

2 TEACH

Materials:
Pizza Feast Take-Home Book, Student Edition, pages 265–266; teacher-prepared blend cards

Discuss the *Pizza Feast* Take-Home Book with ESL learners and review words containing consonant blends and *y* as a vowel.

➤ Assist children in making their Take-Home Books.

➤ Have each child pick a blend card and scan the story for words that begin or end with *spr, st, sl, ng, pr, fl, lt, cr, sp, sm,* or *gr.*

➤ Introduce less-familiar story words such as *water, dough, sauce, cheese, toppings,* and *different.*

★ *For specific notes on various home languages, see pages xiii–xvii of this Guide.*

3 PRACTICE

Materials:
Pizza Feast Take-Home Book

Determine which skills your ESL learners need to practice and implement the Take-Home Book accordingly.

➤ For children who need additional support with pronunciation, read the story aloud and review target or problem sounds.

➤ Build vocabulary by asking volunteers to explain story words.

➤ Confirm comprehension with content-related questions. Discuss the Talk About It question in small groups.

4 APPLY

Materials:
Construction paper, markers, crayons, tape or paste

Provide ESL learners with additional practice by having them create a pepperoni blend pizza.

➤ Cut large circles from construction paper. Have children color the sauce red. They can cut out small pieces for toppings and paste them to the pizza.

➤ Supply each ESL learner with five smaller circles ("pepperoni"). Assign specific blends or *y* sounds; have children print one target word on each slice of pepperoni and attach it to the pizza.

➤ Have ESL learners produce target words independently at first; allow them to use visual clues from the Student Edition, if required.

5 ASSESS

Materials:
Pizza Feast Take-Home Book; teacher-prepared worksheet

Prepare a worksheet of 3–5 fill-in sentences from the story for ESL learners to complete, using blends in context. Ask children to give a brief oral summary of the story. Hand out worksheets. Allow children to use the Take-Home Book to find the missing words on their own. Ask children to form pairs and read their completed sentences aloud to one another. Assess written and oral work.

Book Corner

MORE PHONICS PRACTICE

Set aside class time to read trade books with ESL learners. Preview these books and do a first reading to children.

SALLY'S SPACESHIP by Susan McCloskey. Ready Readers, Stage 2 (Modern Curriculum Press, 1996)

A SKUNK IN CAMP by Dr. Alvin Granowsky. Phonics Practice Readers (Modern Curriculum Press, 1986)

Technology

AstroWord

Have ESL learners work in pairs or small groups on the AstroWord Notebook and Letter Board, found on the *AstroWord Consonant Blends and Digraphs* (Module 6) CD-ROM. Give ESL learners and their English proficient peers a specific task, and have them create a list of words they learned using consonant blends and *y* as a vowel. Check word lists and monitor progress for equal participation.

Lesson 129
Reviewing Consonant Blends and *y* as a Vowel

INFORMAL ASSESSMENT OBJECTIVES

Can children

✔ identify picture names and words that contain blends?

✔ read words that contain blends and *y* as a vowel?

1 INTRODUCE

Materials:
Self-adhesive notes; Unit 4 Checkup worksheet, Student Edition, page 267

Assess ESL learners' ability to recognize words with consonant blends and *y* as a vowel using practical classroom examples.

➤ Give each ESL learner a self-adhesive note on which you have written a blend.

➤ Tell children to stick their notes on classroom objects whose names model their blend sounds. Have volunteers name the objects aloud.

➤ As a group, review picture clue names aloud before beginning the activity on page 267. Allow ESL learners who are unsure to work with an English-proficient peer on items 1–6. Review together; then ask them to complete items 7–12 individually. Check answers orally as a class.

2 PRACTICE

Materials:
Student Edition, page 268

Reviewing the words in the activity word list will greatly facilitate ESL learners' completion of the worksheet on page 268.

➤ After ESL learners complete items 1–6 independently or in pairs, have them go back and underline any consonant blends in the distractors.

➤ As you review answers, ask that ESL learners read aloud the answers they chose and the distractors.

Book Corner

MORE PHONICS PRACTICE

Set aside class time to read trade books with ESL learners. Preview these books and do a first reading to children.

THE RIVER GROWS by Gale Clifford. Ready Readers, Stage 2 (Modern Curriculum Press, 1996)

LES IS LAST by Marjorie Eberts and Margaret Gisler. Phonics Practice Readers (Modern Curriculum Press, 1986)

Assessment Strategy Overview

Throughout Unit 5 you have opportunities to assess ESL learners' abilities to read and write words with inflectional endings, consonant digraphs, and contractions. These skills may be challenging for ESL learners. Note pronunciation difficulties but assess children's work based on their abilities to distinguish the endings, the digraphs, and the contractions when pronounced by a native speaker.

FORMAL ASSESSMENT

Before you start Unit 5, administer the Unit 5 Pretest, found on pages 269e–269f of *MCP Phonics Teacher Resource Guide*. Children's scores will help you assess their knowledge base before beginning the unit and alert you to areas for further support. Complete the Student Progress Checklist on page 269i. Based on their responses to the Unit 5 Pretest, note with which phonics concepts children are struggling. Monitor performance.

♦ Before administering the Pretest, preview picture clues on page 269e so that children are familiar with the picture names. They can focus on matching the answer choices to the picture clues.

♦ Preview the contractions and inflectional endings on page 269f by writing on the board the complete words that make up the contractions, and the words without the inflectional endings. Then have children match the contractions to the complete words on the board and pronounce the contractions and inflectional endings chorally.

INFORMAL ASSESSMENT

Review pages, Unit Checkups, and Take-Home Books are effective ways to evaluate children's progress. Following are other suggestions for informal ways to assess children's understanding of the concepts.

♦ Bring to class props that use the target sounds on page 269e. Say and write each word as you identify it. Have children identify the letters that stand for the sounds of each consonant digraph.

PORTFOLIO ASSESSMENT

Portfolio Assessment opportunities are identified by the logo shown here. In addition to collecting the pages mentioned on page 269c, gather other children's work for comparison and evaluation at critical periods in the unit, as indicated below.

♦ **Initial practice** Encourage ESL learners to use the level of language at which you and they feel they are comfortable to add to portfolios. Analyze entries on a regular basis to identify areas of strength and weakness. Based on ESL learners' work, provide extra practice.

♦ **Midunit classwork** Have each ESL learner create a personal Language Bank of words and phonics skills that include self-correction of misunderstood concepts. Assess "books" to determine areas that need reinforcement and tailor practice opportunities to meet these.

♦ **Final products or projects** Review ESL learners' progress in completing the Curriculum Connections Portfolio activities in the *MCP Phonics Teacher Resource Guide*. Compare later entries to earlier work. Use the Student Progress Checklist on page 269i to assess areas of difficulty.

STUDENT PROGRESS CHECKLIST

Photocopy and attach the checklist on page 269i of *MCP Phonics Teacher Resource Guide* to each child's portfolio. Evaluate growth and areas of weakness from your assessment tools. Use the strategies and activities in this Guide to build a strong phonics foundation for your ESL learners.

Administering and Evaluating the
Pretest and Posttest

➤ Read the information on page 269d of *MCP Phonics Teacher Resource Guide*. Answers for the Pretest and the Posttest are provided on page 269d.

➤ Record test results on the Student Progress Checklist on page 269i after children complete the Pretest.

➤ Record results again after children take the Posttest.

➤ Compare the results of the two tests.

➤ Use the Performance Assessment Profile at the bottom of page 269d to help you draw conclusions about children's performances. Opportunities to reteach each specific skill in the unit are identified by page number.

TEST OBJECTIVES

The objectives of both the Unit 5 Pretest and the Posttest of *MCP Phonics Teacher Resource Guide* are to correctly use words with inflectional endings, consonant digraphs, and contractions. ESL learners may find that some structures in English are not customary in their native languages (especially Asian languages). Have children practice saying the picture clues aloud as you stress the target sound aloud and matching contractions to the complete words that make up the contractions. Reinforce with frequent reading and spelling opportunities throughout the unit.

UNIT 5 PRETEST, pages 269e–269f

Page 269e of *MCP Phonics Teacher Resource Guide* focuses on identifying and naming picture clues that contain consonant digraphs. Implement any of the following suggestions prior to assigning the Pretest.

◆ **Practice test-taking skills.** Some ESL learners may not recognize the picture clues on page 269e and, therefore, cannot pronounce the word names on their own. Ask them to listen to a picture name as you say it aloud and demonstrate with realia or a photograph of the item. Have children repeat after you. Follow this process for items 1–12.

◆ **Adjust pacing.** Some ESL learners may feel intimidated by children who appear to complete the tests more quickly or more easily than they do. Conduct the Pretest in small groups with children who need special pacing and provide frequent encouragement and support for their efforts.

◆ **Analyze results.** Depending on their levels of English proficiency, some ESL learners may not test well. Use the Pretest results as a measure for growth. Provide frequent opportunities for individual children to practice the phonics skills with which they are either unfamiliar or demonstrate difficulty.

Page 269f focuses on inflectional endings and contractions and requires children to read full sentences and insert the correct choice. You may wish to incorporate these strategies as you assign the test.

♦ **Read the prompts aloud to ESL learners.** Items 13–20 require children to read the hints. If necessary, read them aloud to ESL learners and pantomime the meanings for children to respond to. Then have them discriminate among the answer choices for the best answer choice.

♦ **Preview answer choices.** Use word lists that include the complete words that make up the contractions and the words without the inflectional endings, charts, and Book Corner literature suggestions to provide pretest practice. This will familiarize your ESL learners with the structures and the rules behind them.

♦ **Work in groups.** If the Pretest on page 269f appears to be too overwhelming for some ESL learners, work in small groups or one-on-one and read aloud, or have children read the answer choices. Provide prompts and support as determined by children's ability levels.

♦ **Work one-on-one.** Children who are unable to read print independently in English can complete the activities orally with you, during class or at a separate time. At a later time, work on developing print fluency.

Check ESL learners' scores on the Unit 5 Pretest on page 269f. Confirm areas of difficulty and adapt test-taking strategies as needed. You may wish to use these suggestions for ESL learners as they complete pages 269g–269h.

♦ **Confirm children understand directions.** Read aloud the directions for each page and ensure that children know how to proceed. Model what they are expected to do, working one-on-one with ESL learners who need focused attention.

♦ **Eliminate overwhelming tasks.** Even by the end of the unit, some ESL learners may be unable to read well enough in English to complete page 269h alone. For children who experience difficulties, read each incomplete sentence aloud (and answer choices, if necessary) and emphasize the inflectional ending or contraction. Prompt children who are uncertain of their responses. Or conduct the test orally, allowing ESL learners to give verbal responses.

♦ **Create context.** Some children may be distracted by the "text heaviness" of page 269h. Point out that the sentences all form a story. Summarize the sequence of events in the story so children can follow the action. Then, read each sentence aloud. Read the answer choices aloud to children and guide them to select the best choice.

Spelling Connections

Pages 269j–269k of *MCP Phonics Teacher Resource Guide* provide a collection of ideas and opportunities to actively incorporate spelling into your phonics program. It is recommended that ESL learners reach the intermediate fluency level of English proficiency before focusing on spelling.

✳ **Anticipate problem words.** Anticipated areas of difficulty for children who speak Spanish, Korean, Hmong, Khmer, Russian, or Vietnamese are noted by a star in the Informal Assessment Objectives box at the beginning of each lesson in this Guide. You may wish to refer to these notes as you progress through specific lessons, especially as you make the link between oral and written language. These notes include letters, sounds, language structures, and positions of letters in words that may not exist, may be spelled differently, or may sound different in the native language of your ESL learners.

✳ **Develop personalized dictionaries.** Encourage children to add to their lists of new words those with which they have difficulty or are unfamiliar. Accustom children to writing new words on their lists. Review regularly with ESL learners and have children sound them out and spell them for you, first by sight-reading, then from memory. Have them draw or cut-and-paste a picture of each word on individual pages and print the word name beneath each picture.

✳ **Provide frequent minilessons.** Repeated misspellings often indicate children do not understand how to spell words correctly. Provide ESL learners with customized minilessons in which they can be taught phonics skills. First, provide examples of words. Then explain a rule that is a source of misspellings. Provide written, oral, and physical (gestures, pantomimes) reinforcements and examples. Supplement with practice in the form of short drills, writing charts, and opportunities to write independently in spelling dictionaries, journals, and so on.

✳ **Enhance meanings with visuals.** To ensure a link between oral speech and the written form of words, speak in simple, complete sentences and at a natural, but not exaggerated, pace. Have children connect the visuals, the sounds, and the spelling words by posting throughout your classroom picture clues with the spelled words beneath them. Use the picture clues to introduce, model, and prompt meanings. Then cover up the printed words to assess spelling mastery and conduct an oral or a written spelling test of new spelling words in the unit.

✳ **Link sounds and print.** Incorporating listening tools such as audiotapes and CDs provides additional modalities through which ESL learners can acquire English. Have children work with partners to say the spelling words into a tape recorder. Have children record the words they hear. Have ESL learners check their work against their Unit Spelling lists.

✳ **Read it, write it, remember it.** Encourage ESL learners to commit spelling to memory. Ask ESL learners to copy the words from the Unit Word List onto individual index cards. Have them study four or five words daily at frequent intervals—before recess and lunch, during center time, at home, and during other routine activities, such as during homework or bathing.

✳ **Conduct oral spelling drills.** Use oral repetition, as a large group or in smaller groups, at a listening station. Provide quick drill opportunities to reinforce similarities, differences, or other word associations.

✳ **Make writing fun.** Use fun writing mediums such as shaving cream, paints, clay, twine and sandpaper, and sand to practice spelling new or unfamiliar words. Children will have fun with the materials and enjoy writing the words you ask them to spell. Correct spelling before children "erase" their responses.

✳ **Incorporate games and flashcards into spelling practice.** Have ESL learners copy the words from the word list onto individual flashcards. Distribute words in specific letter patterns to small groups of children. Have children take turns playing "teacher" and quizzing the other group members orally on the words in their set. After all the children have had a chance to spell each word in a set, exchange with another group.

✳ **Practice taking dictation.** Model the activity with words children already know and can spell. Preteach new words a few at a time, using visuals, props, gestures, and contexts to enhance meanings. Write the words for children and allow them to trace each one as they sound it out aloud. Then continue with Steps 1–3 of the Introduction on page 269j.

✳ **Incorporate journal writing in your class.** Encourage ESL learners to free-write in English and to use spelling words as prompts for free expression. Have children review their journal writings with you one-on-one and decorate their pages with artwork, photos, pictures, or realia.

Blackline Master 38 (page 269k) contains 16 words grouped by inflectional endings, consonant digraphs, and contractions. For ESL learners, introduce the words and their meanings, in each group separately, three or four at a time, through visuals or realia. Provide ample practice over time and contextual background when introducing the words.

Unit 5

Phonics Games, Activities, and Technology

Pages 269l–269n of *MCP Phonics Teacher Resource Guide* provide a collection of ideas to actively engage children as they develop phonics skills. Many of the activities provided on these pages can be implemented with little or no modification for children whose native languages are not English. However, be alert to pictures clues that are unfamiliar in contexts or in their names. Multistep directions may also be difficult for some ESL learners to understand or follow. You may need to take longer time and make sure children understand one step before moving onto the next step.

To ensure comprehension of activity directions, speak in simple, complete sentences and at a natural, not exaggerated, pace. Incorporating visuals and props, audiotapes and CDs provides additional contexts and clues for new learners of English. For activities that require a written response, determine whether children have sufficient command of written print to complete the activities. Be aware that some children may write in cursive letters.

● **Yesterday** (page 269l) and **Flip My Lid** (page 269n) can be made more visual for ESL learners by posting a time chart, or continuum, in class. On 2 different colored sheets of construction paper, each about 3 feet long (and with arrows at left) write *Yesterday* and *Today*. Under *Yesterday* write *-ed* and under *Today* write *-ing*. Use the chart as a prompt for sequence of action and the corresponding inflectional endings.

▲ **Sneaky *H*** and **Alliterative Sentences** (page 269l) may be difficult for ESL learners to complete orally or with the class. In small groups, have children rewrite the words and then underline or recolor the consonant digraph. Ask them to read the list of original words; then read the new words. Last, have children read the word followed by the new word. Model correct pronunciation and have ESL learners repeat after you.

◆ **Contraction Slides** (page 269l) and **Contraction Action** (page 269m) are practical activities for ESL learners, most of whom are unfamiliar with contractions. Encourage ESL learners to use these manipulatives whenever they need to check their own work.

■ **Special Word Wall** (page 269l) can include ESL learners' personalized spelling lists or journal words. Encourage each ESL learner to add one or more words to the word wall every day of the unit. Schedule a few minutes each day for children to use these words in sentences or phrases so they become accustomed to hearing and using them actively in English. Suggest to ESL learners that they use the word wall as a prompt when they play **Word Clues** (page 269m).

- *CH* **Sandwiches**, **Digraph Necklaces**, and *SH* **Shelf** (page 269m) can be completed successfully by having ESL learners work in pairs. Have children take turns using reference materials, such as the Unit Word List, personalized dictionaries, journals, or Book Corner literature references as sources for words containing the target consonant digraphs.

- ▲ **Action words** (page 269n) require that ESL learners have a strong vocabulary of action verbs. Prompt with flashcards and picture clues cut out from magazines, or photographs that model actions memory of words ESL learners may have been introduced to but have forgotten. To reinforce meanings, take turns acting out the action words they generate as the group says, "_____ is _____ing."

Technology

Use children's interest in technology to their advantage in learning English. If possible, allow ESL learners to work in small groups at the computer before or after class or during center time, using the specific *AstroWord* CD-ROM Modules suggested in each lesson. Preview skill levels and supervise the groups directly to eliminate frustration and to guide phonics development. You may wish to add your observations to the Student Progress Checklist, found on page 269i, of *MCP Phonics Teacher Resource Guide*, as well as use the software suggested on page 269n to provide additional phonics practice for ESL learners.

Lessons 130–131
Inflectional Endings *-ed* and *-ing*

INFORMAL ASSESSMENT OBJECTIVES

Can children

✔ form new words by adding *-ed* and *-ing* to base words?

✔ identify base words that end in *-ed* and *-ing*?

✔ identify a word with the ending *-ed* or *-ing* to complete a sentence?

★ *Native speakers of Spanish, Russian, Chinese, and many other languages may mispronounce /n/ for /ng/ and /ed/ for /d/. Practice the following pairs with children who demonstrate pronunciation difficulty:* sin, sing; thin, thing; sun, sung.

---

1 INTRODUCE

Materials:
Student Edition, page 271; Blackline Master 39, *MCP Phonics Teacher Resource Guide,* page 269o; index cards; book from the Book Corner

Use auditory and visual support to introduce the concept of word endings and inflectional meanings to ESL learners.

➤ Explain that endings change the meanings of words. Read the rhyme aloud and show *rained* and *raining* as examples.

➤ Have ESL learners read words with inflectional endings in the rhyme. Have them cover each ending and read the base word aloud. Accustom them to visualize the base word and the ending separately.

➤ Prepare cards from Blackline Master 39 and two ending cards (*-ing, -ed*). Have ESL learners use the cards to form and read words.

➤ Using a book from the Book Corner, ask ESL learners to locate target words in a paragraph or page you select.

2 TEACH

Materials:
Chart paper

Offer ESL learners one-on-one support on inflectional endings.

➤ On chart paper, review present and past tenses of *to be*; verify correct usage with different subjects (*you are,* not *you am*). Have ESL learners generate their own sentences to practice the forms.

➤ Point out that *-ing* forms of verbs are used with *to be.* Use several *I go/I am going* sentences to illustrate. Separately, teach *I am going/I was going.*

➤ With *-ed* past tenses, verify they discriminate between *ask, asked; bump, bumped;* asking them to raise hands as you give examples.

➤ Stress the pronunciation of an additional syllable on base words that end in *d* or *t,* as in *paint, painted; want, wanted; end, ended.*

★ *For specific notes on various home languages, see pages xiii–xvii of this Guide.*

3 PRACTICE

Materials:
Student Edition, pages 271–273; 4 × 6 card

Use pages 271–273 to practice the lesson strategies and objectives and to assess ESL learners' progress with inflectional endings.

➤ Have ESL learners orally identify the picture clues and base words as a group before completing page 271 individually.

➤ Model page 272 by printing the cue words (*jumped, reading, melted, cooking*) on the board. Cover endings one at a time with a 4 × 6 card as you circle the base words.

➤ For children who are challenged by the worksheet on page 273, teach them the rule, *-ing* words are used with *was* and *were,* and have them look for those clues in each sentence.

4 APPLY

Materials:
Yesterday activity, *MCP Phonics Teacher Resource Guide*, page 269l; paper; pencil

Adapt the Yesterday activity on page 269l to practice both *-ed* and *-ing* word endings with ESL learners.

➤ Ask ESL learners to name seven to ten action words they know. If children have difficulty generating words, pantomime actions and ask them to supply the words.

➤ Write, or have ESL learners write, the words on the board.

➤ Conduct the activity on page 269l. As children exhibit mastery, include other past-tense indicators, such as *last night* and *last week.*

➤ Repeat the activity using base words + *-ing* in sentences such as "Right now I jump. Right now I am jumping."

5 ASSESS

Materials:
Student Edition, page 274

Verify ESL learners' ability to pronounce inflected verbs clearly. Have ESL learners work in groups to pronounce the verb choices on page 274 and then complete items 1–7. To summarize understanding of the rules, have children use the different forms of words (including base words) in original sentences or supply missing words in sentences you generate.

Book Corner

MORE PHONICS PRACTICE

Set aside class time to read trade books with ESL learners. Preview these books and do a first reading to children.

A LOT HAPPENED TODAY by Judy Nayer. Ready Readers, Stage 5 (Modern Curriculum Press, 1996)

THE CHICK THAT HATCHED by Dr. Alvin Granowsky. Phonics Practice Readers (Modern Curriculum Press, 1986)

CITY RHYTHMS by Judy Nayer. Discovery Phonics Readers (Modern Curriculum Press, 1992)

Lesson 132
Consonant Digraph *th*

INFORMAL ASSESSMENT OBJECTIVES

Can children

✔ identify pictures whose names begin with the digraph *th*?

✔ distinguish between the sounds of *th* and *t* in picture names?

★ *Some ESL learners may confuse the sounds of* th *and* t, *but more likely may have difficulty distinguishing the initial unvoiced* th *of* thin *and* f (fin), *or voiced* th (then) *and* d (den). *Assess each child's pronunciation and offer listening and speaking practice with specific word pairs, like* three, free; than, fan; *and so on. Speakers of some Asian languages won't pronounce the* th *since it doesn't exist in these languages.*

---

1 INTRODUCE

Materials:
Chalkboard; mirrors from a science kit (optional)

Determine ESL learners' ability to produce the target sounds correctly and practice production and recognition by using target vocabulary.

➤ Work initially on correct sound production, making sure ESL learners place their tongues between their top and bottom teeth. You may wish to have children look in a mirror to visually see where their tongues are when correctly pronouncing the *th* sound.

➤ Have ESL learners pronounce target words in parts. Print words on the board and cover the *th*: *umb, thumb; ree, three;* and so on.

➤ Point out the second (voiced) sound of *th* and have children read/repeat: *this, that, the, then, them.*

2 TEACH

Materials:
Student Edition, page 275; Rhyme Poster 42 (optional); game markers

Continue practicing pronunciation recognition of *th* while teaching spelling of lesson vocabulary.

➤ Assess ESL learners' ability to hear the difference between *th* and similar sounds. Say word pairs such as *this, dish; thread, tree;* and *ten, them* and have children raise their hands when they hear *th*.

➤ Have ESL learners name aloud the picture clues on page 275. Ask them to cover with markers pictures whose names begin with the sound of *th*.

➤ Have children say the rhyme after you. Ask them to find and underline target words. Ask ESL learners to say the rhyme again, in pairs or individually.

★ *For specific notes on various home languages, see pages xiii–xvii of this Guide.*

3 PRACTICE

Materials:
Student Edition, page 275; Phonics Picture Cards (numbers 36, 82, 101, 154–156)

Use the worksheet on page 275 and a sorting sounds activity to determine ESL learners' progress with recognition of the initial digraph *th*.

▶ Display the Picture Cards face up in a grid. Ask ESL learners to say the picture names and then sort the cards into two piles according to beginning sounds.

▶ Using page 275, say a word and have ESL learners point to the correct picture clue. After reviewing several items at random, have ESL learners complete the activity individually. Together with a volunteer verify responses aloud with the group.

4 APPLY

Materials:
Chalkboard; index card; Sneaky *H* activity, *MCP Phonics Teacher Resource Guide*, page 269l

Adapt the Sneaky *H* activity for additional practice with the digraph *th*.

▶ Print *th* on an index card. Print several *t* words on the board and have ESL learners read them aloud. Cover the initial *t* with the *th* card and read the new word. Words are *tin, ten, tree, tick,* and *torn*.

▶ Repeat with *h* words such as *hat, hen, hem, his,* and *hose*. Continue with words with a final *t*, such as *bat, wit,* and *mat*.

▶ Pick three or four other *th* words and encourage ESL learners to use them in oral sentences.

5 ASSESS

Materials:
Student Edition, page 276; teacher-prepared worksheet (optional)

Verify that ESL learners can pronounce *th* clearly and spell *t* versus *th* words correctly. Review sound-to-spelling distinctions with the activity on page 276. Further practice pronunciation by having ESL learners review answers aloud. Prepare a worksheet similar to the one on page 276 to practice discriminating between *th* and *f* or *d*, based on children's needs.

MORE PHONICS PRACTICE

Set aside class time to read trade books with ESL learners. Preview these books and do a first reading to children.

FIVE LITTLE DINOSAURS by Fay Robinson. Ready Readers, Stage 2 (Modern Curriculum Press, 1996)

BETH'S BATH by Dr. Alvin Granowsky. Phonics Practice Readers (Modern Curriculum Press, 1986)

AstroWord

Ask groups of ESL learners and native speakers of English to explore the activities included on the CD-ROM *AstroWord Consonant Blends and Digraphs* (Module 6). Encourage them to work together to complete activities that interest them. Offer support, monitor group progress, and ask directed questions about the sounds of the digraph *th*.

Lesson 133
Consonant Digraph *wh*

INFORMAL ASSESSMENT OBJECTIVES

Can children

✔ identify pictures whose names begin with the digraph *wh*?

✔ distinguish between the *th* and *wh* digraphs?

★ *Native speakers of Japanese, Korean, Spanish, Tagalog, and Vietnamese may confuse the initial* h *sound with the digraph* wh. *Have them practice with word pairs such as* when, hen; wheel, heel; *and* white, height.

1 INTRODUCE

Materials:
Chalkboard; Rhyme Poster 43 (optional)

Evaluate each ESL learner's pronunciation of *wh*, compared with other initial sounds the child has mastered.

➤ Print *wh* and several *wh* consonant digraph words on the board, or use the Rhyme Poster. Say each and have children repeat.

➤ Have ESL learners pronounce target words in parts as you cover the initial *wh*: *eel, wheel; ip, whip;* and so on. Note that the /w/ as well as the /hw/ pronunciations of digraph *wh* are both considered correct in standard American English. If ESL learners are challenged and unable to clearly reproduce /hw/ or are pronouncing strictly /h/, allow the /w/ pronunciation; saying *where* like *wear* is understood, while pronouncing *hair* changes the meaning.

2 TEACH

Materials:
Student Edition, page 277; Rhyme Poster 43 (optional); markers

Reinforce pronunciation and recognition of *wh* while acquainting children with lesson vocabulary.

➤ Read aloud the rhyme and pantomime the action as you explain it. Ask children to read the rhyme aloud. Work toward distinction between /w/ *wind* and /hw/ *whip*, but do not "over-correct" comprehensible pronunciation.

➤ Remind those pronouncing /w/ that the words are written with *wh*. Assess aural discrimination between the target sound and similar sounds using a "same or different" activity. Say pairs of words such as *wet, wheat; wheel, whale;* and *white, house.*

➤ Assist ESL learners in naming aloud the picture clues on page 277. Begin with shorter words and build up to more challenging vocabulary. Play bingo, having children cover target words with markers as you, or a volunteer, say them aloud.

198

★ *For specific notes on various home languages, see pages xiii–xvii of this Guide.*

3 PRACTICE

Materials:
Student Edition, pages 277–278; Teacher-prepared worksheet

Have ESL learners practice saying and writing lesson vocabulary as they discriminate similar beginning sounds.

➤ Prepare a worksheet using incomplete words from the rhyme and the lesson activities with initial *wh*, *w*, and *th* and have children work in pairs to complete it.

➤ Review the worksheet aloud as a group. Have children identify the digraph that stands for the beginning sound of the words they completed. Have them say the words aloud together.

4 APPLY

Materials:
Ch Sandwiches activity, *MCP Phonics Teacher Resource Guide*, page 269m; construction paper, markers, paste or tape

Adapt the *Ch* Sandwiches activity on to practice *wh* interrogative words.

➤ Distribute art supplies and have ESL learners make sandwiches, as described on page 269m.

➤ Print the word endings *-ere*, *-at*, *-en*, and *-y* on the board. Ask ESL learners to print complete words that begin with *wh* on their sandwiches.

➤ Review the words aloud, then practice words in context by asking a series of sandwich-related questions, such as *Where do you make sandwiches?* and *What kind of sandwich do you like?*

5 ASSESS

Materials:
Student Edition, page 278; Phonics Picture Cards (numbers 16–18, 40, 41, 84, 157–159); paper bags

Assess each ESL learner's pronunciation and recognition of the digraph *wh*. Label each of three bags *wh*, *w*, *h*. Ask children to sort the Phonics Picture Cards into the correct bag according to the beginning sound of each picture's name. Review the sounds of *wh* and *th* before completing page 278 as a group. Check for correct spelling.

Book Corner

MORE PHONICS PRACTICE

Set aside class time to read trade books with ESL learners. Preview these books and do a first reading to children.

HUMPBACK WHALES by Anna Kijak. Ready Readers, Stage 2 (Modern Curriculum Press, 1996)

THE WHITE WHALE by Dr. Alvin Granowsky. Phonics Practice Readers (Modern Curriculum Press, 1986)

Technology

AstroWord

Some ESL learners will benefit from additional practice provided by the CD-ROM *AstroWord Consonant Blends and Digraphs* (Module 6). Encourage native speakers of English and ESL learners to work together to complete the Easy level of *Word Sort*, in which children help alien creatures sort picture clues according to digraph and blend sounds. Offer assistance as you monitor progress.

Lesson 134
Consonant Digraph *sh*

INFORMAL ASSESSMENT OBJECTIVES

Can children

✔ identify pictures whose names begin with the digraph *sh*?

✔ distinguish between the sounds of *sh* and *s* in picture names?

★ *Children whose first language is Spanish or Tagalog will likely assimilate* sh *and* ch. *Native speakers of Cantonese, Khmer, Vietnamese, Hmong, or Korean may confuse* sh *with* s, ch, *or the /zh/ sound of* s *in* measure. *Practice in small groups with* cheap, sheep; chew, shoe; chair, share; *and* chip, ship.

1 INTRODUCE

Materials:
Rhyme Poster 44
(optional);
chalkboard, mirror

Identify ESL learners' abilities to produce the target sounds correctly and to practice production and recognition using lesson vocabulary or the Rhyme Poster.

➤ Print *s* and *sh* on the board. Point out the difference in sounds with word pairs, such as *sell, shell; sip, ship;* and *sort, short.*

➤ Work initially on having children produce the correct sound, making sure they do not place top and bottom teeth together as with /s/. Model how to form the sound. Then have children look in a mirror while they produce /sh/.

➤ Have children pronounce target words in parts. Print words on the board and cover the *sh: ell, shell; ade, shade;* and so on.

2 TEACH

Materials:
Student Edition,
page 279; Rhyme
Poster 44
(optional); game
markers

Continue having children recognize the initial digraph *sh* while teaching spelling of lesson vocabulary.

➤ Assess children's ability to hear the difference between the target sound and similar sounds by using a "same or different" activity. Use word pairs such as *shoe, chin; shell, shop;* and *seat, sheet.*

➤ Have ESL learners name aloud the picture clues on page 279. Ask them to cover pictures that begin with the target sound with markers.

➤ Have children say the rhyme after you model it. Ask volunteers to scan for and circle *sh* words. Have ESL learners say the rhyme again as additional practice with reading recognition and pronunciation.

★ *For specific notes on various home languages, see pages xiii–xvii of this Guide.*

3 PRACTICE

Materials:
Student Edition, page 279; Phonics Picture Cards (numbers 34, 35, 67, 164–166)

Use the worksheet on page 279 and a sorting sounds activity to determine ESL learners' progress with recognition of the initial digraph *sh.*

➤ Arrange Picture Cards face up in a grid. Ask ESL learners to sort the cards into two piles according to beginning sounds.

➤ Using the activity on page 279 as a game board, say a word and have ESL learners point to the correct picture clue. Ask them to complete the activity individually, as they did for *wh* on page 277.

4 APPLY

Materials:
Sh Shelf activity, *MCP Phonics Teacher Resource Guide*, page 269m; construction paper; tacks; markers; magazines

Prepare an *Sh* Shelf bulletin board for ESL learners to decorate with objects beginning with the target sound.

➤ Have children work in pairs to draw or clip pictures of *sh* words from magazines.

➤ Ask ESL learners to say the name of each item and to write it clearly as a label. Provide assistance as needed.

➤ Review the names of the objects aloud and have ESL learners use these words in their own sentences about their picture choices.

5 ASSESS

Materials:
Student Edition, page 280

Review sound-to-spelling distinctions of *s* versus *sh* words with the activity on page 280. Read aloud, or have volunteers read, the name of each picture clue and correct pronunciation if necessary. As a group, have ESL learners print *sh* or *s* and trace the whole word.

MORE PHONICS PRACTICE

Set aside class time to read trade books with ESL learners. Preview these books and do a first reading to children.

SHELL SHOPPING by Deana Kirk. Ready Readers, Stage 2 (Modern Curriculum Press, 1996)

SHAG AND SHEP by Dr. Alvin Granowsky. Phonics Practice Readers (Modern Curriculum Press, 1986)

LITTLE BUNNY'S LUNCH by JoAnne Nelson. Discovery Phonics (Modern Curriculum Press, 1993)

AstroWord

Some ESl learners will benefit from additional practice and feedback using the CD-ROM *AstroWord Consonant Blends and Digraphs* (Module 6). Encourage native speakers of English and ESL learners to work on *Make-a-Word,* where children help alien creatures create words based on a picture clue. Monitor each group's progress.

Lesson 135
Consonant Digraph *ch*

INFORMAL ASSESSMENT OBJECTIVES

Can children

✔ identify pictures whose names begin with the digraph *ch*?

✔ distinguish between the sounds of *ch* and *c* in picture names?

★ *Children whose home languages are Cantonese, Vietnamese, Khmer, Korean, or Hmong may confuse* ch *with* sh, *or initial* j. *Offer additional oral/aural practice, having them clearly pronounce* chair, share; chip, ship; chilly, jelly; cheap, jeep; *and so on.*

1 INTRODUCE

Materials:
Chalkboard, paper, pencils

Assess whether children can discriminate initial *ch* from *sh* or *j*; then begin building target vocabulary.

➤ Print words containing the beginning sounds of *th, wh, sh, ch* on the board; review the sound of each digraph with ESL learners. Point out the new digraph *ch* and reinforce the sound. Have children follow your oral model.

➤ Write *cheer* on the board. Ask a volunteer to define/demonstrate its meaning. Have children repeat, focusing on the initial *ch*.

➤ Tell children you will say a word. If they hear the sound of *ch* at the beginning of the word, they should cheer. Include *chin, jet, check, share, chalk, chair, sheet, cheese, jog,* and *cherry*.

➤ Write target words on the board after the activity. Have ESL learners read them aloud and copy the list in their dictionaries. Encourage children to illustrate the words.

2 TEACH

Materials:
Student Edition, page 281; Rhyme Poster 45 (optional)

Contrast the sound and spelling of *ch* against other *h*-controlled digraphs and words with initial *c*.

➤ Print word pairs on the board and demonstrate their meanings. Reinforce the previously learned digraphs. Word pairs include *think, chick; whale, chair; ship, chip; cat, chat;* and *cow, cheese.*

➤ Have ESL learners find target words in the rhyme and read them aloud. In pairs, or small groups, have children read the rhyme to each other. Monitor for pronunciation and word recognition.

★ *For specific notes on various home languages, see pages xiii–xvii of this Guide.*

3 PRACTICE

Materials:
Student Edition, page 281; realia that models initial *ch* sound; self-stick note

Practice naming visuals that model the initial *ch* sound in preparation for the activity on page 281.

➤ Display five objects with initial *ch*. Write each name on the board.

➤ Ask ESL learner volunteers to copy each word on a self-stick note and place their labels beneath the object each word names.

➤ Have children name aloud all the picture clues on page 281. Prompt and provide pronunciation assistance as needed.

➤ Ask children to complete page 281 individually and review answers aloud together. Ask volunteers which blends stand for the beginning sound of pictures they did not circle. Review answers.

4 APPLY

Materials:
Blend Chains activity, *MCP Phonics Teacher Resource Guide*, page 239n; construction paper; markers; tape or paste

Refer to the Unit 4 Blend Chains activity on page 239n of the *MCP Phonics Teacher Resource Guide* and have ESL learners prepare a chain using words with *ch*.

➤ Brainstorm with ESL learners possible words for their chains. Encourage them to select vocabulary from the lesson.

➤ For additional known vocabulary, suggest words that end with *ip*, *eat*, *ime*, *ill*, and *ase*.

➤ Join the links of the chain together to decorate the classroom.

5 ASSESS

Materials:
Student Edition, page 282

Review the difference between *ch* and *c* before ESL learners complete page 282 individually. As children work through the activity, assess in which areas they need additional practice or instruction. Customize your review of answers to each child's specific needs, such as reading words aloud, using words in context, rewriting *ch* words, and so on.

Book Corner

MORE PHONICS PRACTICE

Set aside class time to read trade books with ESL learners. Preview these books and do a first reading to children.

SOMETHING TO MUNCH by Judy Carlson. Ready Readers, Stage 2 (Modern Curriculum Press, 1996)

CHUCK'S LUNCH by Dr. Alvin Granowsky. Phonics Practice Readers (Modern Curriculum Press, 1986)

Technology

AstroWord
Once children begin mastering lesson content, have them work in pairs or small groups on the CD-ROM *AstroWord* Notebook and Letter Board, found on the *AstroWord Consonant Blends and Digraphs* (Module 6). Assign group members to create lists of words they learned using the *ch* digraph. Check word lists for completeness and accuracy. Monitor progress for equal participation.

Lesson 136
Consonant Digraph *kn*

INFORMAL ASSESSMENT OBJECTIVES

Can children

✔ identify pictures whose names begin with the digraph *kn*?

✔ identify sentences that describe pictures?

★ *ESL learners whose home language is Spanish, Cantonese, or Haitian Creole may be unfamiliar with the digraph kn. Point out that although the /k/ is silent, children need to learn words that begin with /kn/. Contrast* **knife, night; knot, not;** *and* **knee, need.**

1 INTRODUCE

Materials:
Chalkboard;
construction paper;
Student Edition,
page 283

Begin with sound-to-letter recognition and confirm that ESL learners independently make the sound /n/ for the digraph *kn*.

➤ Introduce spelling of high-frequency words beginning with *kn*. Print *kn* on construction paper and write word endings (*ife, ot*, and so on) on the board. Have children form and read aloud each word. Explicitly point out the unique spelling pattern of *kn* and the silent /k/ when pronounced.

➤ Assist ESL learners in naming the picture clues on page 283. Model writing words as pictures are named. Have children copy words.

➤ Use the word pairs *not, knot; no, know;* and *night, knight* to stress that even though the words sound the same, they are spelled differently and have different meanings. Reinforce as needed.

2 TEACH

Materials:
Student Edition,
page 283; Rhyme
Poster 46
(optional); Phonics
Picture Cards
(numbers 20, 26,
27, 56, 98, 99)

Focus on spelling and initial *n* sound of words beginning with the digraph *kn*.

➤ Practice the *n* sound of *kn* with the rhyme. Have children locate target words and read them in context. Verify pronunciation.

➤ Reinforce the separate sounds of letters *k* and *n* using the Picture Cards listed. Model pronunciation and have children repeat.

➤ For ESL learners who are confused by *kn* for the initial /n/, explain that the *k* stands for no sound; help children recall that this is the case with second (silent) vowels in words containing long vowel sounds. Examples include *nail, sale, fruit,* and *beat*.

➤ If children confuse initial *kn* with final *nk*, point out the difference using known words, such as *sink, junk, knit,* and *knee*.

★ *For specific notes on various home languages, see pages xiii–xvii of this Guide.*

3 PRACTICE

Materials:
Student Edition, page 283; Auditory Learners section, *MCP Phonics Teacher Resource Guide*, page 284

Use the activity for Auditory Learners and the worksheet on page 283 to assess recognition of the initial digraph *kn*.

➤ As you complete the activity for Auditory Learners, incorporate familiar high-frequency words that begin with *n*, such as *need, now, name, nice*, and *noise*.

➤ Using page 283, begin as a group with ESL learners to read words aloud and circle initial letter sounds. Have children finish the activity individually as you circulate and provide support.

➤ Have children rewrite all *kn* words on page 283 (including the rhyme) to reinforce correct spelling. Pronounce the words aloud.

4 APPLY

Materials:
Sneaky *H* activity, *MCP Phonics Teacher Resource Guide*, page 269l; posterboard, index cards

Adapt the Sneaky *H* activity for additional practice with the digraph *kn*.

➤ Print *kn* on one index card and *n* on another. Create a set for each child.

➤ Print several *kn* and *n* word endings on the board. Ask ESL learners which card is needed to complete each word. Have them read the words aloud. Reinforce pronunciation. Endings include (*kn*) *ife, it, ee, ock, ow*; (*n*) *ose, ag, eat, ame*, and *ine*.

➤ Encourage ESL learners to say the words in short sentences.

5 ASSESS

Materials:
Student Edition, page 284

Verify that ESL learners pronounce and spell words with the digraph *kn* correctly and can read them in context. Review sound-to-spelling distinctions with the activity on page 284. First complete the activity orally. Then assess pronunciation by covering the picture clues and having ESL learners read the sentences aloud. Then have them individually complete the page. Review to correct misconceptions.

Book Corner

MORE PHONICS PRACTICE

Set aside class time to read trade books with ESL learners. Preview these books and do a first reading to children.

KNOCK, KNOCK! by Dr. Alvin Granowsky. Phonics Practice Readers (Modern Curriculum Press, 1986)

VAN'S SANDWICH by Dina Anastasio. Discovery Phonics (Modern Curriculum Press, 1994)

Technology

AstroWord

Some ESL learners will benefit from additional practice and linguistic interaction, such as that provided by the CD-ROM *AstroWord Consonant Blends and Digraphs* (Module 6). Encourage groups of children to work together to complete the Easy level of *Word Sort*, in which children help alien creatures sort picture clues. Offer assistance while monitoring progress.

Lessons 137–138
Reviewing Consonant Digraphs

INFORMAL ASSESSMENT OBJECTIVES

Can children

✔ identify words that begin with the digraphs *th, wh, sh, ch,* and *kn* to complete sentences?

✔ identify pictures whose names begin with the digraphs *th, wh, sh, ch,* and *kn*?

---

1 INTRODUCE

Materials:
Phonemic Awareness activity, *MCP Phonics Teacher Resource Guide,* page 285; chart paper; colored markers

Adapt the Phonemic Awareness activity to assess ESL learners' ability to identify digraphs in words and picture names.

➤ Ask ESL learners to brainstorm the digraphs they remember from lessons 132–136. List the digraphs on chart paper. Add missing digraphs to the list.

➤ Print familiar words or word endings on the board. Remind ESL learners that digraphs can appear in many positions within a word. Have children say each word and identify the digraph by underlining it with a colored marker.

➤ Have volunteers review their Unit 5 Word List to add other words to the list for classmates to pronounce and locate the digraphs.

2 TEACH

Materials:
Realia that models the sound of words with digraphs, colored chalk

To make ESL learners aware of new words with digraphs that they will encounter, point out the digraphs *th, sh,* and *ch* in positions other than the initial word position.

➤ Create a list of words ESL learners are likely to know that contain *th, sh, ch* in middle or ending positions, such as *lunch, fish, with, mother, father, dish,* and *catch.*

➤ Use incomplete context sentences to elicit target words, such as *At 11:30 we eat our ___.*

➤ Reinforce the two sounds of digraph *th* (*father, cloth*). Print a series of words on the board that have this digraph. If necessary, add a quick sketch next to the word or show objects whose names contain the target sounds to ensure comprehension. Have children practice saying the words aloud, following your pronunciation model if needed.

★ *For specific notes on various home languages, see pages xiii–xvii of this Guide.*

3 PRACTICE

Materials:
Student Edition,
pages 285–288

Provide additional practice with digraphs for ESL learners by adapting the Student Edition worksheets in the following ways.

➤ Adapt page 285 by reading completed sentences 1–6 to the group before assigning children to go back and circle the words individually. Review in groups, reading each sentence aloud.

➤ For ESL learners who are unfamiliar with riddles, change each item on page 286 to a direct question, such as "What has hair called wool and can be white, brown, or black?"

➤ Name the six picture clues on page 287 for children; then match as a group activity. Say each word clue aloud for children to print on the lines. Have children complete page 288 individually, after you read or have children read the directions aloud.

4 APPLY

Materials:
Special Word Wall
activity, *MCP Phonics
Teacher Resource
Guide*, page 269l;
bulletin board,
construction paper,
colored markers

Create a Special Word Wall as described on page 269l to practice recognition and spelling of words with initial digraphs.

➤ Each time ESL learners find words containing consonant digraphs, give them shapes cut from colored paper. Have them print each word on a shape and attach it to the Word Wall.

➤ Use the completed bulletin board as a tool for reviewing the digraph sounds, the words, and the meaning of each.

5 ASSESS

Materials:
*MCP Phonics
Teacher Resource
Guide*, page 288;
Letter Cards; word
list

Have each ESL learner work with a more English-proficient partner on the spelling activity, found on page 288. Prepare a list of ten known words beginning with the digraphs to be reviewed. Have children take turns being the "teacher" who dictates and the child who spells each word on the list, using the Letter Cards.

Book Corner

MORE PHONICS PRACTICE

Set aside class time to read trade books with ESL learners. Preview these books and do a first reading to children.

STAN PACKS by Frances Minter. Ready Readers, Stage 2 (Modern Curriculum Press, 1996)

CHIMP CHUMS by Marjorie Eberts and Margaret Gisler. Phonics Practice Readers (Modern Curriculum Press, 1986)

Technology

AstroWord

Some ESL learners will benefit from additional practice and linguistic interaction, such as that provided by the CD-ROM *AstroWord Consonant Blends and Digraphs* (Module 6). Encourage native speakers of English and ESL learners to work together on *Listen & Write,* in which children listen to clues and write the appropriate responses. Offer assistance while monitoring progress.

Lesson 139
Endings and Digraphs

INFORMAL ASSESSMENT OBJECTIVES

Can children

✔ spell and write words with inflected endings and digraphs?

✔ write about a funny incident?

1 INTRODUCE

Materials:
Cassette tape of different sounds (optional)

Encourage ESL learners to share stories about a time they heard a strange noise. Talk about words that express sounds.

➤ Have volunteers talk about the lesson topics.

➤ Make a homemade tape for the class; use sounds like *knock, thump, splash*, and so on. Stimulate children's imaginations and encourage input by playing the tape and asking ESL learners to identify the sounds they hear.

➤ Give children a brief overview of the story they will be reading.

2 TEACH

Materials:
Student Edition, page 289

Review digraph words, focusing on those used in the story. Have children read "Thump and Chomp."

➤ Ask ESL learners to read the story aloud as a group. Have volunteers summarize what happened. Ask questions that model correct pronunciation to reinforce the sounds. Model by reading first, then repeat as a chorus line by line.

➤ Have children write on the board words from the story that contain digraphs and endings.

➤ Have volunteers circle the letters that stand for the initial sounds. As a group, say the words and confirm the digraphs.

➤ Review the unfamiliar words *Sheri, school, said*, and *muddy*.

➤ Read the story aloud in small groups. Discuss the Think! question.

★ *For specific notes on various home languages, see pages xiii–xvii of this Guide.*

3 PRACTICE

Materials:
Student Edition,
page 289

Practice endings and digraphs by having ESL learners complete the worksheet in pairs.

➤ Ask each ESL learner to contribute one thing she or he remembers about "Thump and Chomp." Assist with content recall by asking related questions. Restate to reinforce pronunciation.

➤ Have pairs complete sentences 1–4 on page 289; then have them read the completed sentences to one another.

➤ With ESL learners who need additional support, reread the story one-on-one and summarize the page in front of you. Then ask questions that elicit the responses for sentences 1–4. Confirm comprehension of concepts as well as pronunciation.

4 APPLY

Materials:
Flip My Lid activity
and Blackline Master
39; *MCP Phonics
Teacher Resource
Guide*, pages
269n–269o;
cardboard; marker

Have small groups of children play Flip My Lid to practice forming new words with inflected endings.

➤ Reproduce Blackline Master 39 and cut the cards apart. Make the ending disk as described on page 269n.

➤ Have ESL learners practice pronouncing and using the words they form in original sentences. Help children understand the meanings of words as needed.

5 ASSESS

Materials:
*MCP Phonics
Teacher Resource
Guide*, pages 269k
and 290

Give a spelling test using the Unit 5 Word List and the spelling words on page 290 to assess ESL learners' progress with endings and digraphs. Say each word, repeat it, read the context sentence, and say the word again. Monitor how children are managing the task. Give immediate feedback as needed.

Book Corner

MORE PHONICS PRACTICE

Set aside class time to read trade books with ESL learners. Preview these books and do a first reading to children.

RUSH, RUSH, RUSH by Diane Engles. Ready Readers, Stage 2 (Modern Curriculum Press, 1996)

THREE PALS by Marjorie Eberts and Margaret Gisler. Phonics Practice Readers (Modern Curriculum Press, 1986)

Technology

AstroWord

Invite children to complete some of the intergalactic activities on the CD-ROM *AstroWord Consonant Blends and Digraphs* (Module 6). Ask small groups of English-speaking children and ESL learners to work together as you focus their efforts on continued practice with unit content. Monitor groups for equal participation and progress.

Lesson 140
Reviewing Endings and Consonant Digraphs

INFORMAL ASSESSMENT OBJECTIVE

Can children

✔ read words with inflected endings and consonant digraphs in the context of a story?

1 INTRODUCE

Materials:
Books and photos showing different types of weather and clouds

Remind ESL learners that the theme for Unit 5 is Whatever the Weather. Assess their contextual backgrounds regarding weather in preparation for reading the Take-Home Book. Clarify unfamiliar weather patterns with simple explanations, gestures, and visuals.

➤ Hold up pictures of specific weather scenes, such as rain and snow. Have ESL learners identify each. Prompt or provide context or background, since some children may be unfamiliar with certain weather patterns.

➤ Ask children what types of weather they enjoy or dislike most. Invite ESL learners to tell what kinds of activities they participate in on rainy, snowy, or windy days. Record their responses on a chart.

2 TEACH

Materials:
Clouds Take-Home Book, Student Edition, pages 291–292; teacher-prepared digraph and ending cards

Picture walk the *Clouds* Take-Home Book with ESL learners and review words containing consonant digraphs.

➤ Assist children in making their Take-Home Books.

➤ Read the story to children.

➤ Choral read by sentences.

➤ Have each child pick a card and scan the story for a word that begins or ends with the target sound. For inflected endings, have them identify the base words. Have children write the words they find.

➤ With more proficient ESL learners, you may wish to review briefly words with blends (from the previous unit), including *clouds, almost, sky,* and *bring.*

➤ Prompt less-familiar story words, such as *weather, would, touch, heavy,* and *change.* Model their meanings.

★ *For specific notes on various home languages, see pages xiii–xvii of this Guide.*

3 PRACTICE

Materials:
Clouds Take-Home Book

Assess which skills your ESL learners need further practice in and adapt activities with the Take-Home Book accordingly.

➤ Build vocabulary by asking volunteers to explain story words.

➤ For children who need additional pronunciation support, read the story aloud and review target or problem sounds. Have them tape their reading of the story for your review.

➤ Check comprehension with content-related questions. Discuss the Talk About It question on page 8 in small groups.

4 APPLY

Materials:
White and blue construction paper, markers, crayons, tape or paste

Provide ESL learners with additional unit practice by having them create digraph clouds in small groups.

➤ Have ESL learners cut cloud shapes from white paper and paste them to blue paper, on which you have printed a digraph or ending in one corner.

➤ Ask each child to print one word containing that digraph or ending inside the cloud. Divide the class into small groups. Children pass their clouds to another peer in the group to add a word.

➤ Have children produce target words independently, using visual clues from the Student Edition or their Unit 5 Word List.

➤ Display pages. Have children take turns reading each other's contributions. Correct pronunciation and misconceptions.

5 ASSESS

Materials:
Clouds Take-Home Book

After rereading the Take-Home Book, ask ESL learners to write a brief summary of the story with a more English-proficient partner. Have the ESL students read the summaries aloud to the class. Assess participation by asking each member of the pair context questions.

Book Corner

MORE PHONICS PRACTICE

Set aside class time to read trade books with ESL learners. Preview these books and do a first reading to children.

DRAGON LUNCH by F. R. Robinson. Ready Readers, Stage 2 (Modern Curriculum Press, 1996)

WIN WHITE'S HOME by Marjorie Eberts and Margaret Gisler. Phonics Practice Readers (Modern Curriculum Press, 1986)

Technology

AstroWord

Ask ESL learners and native speakers of English to explore the activities included on the CD-ROM *AstroWord Consonant Blends and Digraphs* (Module 6). Encourage children to work together to complete activities that interest them. Assign specific tasks to those who need additional practice with lesson content. Monitor each group for equal participation and progress.

Lesson 141
Contractions with *will* and *is*

INFORMAL ASSESSMENT OBJECTIVE

Can children

✔ identify and form contractions for word pairs with *will* and *is*?

★ *Many character-based languages, such as Chinese, do not form contractions with subject + verb/modal, while native speakers of Spanish will understand the concept. Look for pronunciation difficulties between long and short vowel sounds in contractions. Practice she'll, shell; I'll, ill; and we'll, well.*

---

1 INTRODUCE

Materials:
Student Edition, pages 293–294; colored chalk; chalkboard

Identify ESL learners' knowledge of contractions by focusing efforts on formation. Teach the word "contraction" meaning "short cut".

➤ Explain to ESL learners that the words *will* and *is* can be shortened and attached to the word that comes before it.

➤ Print *I will* on the board. Have each ESL learner read the phrase.

➤ Erase the *wi* and fill in an apostrophe, using colored chalk. Model pronunciation and have ESL learners repeat.

➤ Print *I will* once again. Have a volunteer form the written contraction as you did. Repeat for all children.

➤ Continue, working with all the forms on pages 293–294.

2 TEACH

Materials:
Student Edition, pages 293–294; Rhyme Poster 47 (optional)

Assess ESL learners' phonemic awareness by having them form and use contractions with *will* and *is* in sentences.

➤ Stress that only certain word pairs combine to form contractions.

➤ Print *They'll* and *I'll* on the board. Ask ESL learners to pronounce each and tell you from which words they are formed.

➤ Instruct children to locate these words in the rhyme on page 293.

➤ Read the rhyme aloud; focus on the same meaning of *they'll/they will* and *I'll/I will*. Repeat this strategy with *is* on page 294.

➤ Print several target phrases on the board, such as *she will, he is,* and *it will*. Ask volunteers to write the contracted form of each next to the long form.

➤ Assist children in creating sentences using the contractions they formed. Erase long forms and contractions and repeat.

★ *For specific notes on various home languages, see pages xiii–xvii of this Guide.*

3 PRACTICE

Materials:
Teacher-prepared worksheets

Practice target lesson objectives by providing additional practice with forming contractions, first in isolation and then in context.

➤ Prepare two worksheets of five items each where children take two words and print the correct contracted form, such as *she is, she's*.

➤ For oral practice and review, have ESL learners use the contractions correctly in a sentence.

➤ Assess each ESL learner's mastery of lesson content. Review specific contractions, as needed.

4 APPLY

Materials:
Two number cubes, masking tape, marker, counters, index cards

Working in pairs play a contraction game to get ESL learners thinking about and actively using the contractions *will* and *is*.

➤ Print *will* and *is* on two index cards.

➤ Cover each number cube with masking tape. Write *I, you, he, she, they, we* on the sides of one (for the *will* card); write *he, she, it* on two sides each of the other (for the *is* card).

➤ Display one card at a time. Have children toss the number cube and form the correct contraction. Correct answers earn a point.

➤ For a second point, ask ESL learners to use each contraction in a sentence. Repeat play with both cubes.

5 ASSESS

Materials:
Student Edition, pages 293–294

After you read directions aloud and model the first items, have ESL learners complete pages 293–294 individually. Then, working with a more English-proficient partner, children can correct their activity sheets. In small groups, correct any misconceptions. Verify correct pronunciation of each contraction. Monitor children's work.

Book Corner

MORE PHONICS PRACTICE

Set aside class time to read trade books with ESL learners. Preview these books and do a first reading to children.

WHEN I GO SEE GRAM by Bonnie Ferraro. Ready Readers, Stage 3 (Modern Curriculum Press, 1996)

THE BUSY FOREST by Shirley Boydstun. Winners' Circle (Modern Curriculum Press, 1995)

ERIK AND THE THREE GOATS by Gale Clifford. Ready Readers, Stage 3 (Modern Curriculum Press, 1996)

Lesson 142
Contractions with *am*, *are*, and *not*

INFORMAL ASSESSMENT OBJECTIVE

Can children

✔ identify and form contractions for word pairs with *am*, *are*, and *not*?

★ *Some ESL learners may be unfamiliar with the wide use of contractions in English. Provide frequent models as well as oral and written practice opportunities. Spanish speakers may recognize contractions* del *and* al (de el *and* a el); *French speakers will note* j'ai (je *and* ai).

1 INTRODUCE

Materials:
Student Edition,
pages 295–296;
colored chalk;
chalkboard

Assess ability to form contractions with *be* and *not* with an oral activity.

➤ Explain to ESL learners that the words *am, are,* and *not*, like *will* and *is,* can be shortened and attached to words that come before them. These "short forms" are called contractions. Give whole sentence examples of how to use the shortened form.

➤ Review subject and verb forms of *to be*; reinforce contractions *he's, she's,* and *it's* as you say them and give examples.

➤ Print *I am.* Have each ESL learner read the phrase. Erase the *a* and fill in an apostrophe, using colored chalk. Model pronunciation.

➤ Print *I am* once again. Ask an ESL learner volunteer to form the contraction as you did. Repeat with *you/we/they are.*

➤ Follow a similar procedure to introduce contractions with *not.*

2 TEACH

Materials:
Chalkboard

Have ESL learners begin forming and using contractions with *am, are,* and *not* orally in context sentences.

➤ Focus on using *am, are,* and *not*; reinforce that not all words can be combined in contractions.

➤ Practice *won't*, the only irregularly formed contraction in this lesson.

➤ Point out that only two words can be contracted. Some ESL learners might eliminate the middle element in phrases using *not*, forming *he'nt* for *he is not*, and so on.

➤ For children with greater comprehension, point out that some phrases with *not* can be contracted two different ways, *she is not, she's not, she isn't.* Practice with *he is not* and *it is not* by writing the phrases and having children form contractions.

★ *For specific notes on various home languages, see pages xiii–xvii of this Guide.*

3 PRACTICE

Materials:
Student Edition, pages 295–296

Use the lesson worksheets as a practice and assessment opportunity for ESL learners' progress with forming and understanding contractions.

➤ Read directions aloud and have ESL learners review the green word boxes along with you. Ask children to complete each page individually, asking for assistance if needed.

➤ Working with a more English-proficient partner, children can read and correct their activity sheets. Monitor children's work.

➤ In small groups, review progress together and correct any misconceptions. Verify understanding and correct pronunciation of each contraction. Provide additional oral and written practice, as appropriate.

4 APPLY

Materials:
Contraction Action activity, *MCP Phonics Teacher Resource Guide,* page 269m; Slips of paper or index cards, marker

Ask ESL learners and English-proficient peers to play the Contraction Action activity to practice lesson content.

➤ Prepare cards with word pairs, as described on page 269m of the *MCP Phonics Teacher Resource Guide.*

➤ Have children take turns playing both roles in the game.

➤ In another session, have children use cards with contractions printed on them. Ask them to read the contraction as two separate words.

5 ASSESS

Materials:
Textbooks and readers from other subjects; chart paper

Assist ESL learners in selecting from readers or grade-appropriate resources you have gathered. Have them locate and, on the chart paper, make a class list of contractions they find. As a group, direct children to then identify the word pairs that form the listed contractions. Review the class list orally.

Book Corner

MORE PHONICS PRACTICE

Set aside class time to read trade books with ESL learners. Preview these books and do a first reading to children.

THAT CAT by Polly Peterson. Ready Readers, Stage 3 (Modern Curriculum Press, 1996)

IF I COULD by Judy Nayer. Discovery Phonics (Modern Curriculum Press, 1992)

BLUE SUE by David McCoy. Ready Readers, Stage 3 (Modern Curriculum Press, 1996)

Lesson 143
Reviewing Contractions

INFORMAL ASSESSMENT OBJECTIVE

Can children

✔ identify sentences that illustrate pictures and contain contractions?

★ *Native speakers of Chinese, Japanese, Korean, or Vietnamese who had difficulty pronouncing /l/ versus /r/ may need additional support and oral/aural practice with the pairs you'll, you're; we'll, we're; and they'll, they're.*

1 INTRODUCE

Materials:
Chalkboard

Assess ESL learners' comprehension of formation and usage of contractions by reviewing at random contracted forms with *will, not,* and various forms of *to be.*

➤ Print several word pairs with these word forms on the board.

➤ Have ESL learners read the word pairs aloud. Correct pronunciation as needed.

➤ Ask a volunteer to write the corresponding contraction for each word pair and read it aloud. Have the group repeat. Ask for volunteers to form a sentence with each contraction.

➤ Repeat with different word pairs.

2 TEACH

Materials:
Photos or pictures clipped from magazines, paper and pencil

Expand the review of contractions by having ESL learners rewrite sentences and form contractions with target word pairs.

➤ Bring to class five to eight pictures of different, but familiar, daily activities. Plan short captions for each, using target word pairs: *He will wash his hands; Ana cannot play;* and so on.

➤ Print each caption sentence on the board and display the corresponding picture. Ask volunteers to read the caption sentence aloud. Repeat to correct pronunciation errors.

➤ Ask another child to circle the words that can be contracted; have children write the contractions on their papers. Review aloud.

➤ Ask each ESL learner to say a sentence using one of the contractions.

★ *For specific notes on various home languages, see pages xiii–xvii of this Guide.*

3 PRACTICE

Materials:
Student Edition, pages 297–298; highlighter marker

Assess ESL learners' ability to read and use contractions in context before completing the activities in writing.

➤ Have ESL learners take turns reading aloud to the group the sentences on their pages.

➤ Ask children to say each contraction and tell which two words form it. Have children highlight the contractions with a marker.

➤ Have children take turns rereading the sentences to each other in pairs or in small groups.

➤ Ask children to complete page 297, working with a peer partner. Encourage them to try to complete page 298 individually.

4 APPLY

Materials:
Digraph Necklaces activity, *MCP Phonics Teacher Resource Guide*, page 269m; pasta, yarn, or string; fine-tipped markers

Adapt the Digraph Necklaces activity to provide additional practice with contractions.

➤ Ask ESL learners to make a necklace using any 4–5 contractions they have learned, if possible without using visual or oral clues.

➤ Ask volunteers to read the words on their necklaces aloud as you copy them on the board. Have children tell which two words are used in each contraction. Write these next to the contraction.

➤ Allow children to wear their necklaces and ask one another questions using the contractions on their necklaces.

5 ASSESS

Materials:
Photos or pictures clipped from magazines, paper and pencil

Recycle the photos used in the Teach activity of this Guide. Display a visual and say a target word pair (*he will*). Have children say an appropriate sentence for each picture clue, using the word pair to form a contraction. Repeat, customizing the activity to practice pronunciation, recognition, and written practice with contractions.

Book Corner

MORE PHONICS PRACTICE

Set aside class time to read trade books with ESL learners. Preview these books and do a first reading to children.

A STEW FOR EGOR'S MOM by F. R. Robinson. Ready Readers, Stage 3 (Modern Curriculum Press, 1996)

COUNT TO TEN by Amy Anderson. Winners' Circle (Modern Curriculum Press, 1995)

LOOKING FOR ANGUS by Cass Hollander. Ready Readers, Stage 4 (Modern Curriculum Press, 1996)

Lesson 144
Endings, Consonant Digraphs, Contractions

INFORMAL ASSESSMENT OBJECTIVES

Can children

✔ spell and write contractions and words with endings and consonant digraphs?

✔ write a weather report using spelling words?

1 INTRODUCE

Materials:
Unit 5 Word List (one per child), *MCP Phonics Teacher Resource Guide,* page 269k; highlighter markers

Orally assess ESL learners' mastery of the unit strategies.

➤ Divide the class into three groups: endings, digraphs, and contractions. Move among the groups to direct progress.

➤ Have children highlight the section of their Unit 5 Word List that corresponds to their group.

➤ Have children use each word in their section of the Word List in an oral sentence. Have the group members confirm accuracy by indicating thumbs-up or thumbs-down. Confirm accuracy.

➤ Have groups move to the next section and repeat the activity until all categories have been practiced.

➤ Note areas of weakness for more individualized practice.

2 TEACH

Materials:
Posttest on pages 269g–269h and Student Progress Checklist, page 269i of the *MCP Phonics Teacher Resource Guide*

Confirm understanding of unit content, tailoring further practice to the needs of individual ESL learners.

➤ Assign the Posttest on pages 269g–269h, following suggestions on pages 202–203 of this Guide. Record progress on the Student Progress Checklist.

➤ Tailor additional oral practice opportunities for individual ESL learners based on Posttest scores. Practice as follows.

➤ *Pronunciation:* Model word pairs (*they're, they'll*) or groups with common digraphs (*think, bath*) for children to say after you.

➤ *Contractions:* On the board, list contractions to rewrite as two words, and vice versa. After children write the changed form, review and have them practice using assigned words in oral sentences.

➤ *Endings:* Create sentences and, one at a time, say them aloud to ESL learners. Have children restate the sentences, using the inflected verb forms. Use printed prompts as necessary.

★ *For specific notes on various home languages, see pages xiii–xvii of this Guide.*

3 PRACTICE

Materials:
Student Edition, page 299; two number cubes

Practice the unit concepts by having ESL learners complete the worksheet in pairs.

➤ Have ESL learners say the Word List aloud. On the chalkboard, make a three-columned chart for endings (-*ed* and -*ing*), digraphs, and contractions. Help the group classify the words.

➤ Complete page 299 in small groups. Summarize for children the rule for each section and give oral and written examples. Then have children work together to complete items 1–3, 4–5, 6–10, and 11–12. Verify answers.

➤ To demonstrate understanding, have children toss one or both of the number cubes. Have each say a sentence corresponding to the worksheet item.

4 APPLY

Materials:
Index cards, marker

Practice unit content by doing word changes using words from the Unit 5 Word List.

➤ Print each spelling word on a separate card. Pile face down.

➤ Have a volunteer draw a card and read the word aloud.

➤ Assign a specific change. For example, for the word "spilled," say the base word and then add -*ing* (-spilling). Model several times on the board.

5 ASSESS

Materials:
Student Edition, page 300; *MCP Phonics Teacher Resource Guide*, page 300

Brainstorm ideas aloud with ESL learners before assigning a written weather description in which they include the target skills. For less-proficient children, create a Language Experience description with you serving as the scribe and support for attempted communication. After checking ESL learners' papers, have them read their descriptions aloud to the class. Verify usage and pronunciation.

MORE PHONICS PRACTICE

Set aside class time to read trade books with ESL learners. Preview these books and do a first reading to children.

THE ANT by Anne Miranda. Ready Readers, Stage 2 (Modern Curriculum Press, 1996)

REACHING INTO SPACE by Barbara Reeves. Discovery Phonics (Modern Curriculum Press, 1993)

AstroWord

Have ESL learners work in small groups on the *AstroWord* Notebook and Letter Board, found on the CD-ROM *AstroWord Consonant Blends and Digraphs* (Module 6). Have children create a list of words from the CD-ROM that use consonant digraphs, contractions, and/or inflected endings. Check word lists and monitor progress for equal participation.

Lesson 145
Reviewing Endings, Digraphs, Contractions

INFORMAL ASSESSMENT OBJECTIVE

Can children

✔ read contractions and words containing consonant digraphs and inflectional endings in the context of a story?

1 INTRODUCE

Materials:
Books containing pictures of types of weather or different seasons

Remind ESL learners that the theme for Unit 5 is Whatever the Weather. Prepare children for reading the Take-Home Book by talking about weather and the different seasons, with which ESL children may be unfamiliar.

➤ Write the names of the seasons on the board.

➤ Hold up a picture of a weather scene, such as snow or fog, and use simple words and gestures to describe it. Have ESL learners match the names to the pictures, based on your descriptions. Repeat for different seasons.

➤ Invite ESL learners to talk about the types of weather they enjoy or dislike most. Have children say what kinds of indoor or outdoor activities they participate in on different weather days.

2 TEACH

Materials:
It's Raining Take-Home Book, Student Edition, pages 301–302; colored pens or crayons

Review unit-specific aspects of the *It's Raining* Take-Home Book with ESL learners before you begin to read.

➤ Assist children with making their Take-Home Books.

➤ Read the book to the children.

➤ Choral read by sentences.

➤ Ask children to locate specific types of story words and circle them in a different color for each category: digraphs, contractions, base words, and inflectional endings.

➤ Have pairs look at the picture clues and retell what happens in the story.

➤ Have ESL learners read the story together aloud in groups.

★ *For specific notes on various home languages, see pages xiii–xvii of this Guide.*

3 PRACTICE

Materials:
It's Raining Take-Home Book; Student Progress Checklist, *MCP Phonics Teacher Resource Guide*, page 269i

Use the Student Progress Checklist on page 269i to determine which skills specific ESL learners need to practice and use the Take-Home Book as a resource for practicing the skills.

➤ Build vocabulary by asking pairs of ESL learners to explain story words to one another and to name objects shown in the pictures.

➤ For children who need additional support with pronunciation, have them read the story aloud with a partner. Monitor oral readings and model pronunciation of problem sounds as needed.

➤ Assess comprehension with content-related questions. Discuss the Talk About It questions on page 8 in small groups, using endings, digraphs, and contractions in your sentences.

4 APPLY

Materials:
Index cards

Apply unit content by having ESL learners play a sentence-builder game using cards you prepare.

➤ Make a set of 15–18 cards containing spelling words or short phrases, such as *cooking, when it's raining*, and *at night I can't*.

➤ Shuffle the cards and ask a volunteer to pick one and make an original sentence using the word(s) printed on the card.

➤ Collect cards, mix again, and repeat the activity.

5 ASSESS

Materials:
It's Raining Take-Home Book, teacher-prepared activity sheet

Create an activity sheet for ESL learners to practice verb endings. Divide the sheet into 3 columns: *base word, -ed*, and *-ing*. Have children work together in pairs to locate verbs from the story (such as *raining*), print them in the appropriate column, and then supply the other two forms (*rain, rained*). Verify responses.

MORE PHONICS PRACTICE

Set aside class time to read trade books with ESL learners. Preview these books and do a first reading to children.

LOBSTER FISHING AT DAWN by Robert Newell. Ready Readers, Stage 4 (Modern Curriculum Press, 1996)

SOMETHING IS STRANGE ABOUT PAULA'S NEW FRIENDS by Billy Aronson. Discovery Phonics (Modern Curriculum Press, 1993)

AstroWord
Some ESL learners will benefit from additional practice and linguistic interaction such as that provided by the CD-ROM *AstroWord Consonant Blends and Digraphs* (Module 6). Encourage native speakers of English and ESL learners to work together on *Listen & Write*, in which children listen to clues and write the appropriate responses. Offer assistance as you monitor progress.

Lesson 146
Reviewing Endings, Digraphs, and Contractions

INFORMAL ASSESSMENT OBJECTIVES

Can children

✔ identify picture names that contain consonant digraphs?

✔ identify words that contain inflected endings, digraphs, and contractions to complete sentences?

1 INTRODUCE

Materials:
Student Edition, page 303; self-stick notes

Have ESL learners start with a kinesthetic activity before completing the worksheet on page 303.

➤ Give each ESL learner a set of self-stick notes on which you have printed each of the target digraphs.

➤ Say the name of an object. Tell children to post the correct note on the object. Some class words with digraphs are *chalkboard*, *chair*, *knob*, numerals 3 and 13, *whistle*, *shelf*, *shirt*, and *shade*.

➤ Pair ESL learners with more English-proficient peers to complete items 1–3 on page 303. Review answers, then have children complete items 4–9 individually. Correct answers orally as a group.

2 PRACTICE

Materials:
Student Edition, page 304

Assess ESL learners' abilities to read and write endings, consonant digraphs, and contractions in sentences.

➤ Discuss the items as a group to make sure they understood.

➤ Review target digraphs. Children complete items 1 and 3.

➤ Follow this process for items 2 and 6 (inflected endings) and 4 and 5 (contractions).

➤ Review answers; ask ESL learners to correct their own work and explain corrections.

Book Corner

MORE PHONICS PRACTICE

Set aside class time to read trade books with ESL learners. Preview these books and do a first reading to children.

WHEN BOB WOKE UP LATE by Robin Bloksber. Ready Readers, Stage 2 (Modern Curriculum Press, 1996)

CITY RHYTHMS by Judy Nayer. Discovery Phonics (Modern Curriculum Press, 1992)